W9-AIB-526

ADVENTURE
IN
GLORY

THE SAGA OF TEXAS SERIES

Edited by Seymour V. Connor

THE SAGA OF TEXAS, 1836=1849

ADVENTURE IN GLORY

by SEYMOUR V. CONNOR

Illustrated by Betsy Warren

Steck-Vaughn Company

Austin, Texas

ABOUT THE AUTHOR

SEYMOUR V. CONNOR has been professor of history at Texas Technological College, where he established and directed the Southwest Collection from 1955 to 1963, and where he became editor of publications in 1965. His B.A., M.A., and Ph.D. degrees are from the University of Texas. He has served on the executive councils of the Society of American Archivists, the Texas State Historical Association, and the West Texas Historical Association. While archivist at the Texas State Library he compiled *A Preliminary Guide to the Texas Archives* and edited the three-volume *Texas Treasury Papers* which won an award of merit from the American Association for State and Local History. He was also editor of the *Panhandle Plains Historical Review* (1953-1957), *The West is for Us*, and *Builders of the Southwest*. His writing includes *The Peters Colony of Texas*, *A Biggers Chronicle*, and a large number of articles on Texas and Southwest history in a variety of scholarly journals. As a staff writer, he contributed several hundred short articles to *The Handbook of Texas*. He is general editor of this six-volume Saga of Texas.

Library of Congress Catalog Card Number 65-22119

PREFACE

In this book the history of Texas from 1836 to 1850 is presented in chronological form—as it happened. It is much more difficult to organize and write a book like this chronologically than it is to arrange the material topically. But I believe it makes the book easier to read and the history easier to understand.

The chronological treatment was of great value to me, as a historian, because almost without exception the significant studies of Texas history have been produced on a topical basis, such as German colonization, diplomatic relations, Indian affairs, or even more specialized works about particular episodes or people. Thus, to take these topical investigations and shuffle them together, so to speak, in a proper time sequence, has been a most rewarding and exciting exercise.

Adventure in Glory was fun to write. I lived nearly every day of the period 1836 to 1845 vicariously and really felt several times that I was about to lose my scalp, get shot by a Mexican, or be called out for a duel—which last no doubt I would have been if some of the characters were alive today.

My indebtedness to others is great, especially to other writers of history as I have tried to make clear in the last section of this book entitled "Point of View." I would also like to acknowledge the extra-duty services of Mary Doak Wilson, secretary of the Southwest Collection at Texas Tech, and the generous and encouraging attitude of the administrative officers at Tech.

SEYMOUR V. CONNOR

TABLE OF CONTENTS

1

1836

SUMMER INTERLUDE

ALTERNATELY WEEPING with frustration and screaming with rage, the once-magnificent Antonio López de Santa Anna, President of Mexico and self-styled "Napoleon of the West," lay on his back in a small stateroom aboard the Texas schooner *Invincible*. A little more than two months earlier he had been captured at the Battle of San Jacinto while trying to make his escape in the uniform of a private. With the defeat of his army and the imprisonment of his person, Texas had dramatically and decisively won its independence. What should the Texans do with their prize prisoner?

"Give him a fair trial and hang him!" cried the soldiers. But the statesmen urged his greater value, alive, as a lever for future negotiations with Mexico. So in the immediate aftermath of victory, Texas was torn by factions which seriously threatened to destroy it. The drama unfolding on board the *Invincible* was the climax—and Santa Anna was agonizingly uncertain of its outcome.

Brokenly he sobbed imprecations against his captors and pleaded for his life, as the small group of men around him looked on in amazement and disgust. One of his own officers later wrote that the general's behavior defied description; another eyewitness, Thomas Jefferson Green, entered a lurid account of the whole affair in his journal.

It was a hot, sultry, midsummer afternoon, the second day of June, 1836. A fierce storm of the day before had died to a calm during the morning. Lying at anchor in the mouth of the Brazos River off Velasco, the *Invincible* presented a relatively peaceful appearance to a gathering mob of soldiers and irate citizens on shore. The inescapable heat and sticky salt air were added irritants to tempers already strained to a critical point of tension. In the Mexican general's stateroom, Green recovered his astonishment to reiterate his demand that Santa Anna, together with his secretary and his aide-de-camp, return to shore. And, with another manic outbreak, Santa Anna repeated his refusal: he was too sick to leave his bed— he was dying from an overdose of opium—he would never leave the ship alive. His breath began coming in hoarse, rasping pants, and Green promptly sent for the ship's surgeon who, after a brief examination, assured him that Santa Anna's health was excellent.

From the aide-de-camp, Juan N. Almonte, Green learned that Santa Anna was morbidly afraid of the unruly mob ashore. Had not the bitter shouts of "Remember the Alamo! Remember Goliad!" reached the prisoner's ears? Had he not seen mobs in action in Mexico, where already, only a scant fifteen years after independence from Spain, three governments had been overthrown in violence? Had he, himself, not risen to power by treachery? Little wonder that Santa Anna was afraid.

Green announced firmly that he intended to put Santa Anna in irons to remove him from the ship. The general fell from his bunk moaning and pleading for mercy. Suddenly he seemed to recover his composure and agreed to accompany the Texans ashore. Green quickly got him aboard a small boat which was waiting at the schooner's side. For a short while, Santa Anna remained calm; but as the party neared land, he fell again into a panic of fright, tearfully beseeching his captors to row for the opposite bank.

Amid Santa Anna's cries and the shouts from the Velasco shore, Green unperturbedly continued up the Brazos River toward Quintana, where President David G. Burnet of the *Ad Interim* government of Texas awaited the delivery of the prisoner. Santa Anna was taken from there to Columbia; and when an alleged plot to effect his escape was exposed, he and Almonte were kept in leg irons for nearly two months. Later when a kinder attitude prevailed, Santa Anna and his aide were transferred to a relatively isolated plantation, Orozimbo, where they were treated more like honored guests than prisoners.

The whole episode was filled with elements of shame and some dishonor, not all of which were on the part of the cringing butcher of the Alamo and Goliad. The removal of Santa Anna and his small staff from the *Invincible* was a violation of the Treaty of Velasco, signed two weeks earlier by Burnet for Texas and Santa Anna for Mexico. Even the treaty was shrouded in doubt. It had been violently opposed by many Texans, including members of Burnet's own cabinet; it was, of course, not properly ratified; and Santa Anna's own status as head of the Mexi-

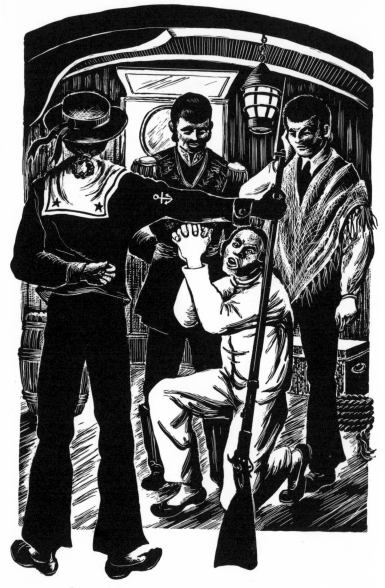

Santa Anna as a Prisoner on the *Invincible*

can government was questionable. In a nation prone to *coups d'etat*, where the constitution lay in utter disregard, His Excellency could hardly expect that his office would not be usurped while he remained a prisoner two thousand miles from his capital.

Overlooking the questionable validity of the treaty and overriding the mounting resentment towards the proposed repatriation of Santa Anna, Burnet had sent the general aboard the *Invincible* with orders to its commander to carry him to Vera Cruz. Before the anchors had been weighed, a violent Gulf storm delayed the departure until Burnet changed his mind. So strong was the sentiment, however, that the ship might not have sailed even had there been no storm. Burnet confessed that his order the next day to remove Santa Anna from the ship was influenced by a "highly popular indignation."

Much of that feeling came from the volunteer soldiers. On the same day that Santa Anna had been sent out to the ship, a strong contingent of volunteers had arrived from the United States under the command of General Green. These men aligned themselves with others who opposed Santa Anna's return to Mexico and virtually forced the shift in policy. To some, Green and his men were little more than kidnappers; to others, they were brigands usurping the authority of the civil government. Still others regarded them as heroes of the day and little less than saviors of Texas, as it was presumed that Santa Anna would violate his pledge to recognize the independence of Texas and return with an army of conquest to avenge his defeat.

In this thought there was much logic. Even then, Mexican leaders were shouting war. The acting President issued a call for a new army to be raised, and General Vicente Filisola was replaced in command by José Urrea, who was pledged to another invasion of Texas. Troops, many of them from the defeated and retreating army, began to gather at the newly established headquarters at Matamoros. Texas commissioners sent there under the terms of the somewhat abused Treaty of Velasco were arrested and held incommunicado. Mexico apparently intended to attempt the reconquest of Texas immediately!

Texas soon learned of these plans. Shortly after Santa Anna's removal from the *Invincible*, Major Isaac W. Burton and a command of twenty mounted men, ranging near Copano Bay, won immortal fame as the Texas Horse Marines by the spectacular capture of three Mexican naval supply ships which were evidently carrying provisions for the proposed invasion. On the morning of June 3, Burton and his men attracted the small boat from one of the Mexican vessels to the shore, ambushed its crew, and returned in their place to the ship which they boarded and captured. Using this ship as a decoy, the Texans later persuaded the commanders of the two other Mexican ships, which sailed into the bay on June 17, to come aboard for a conference. After the captains were taken prisoner, it was a relatively easy matter to obtain the surrender of their vessels. Dividing his men among the three ships to force the compliance of the Mexican officers, Burton brought the captured fleet into Velasco. A bold stroke and a lucky one—for there was an estimated $25,000 in much-needed supplies on the ships, and the Texan commanders were, at the same time, alerted to prepare a defense against invasion.

On June 27, Thomas Jefferson Rusk, who was in command of the Texas army while Houston recuperated from the wound which he had received at San Jacinto, publicly called on the people of Texas to rally to defend their newly won independence. All furloughs were cancelled; additional volunteers were enlisted; and by July, the army was estimated to have a strength of nearly 2,500. At the same time, the Mexican command under Urrea at Matamoros had swelled to over 4,000 troops. In reality, however, the Mexicans were not prepared to invade, for they were almost completely without supplies, and a majority of the soldiers were raw, unwilling recruits. Furthermore, the Mexican officers did not know whether to obey the acting President's order to attack or Santa Anna's order to honor the Rio Grande as an international boundary.

But if the Mexican camp was an indecisive shambles, the Texan headquarters was a riot of confusion. Scores of individual companies, each with its own commander and its own ambitions, hardly made a disciplined, cohesive army. Prior to the alarm, Rusk had attempted to resign; this was now held against him as dissatisfaction grew within and without the army. With Houston hospitalized and Rusk out of the way, the coveted post of commander in chief might be open to any one of a dozen or more men. One contemporary observed: "There were very few above the rank of captain who did not aspire to be commander in chief!" At this point, Burnet and his cabinet decided to relieve Rusk and replace him with Mirabeau B. Lamar, who had rocketed to fame in Texas at the Battle of San Jacinto.

Lamar, a Georgian by birth, was from a distinguished family of statesmen and military men. Educated in the classics, he possessed an artistic nature and was an accomplished poet. Prior to his Texas adventure, he had served in his state legislature, had run unsuccessfully for Congress, and had established and edited the Columbus (Georgia) *Enquirer*. His wife's failing health and ultimate death in 1830 was one of the great tragedies in his life. Broken in health and spirit, in 1835 he sold his newspaper and, at the age of thirty-seven, came to Texas with James W. Fannin on a visit. Deciding to migrate permanently, he characteristically threw himself into the life of the Mexican province, and sensing the coming war, he urged that Texas declare its independence from Mexico. Hastily he returned to Georgia to close out his affairs, but with the news of the fall of the Alamo and Goliad, he rushed back to Texas, joining Houston's army, as it retreated from Gonzales toward the coast, with the rank of private. On the day before the Battle of San Jacinto, Lamar's brilliant personal actions virtually saved the cavalry commands of Rusk and Walter P. Layne, who had permitted themselves to be surrounded by the enemy. Lamar was verbally commissioned a colonel and placed in charge of the Texas cavalry the following day. With the cavalry he won greater glory in the charge on Santa Anna's slumbering encampment that fateful afternoon. Ten days later Burnet appointed him secretary of war to succeed Rusk who had replaced Houston as commander in chief. Quick in thought, polished in speech and manner, and decisive in action, Lamar was yet a dreamer by nature and somewhat prone toward the mercurial temperament of an artist. As a member of Burnet's cabinet he was outspoken in demanding the execution of Santa Anna and was one of the leaders of the opposition to that part of the Treaty of Velasco which provided for the release of the Mexican commander.

Motivated in part perhaps by a desire to get Lamar out of the cabinet, and certainly in large measure to provide the army with a more decisive leadership, Burnet appointed Lamar to the rank of major general and named him commander in chief. But rather than settling the army question, this provoked an uproar of protest. On July 14, Lamar reached the main Texan camp where he found the leaders much more occupied with intrigue than with military drill and preparations. News of his appointment had preceded him, so that when he arrived he was met with determined and organized opposition. An informal meeting of officers had adopted resolutions requesting Lamar "not to act in his official capacity of major general" on the ostensible grounds that the cabinet did not have the right to suspend Houston or to dismiss Rusk. This was but the subterfuge of an army on the verge of open rebellion against the civil government. Lamar, apparently believing that it did not represent the true sentiments of the men, determined to put his command to the vote of the whole army.

An open meeting was held at which he and several other leaders made speeches in regard to the matter. The troops were then asked to divide on the question whether to accept Lamar or not, and a majority approaching fifteen-to-one took their positions in the formation against him. Lamar remained in camp another day, seemingly uncertain about whether to assume command or not. He finally referred the question again to a vote of the officers. On the following day, he retired; the army was thus thrown into a much more confused state than before.

Among the popular leaders was Felix Huston, a thirty-six-year-old Kentuckian, who was frequently mentioned, along with General Green, as a favorite replacement for Rusk. Both were newcomers to Texas, Green having arrived but the day before the "kidnapping" of Santa Anna at the head of about 250 volunteers and Huston, about the same time, having arrived with nearly 500 men. The thirty-four-year-old Green was a competent officer, but vain and pompous; he was later to become one of Sam Houston's greatest enemies. Huston, who was reputed to have spent nearly $40,000 from his own coffers on the Texas cause, was an excellent leader as well as an articulate and educated gentleman. Of the two, Huston was the more aggressive. Almost immediately after his arrival in Texas he began demanding an attack on the Mexican forces gathering at Matamoros. The longer the Mexicans delayed their invasion, the more insistent Huston became that the Texans strike first.

The unfortunate affair over Lamar's command benefitted neither Green nor Huston, and so many of the soldiers themselves became discouraged and left the service that by the beginning of August, total army strength was estimated to be substantially less than 1,500 troops. Small detachments were stationed at San Antonio de Bexar and near the mouth of the Nueces River, while Rusk transferred the main camp to Coleto Creek, about fifteen miles from Goliad. Felix Huston, with his 500 volunteers and a few additional recruits, occupied San Patricio. Sam Houston, who might have unified the army and brought it meekly to the heel of the civil government, was convalescent at Nacogdoches and in no condition to take command.

The restlessness of the military leaders was not the only problem with which *ad interim* President Burnet had to cope. Civil conditions, too, were in a turmoil. Money was scarce throughout Texas; few crops had been planted in the spring and early summer of 1836; livestock had strayed and scattered; families who had fled their homes were returning to face nearly destitute conditions; and above all, the *Ad Interim* government lacked the strength and prestige to hold Texas together or to deal with foreign powers, especially Mexico and the United States. The sooner the temporary government could be replaced with a regularly elected constitutional government, the more stable conditions would become.

The *Ad Interim* government was the creation of the Convention of 1836 which had met at Washington-on-the-Brazos between March 2 and March 17 at the blackest hour of the Revolution. This convention had not only written a masterful declaration of independence for Texas, but it had also framed a remarkably effective constitution for the future republic. In keeping with the republican theories of government to which the Texans adhered, the new constitution could not be put into effect until it had been ratified by a vote of the people. This was obviously impossible at that time, however, for Santa Anna was close behind Houston's bedraggled army and hundreds of families were fleeing their homes in terror. Therefore, the framers of the constitution provided for a temporary government to conduct the war. With wholly unwarranted optimism, the convention proposed that constitutional elections be held in December—victory over Santa Anna by that date being presumed.

The victory had been startlingly swift and surprisingly decisive, and the ineffectual *Ad Interim* government had fallen heir to the tempestuous aftermath of the war. In desperation Burnet and his cabinet called for an election prior to the constitutionally appointed time. On July 23, Burnet issued the election proclamation, setting the first Monday of the following September as the date. Three major issues were to be put to the electorate: (1) ratification of the constitution which, if done, necessitated (2) the election of constitutional officers, from President through congressmen, and (3) a mandate to the new government stating the desire of the people of Texas regarding annexation to the United States.

On annexation, the vote was overwhelmingly favorable, and on the ratification of the constitution, there was never any serious question. It was a sound instrument of government in the spirit of liberal American republicanism, providing for a popularly elected President and Vice-President, two houses of Congress with full legislative powers, and a court system, the judges to be elected by both houses of Congress. Each future county was to elect at least one member of the House of Representatives, who must be free, white, male, and over twenty-five years of age, and who could serve a one-year term. Senators, who had to be over thirty, were to serve three-year terms and represent districts based on population. The constitution contained an adequate statement of the rights of man, including such things as trial-by-jury, which the Anglo-American of the mid-nineteenth century had come to look upon as especially sacred. Separation of church and state was emphasized, and the document even prohibited ministers from holding public office or running for Congress. In large measures the Constitution of the Republic of Texas was modelled after that of the republic to the north and east from which most of the Texans had come. The principal difference was that the Texas polity was centralized, local units of government (the counties) deriving their powers from the general government. The United States had a federal government deriving its powers, as James Madison and Thomas Jefferson had somewhat ambiguously put it, "from the people of the several states."

Since the ratification was a certainty in all men's minds, the necessary selection of the "right" men to fill the constitutional offices was the chief feature of the election.

Henry Smith, the fiery provisional governor who had clashed with the Permanent Council in 1835, was one of the first to have his candidacy for the presidency actively advocated by his friends. Smith was an "old Texan" and had served as political chief of the erstwhile Department of the Brazos, as well as the head of the Provisional Government in 1835. Smith's campaign was largely an effort to vindicate his ill-starred career as governor, but Stephen F. Austin entered the election more seriously bent on obtaining the office. Austin—"the Father of Texas," the patient and beloved colonizer, the martyr to Texas liberty who had been imprisoned in 1834 by Santa Anna, and the first commanding general of Texas troops after the outbreak of fighting—had spent the past six months in the United States as a special commissioner (with William H. Wharton and Branch T. Archer) to arouse sympathy and enlist aid for the Texas cause. He returned to Texas in June and to many he seemed the most logical man in the country for the office of chief executive.

Some tried to put Rusk's name forward, but he firmly refused to be considered; Archer permitted his friends to advance his name, but did not actively campaign. A great many called for Sam Houston, the hero of San Jacinto, to run for the office, but for several weeks Houston consistently refused to be considered. On August 10, Burnet wrote the new Texas commissioners in the United States: "The electioneering campaign has opened with some activity and will probably be conducted with a good deal of spirit. Austin is out for the presidency. Archer is talked of by a few. No other candidate has yet passed the curtain."

The campaign was about to resolve into a contest between Austin and Smith when, just eleven days prior to the election, Houston formally accepted the nomination by numerous groups of citizens in various parts of the country. Neither the explanation for his delay nor the reason for his final acceptance is completely clear. A great natural leader, he frequently refused to explain to his followers the motives for his decisions. He preferred to be a little mysterious, a little enigmatic, a little ambiguous—and as a result he was darkly glamorous, raising himself in the public eye, perhaps, a little above the ordinary mortals. Thus it had been in Tennessee when, in the tragedy of his dissolving marriage to Eliza Allen and in the face of intolerable criticism, he had, without a word, resigned from his office as governor of the state and abandoned one of the most promising political careers of the time. Thus it had been when he first came to Texas in 1832, an alleged secret agent of Andrew Jackson and so non-communicative about his intentions that amateur historians forever after have credited Jackson and Houston with hatching some gigantic conspiracy to wrest Texas from Mexico for the United States. Thus, too, it had been on the long retreat to San Jacinto when he had ordered withdrawal upon withdrawal without explanation to his captains, who repeatedly urged him to face the Mexican army. And the mystery of his motives and his decision clouds even the victory on April 21, for his tactics are argued even today as historians speculate whether the victory was an accident or a calculated maneuver. They even debate, with strong evidence on both sides, whether it was Houston who ordered the charge or his rebellious captains who finally grasped the initiative from their commander.

There is no argument, however, that when the fighting began, Sam Houston was in the forefront of the attack. Indeed, his personal courage was so great that it rose above even petty assaults upon his bravery, as when he once refused to fight a duel upon being called a coward. He was an awesome, majestic figure of a man, standing well over six feet tall and in his prime weighing over two hundred pounds. He had strikingly handsome features and a graceful carriage that told of his splendid physical coordination. His gracious manner, his deep humanity, and his high sense of humor charmed both men and women, and his really remarkable intellectual ability won him innumerable constant and consistent admirers. But he had his faults. His three-year stay with the Cherokee Indians earned him the nickname "The Big Drunk," a reputation, deserved or not, which he sustained throughout most of his life. Without doubt he was eccentric, although much of this was feigned since he was surely conscious, for example, of the publicity value of wrapping himself in an Indian blanket when he went to Washington in 1830 as the self-styled ambassador of the Cherokee Nation.

Hence, although he entered the campaign just when it was drawing to a close, it can be no surprise to any that he won an overwhelming victory at the polls, receiving four times as many votes as the other two candidates together. Added to his compelling and magnetic personality was the simple fact that he was the victorious hero of San Jacinto, a role he was forced to exchange for that of midwife at the birth of the new nation. Poor Austin received only 587 votes, fewer even than Smith. Lamar was elected Vice-President over both Rusk, who had reluctantly permitted his name to be used, and Alexander Horton, an early settler in East Texas who had been Houston's aide-de-camp during the San Jacinto campaign.

2

1836

BIRTH OF A NATION

A MONTH FOLLOWING the election on October 3, 1836, the First Congress of the new Republic of Texas assembled at the little town of Columbia to which Burnet had moved the seat of the *Ad Interim* government in September. Located about two miles from the Brazos River in Brazoria County, the town contained a scattering of houses, a few buildings which could be used by the government, and a makeshift hotel. The House and Senate met in separate buildings and passed the first three weeks in organizing themselves amidst almost interminable discussions over minute points of order, the appointment of committees, and the settlement of contested elections. An interested observer might well have despaired for the future of Texas. True, President Burnet delivered a challenging ad-

[16]

dress to both houses on the second day of the session, but the business of organizing proved more interesting to the members than the deplorable state of the country.

A temporary digression interrupted business the third day, when the newly elected sergeant-at-arms became involved in "an affair of honor" just outside the open windows of the House. Pistol shots rang out—several members dived for the floor—startled and angry shouts filled the momentary silence that followed the shooting. A rush to the scene revealed that the pistol balls had gone wild and that no one was injured. The members of the House then settled into a lengthy two-hour discussion of whether their dignity had been abused, and if so, what they were going to do about it. This debate continued into the next day, when the duelists were ordered arrested and tried by the House Judiciary Committee. On the following day the men were released and the sergeant-at-arms restored to office on his plea of self-defense. The House returned to the consuming question of contested elections.

At the end of the third week of the session, on Saturday afternoon, October 22, the two houses met jointly to inaugurate President Sam Houston and Vice-President Mirabeau B. Lamar. Despite the primitive frontier surroundings and the comic opera futility of the preceding three weeks, the inaugural ceremonies were impressive and dignified. Both Houston and Lamar made gracious and meaningful addresses, while Burnet and Lorenzo de Zavala, *ad interim* Vice-President, presented their resignations in writing. On this day the Republic of Texas became a nation.

Houston lost little time in asserting his influence. Whatever anti-Houston feeling may have erupted in later years (and there was a considerable amount of it), there can be little question but that he provided the leadership and the unifying force then so desperately needed. His initial message was designed to turn Congress toward the important business of the country, and his appointments to the cabinet were calculated to put an end to disharmony and factionalism.

To his opponents in the election he gave the principal positions: Austin, secretary of state; and Smith, secretary of the treasury. Rusk, the chief contender for the vice-presidency who had received nearly half as many votes as Lamar, was made secretary of war. Samuel Rhoads Fisher, an outspoken supporter of Austin during the campaign, was named secretary of the navy—an appointment Houston would regret before many months had passed. James Collinsworth, one of Houston's own supporters, was offered the post of attorney general. Although he was confirmed by the Senate, Collinsworth declined the appointment for personal reasons. A month later Houston gave the post to James Pinckney Henderson, a recent immigrant to Texas who would later serve as secretary of state and minister to France, and who was destined to become Texas' first governor ten years hence.

On the whole, the selections were excellent ones, especially the first three. Rusk, who had served previously in the war department post and had commanded the army during Houston's absence after San Jacinto, was the best hope (other than Houston himself) for controlling the still restless volunteers. Smith, quarrelsome and contentious as he may have been, was of undoubted sincerity and integrity—a perfect watchdog for the fiscal records of the Republic, which in fact had been safely in his possession since his controversial term as governor. And finally, no man was better suited than Austin, the new secretary of state, to handle the two immediate prob-

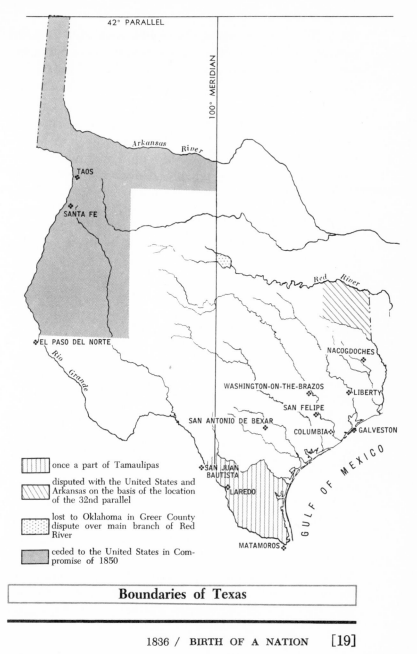

42° PARALLEL

100° MERIDIAN

Arkansas River

TAOS

SANTA FE

EL PASO DEL NORTE

Rio Grande

Red River

NACOGDOCHES

WASHINGTON-ON-THE-BRAZOS

LIBERTY

SAN FELIPE

SAN ANTONIO DE BEXAR

COLUMBIA

GALVESTON

SAN JUAN BAUTISTA

LAREDO

GULF OF MEXICO

MATAMOROS

once a part of Tamaulipas

disputed with the United States and Arkansas on the basis of the location of the 32nd parallel

lost to Oklahoma in Greer County dispute over main branch of Red River

ceded to the United States in Compromise of 1850

Boundaries of Texas

lems: the delicate negotiations involving the prisoner Santa Anna and the pleading for recognition of the independence of Texas.

Recognition by the United States was the most vital issue confronting Houston's government, for until recognition was conceded, the world would continue to look upon Texas as merely a rebellious Mexican province. To establish its credit, to borrow money by the sale of bonds, to give credence to its land grants, and generally to give people faith in the reliability of its acts, the Republic needed the status of recognition. Futhermore, annexation, for which the people of Texas had voted nearly unanimously, was impossible until the United States recognized Texas independence, since the annexation of territory still theoretically a part of Mexico would have been an international outrage. The future of the Republic, therefore, hinged on prompt recognition by the United States.

This should have been a simple matter. The United States was philosophically committed to the recognition of *de facto* governments, as its own origins were those of revolution and self-determination. To prove its position, the United States had, in 1821 and 1822, recognized Mexico and the other Latin-American nations almost before the wars of independence from Spain were ended in those countries. Precedent stood strongly for the immediate recognition of Texas.

But two factors caused a delay. First, President Andrew Jackson desired to avoid antagonizing Mexico by acting too hastily. The two nations had been on the brink of war at least twice during his term in office over the question of Mexico's unpaid financial obligations to American citizens. Negotiations with the shifting and unstable government to the south were already sufficiently exasperating without adding to the complications, and Jackson hoped to settle the claims question before he left office. In this he was to be disappointed, for before the year was out the two countries broke off diplomatic relations.

Second of the factors delaying recognition was abolitionist sentiment in the United States which equated recognition with annexation and opposed it because Texas' entrance in the union would upset the balance of slave states versus free states in the Senate. Anti-slavery forces, too, were irreconcilably opposed to any expansion of the South's "peculiar institution." Benjamin Lundy, one of the leading abolitionists, published a fantastic book entitled *The War in Texas*, which alleged that the whole movement for Texas independence was a monumental conspiracy by the slavocracy to introduce a new slave state into the union. Until the November elections were held, neither Jackson nor any other politician in Washington would deliberately stir up this hornet's nest of violent radicalism.

But Texas had friends in Congress, and Jackson was especially eager to acquire the territory for the United States. Once he had tried to buy it from Mexico, but he and his blundering, tactless agent had wounded the sensitive feelings of the Mexican officials. Now, with an eye on the unsettled claims question, on the abolitionists, and on the November elections, Jackson made his policy cautious, proper, and circumspect. After the victory at San Jacinto, Texans were told that it would be premature to consider recognition until the permanence of the Texas government was assured. On July 4, 1836, the United States Congress (each house acting separately) resolved "that the independence of Texas ought to be acknowledged by the United States, whenever satisfactory information should be received that it had, in successful operation, a civil government capable of performing the duties and fulfilling the obligations of an independent power." Henry M. Morfit, a Virginian, was promptly appointed to investigate the "political, military, and civil condition of Texas."

Morfit's reports, a series of ten letters, were on the whole impartial, if unenthusiastic. He arrived in the midst of a turmoil in the Texas army and at a time when gathering Mexican troops at Matamoros were threatening invasion; he remained for several weeks after the Texas election in September. He observed, of course, the desolate situation of the country—nearly half of the settled portion having been ravished by Santa Anna's army. He saw a meager population thinly scattered over the land, a government in conflict with itself, a bankrupt treasury, and a frontier unprotected from Indian depredations. The influx of adventurers, speculators, and soldiers of fortune did not seem to him to bode well for the future relief of these conditions. He pointed out that many thought that "this whole enterprise of independence is a mere speculative scheme, concocted and encouraged for the aggrandisement of a few." In contrast, however, his review of the history of the Texas Revolution was understanding and sympathetic, and he tried to correct the flagrant errors being made in the abolitionist propaganda.

Statistically, Morfit estimated the army at 2,500 troops and predicted its possible increase to four or five thousand. He judged the total population, on the basis of information received from Texans, to be less than 50,000, including some 30,000 Anglo-Americans, 3,500 Mexicans, and 12,000 Indians; but he added that if he were to give his own opinion, the number of Anglo-Americans would be something less than the number Texans boasted of. Financially, he drew a bleak picture, as in fact it was. The government was in debt some $1,250,000 and had little hope of reducing it. Rather, it was to be expected that the government obligations would increase, and there was little reason to anticipate more than a negligible income for some time in the future. As the government was without money or credit, so were most of its citizens. The widespread poverty made it difficult for Morfit to envision opportunity or prosperity. Yet he gave the Texans credit for trying, pointing out that while the United States had delayed nearly twenty years the settlement of its revolutionary accounts, Texas had attempted the collection of revenue for that purpose within a month after the outbreak of fighting.

In the final analysis, Morfit could not, in the "rigid course of duty, which requires a candid statement from the facts," give Texas a hearty recommendation. But politics being what they are and American policy entering its state of suspended animation as it does every fourth year, Morfit's opinion had little effect on the recognition of Texas independence. Soon, however, a formidable obstacle to the negotiations did confront the Texas state department—diplomatic relations between the United States and Mexico were broken off.

On October 15 the Mexican minister to the United States, Manuel E. Gorostiza, withdrew in anger, and three weeks later, the United States minister to Mexico, Powhatan Ellis, called for his passports. Curiously, the reasons for the two ministers' departures had little direct connection. Gorostiza left Washington because of the presence of United States troops under General Edmund Pendleton Gaines at Nacogdoches; Ellis left Mexico because of the insulting and cavalier manner in which the Mexican government treated the claims issue. Both ambassadors seemed to think the only recourse was war.

One of the imponderables—one of the moot, unanswered questions about the Texas Revolution—was the action of General Gaines in the spring of 1836. When Santa Anna's army had invaded Texas, Gaines had gathered United States troops in Louisiana near the Sabine. As Houston had fled to the east, Gaines had moved to the west, ultimately crossing the international boundary and occupying Nacogdoches. Had Houston's real strategy been simply to run for the protecting wing of the United States army? Had Gaines intended to enter the fray against Mexico if Houston failed? Were United States troops held at Nacogdoches after the war as a deterrent to the reconquest of Texas by Mexico? These were Gorostiza's assertions which he published to the world in a remarkable dialectic pamphlet issued in both English and Spanish.

An anonymous member of the United States state department (who has been identified as William A. Weaver) answered the accusations, reiterating the official position and attempting to explain it. In effect, he said, the United States was dedicated to a policy of neutrality in the affair between Texas and Mexico, and under no circumstances would Gaines have interfered in what was then an internal matter of the Mexican republic. However, due to the breakdown of law and order and the actions of Mexican agents in East Texas, the Indians had become threatening, and it was Gaines's obligation first to protect the United States boundary and prevent depredations in Louisiana, and ultimately to send troops into the Indian country after Mexico had failed to take necessary measures to control the hostiles. Gaines claimed that he had not occupied Nacogdoches until July, and then only on Stephen F. Austin's request.

The claims question, which caused the United States minister Powhatan Ellis to leave his post, was much more complex than that of the army crossing the Sabine but, on the other hand, the motives and actions of the parties involved were simpler and more clear cut. For six years, the United States had attempted to negotiate a settlement of the claims of United States citizens against the Mexican government, but each of the successive revolutionary governments of Mexico had brushed aside the question, using evasive diplomatic tactics. Powhatan Ellis, who replaced Anthony Butler in January 1836, was instructed to emphasize the necessity of making some settlement of the issue. Ellis tried but finally, in exasperation over the behavior of Mexican officials, suggested that a stronger policy by the United States would be required. On May 28 Ellis wrote: "The long forbearance of our Government in relation to the numerous outrages on our Commerce has had the most unhappy influences on the Mexican people. They look upon us as either too imbecile, or afraid to indicate our just rights; and hence the continual injuries inflicted upon the persons and property of citizens of the United States. So long, then, as these impressions prevail here, I am deprived of the power of rendering but little service to my countrymen. . . ."

In July, Ellis was instructed to present the question again and to threaten to leave Mexico if the Mexican government did not take some action. Ellis prepared a lengthy brief giving a description and history of the specific claims, which he submitted to the Mexican government. There followed a series of wholly frustrating letters, the Mexican officials once again resorting to delaying tactics. In reply to Ellis' brief, the Mexican foreign minister said that before he could take any action he would have to examine the original documents in each case. Ellis informed him that these had been filed with the Mexican courts five years earlier on the request of a previous foreign minister. Ellis was told that he would have to locate them in the Mexican archives, withdraw them, and cause them to be refiled in the foreign department. Six weeks later he finally got the original documents into the foreign minister's hands. After another delay he was informed that this was not a matter for the foreign office and that he should rewrite the charges to present to the courts. Ellis' protest that the matter had been presented to the courts five years earlier and that he had encountered considerable difficulties in retrieving the documents fell on deaf ears. He then asked for his passport, but the foreign minister would not release it. After several weeks of further exasperating exchanges about the passport, Ellis finally left in disgust without it.

It was in this frustrating game of international poker that Texas had been dealt a hand, but Austin played along. He felt that Texas had the joker in the hole—in the person of Santa Anna. It was possible that if the former dictator were returned to Mexico he could retrieve his lost power; it was possible that he would honor his commitment to recognize the independence of Texas, thus opening the way for United States recognition; and it was possible that he could mediate the three-way dispute and restore diplomatic intercourse. With no other course of action open to them, Houston and Austin decided to accept Santa Anna's long standing offer of mediation. On November 25, escorted by Barnard E. Bee, George W. Hockley, and William H. Patton, Santa Anna and Almonte were sent to Washington to plead the Texas cause with Andrew Jackson. The irony of the situation could hardly escape notice.

Meanwhile, against this backdrop of international complications, Houston and the First Congress of the Republic sought to find the country's domestic salvation. The problems were overwhelming and multitudinous, yet many which would seem important today were scarcely noticed then, while others which the modern mind would dismiss as relatively trivial, occupied much of the time and attention of Congress. The major acts of this first government were concerned with meeting the financial crisis: regulating and paying the army and navy; providing for frontier and emergency defense by creating a force of rangers and a local militia; establishing a system of courts, a post office, and a land office; locating another capital; providing for local government; and defining the boundaries of the Republic. A number of relief acts were passed for the benefit of individuals such as Deaf Smith, who was given his choice of public property in San Antonio for his home; also, a private banking house was chartered.

The chartering of the bank, known as the Texas Rail Road, Navigation and Banking Company, probably provoked the most discussion and debate, which all went for naught, as the company never functioned. The longest act was the one for the regulation of the navy, which minutely described duties and responsibilities of each rank, as well as punishments for crimes and innumerable other minor details. The drafting of this bill was the major contribution of the controversial secretary of the navy. The most serious disharmony arose over the act creating the general land office, which Houston vetoed but Congress passed anyway. Despite the passage of the act, the land office was not established and the problem was inherited by the next Congress. The act affecting the most people was probably the Militia Act which provided for all able-bodied males between seventeen and fifty years of age to be enrolled in militia companies, organized by precincts. These companies were required to meet and drill on the average at least one day every month, each citizen so enrolled having to furnish his own musket, balls, powder, clothing, and other equipment. The act with the greatest longevity was the one which created the Lone Star flag; and the most futile of the acts of the First Congress was one to suppress gambling, which was well established as the most popular amusement of the Republic.

Without doubt, the most important acts dealt with the financial problem. There were several such measures, some attempting to raise revenue through the sale of bonds, notes, and land scrip, and some levying taxes and duties. The attempt to collect taxes proved to be awkward and embarrassing. Not many of the citizens of Texas had any money at all, and those who did usually paid their taxes in treasury warrants of the Provisional or *Ad Interim* governments. Between November 1835 and March 1836, the old Provisional Government had issued approximately $66,000 in drafts and warrants, which were nothing more than pieces of paper promising to pay the specified amount if and when the government ever became solvent. These had been paid to soldiers, sailors, and merchants, and of course soon began to circulate as currency at considerably less than their face value. But when they were used to pay taxes, the Treasury Department had to accept them at par, which reduced the public debt but did not bring any real money into the treasury. Likewise, the *Ad Interim* government had paid its bills with warrants, totalling over one million dollars in value, and soon the Republic was doing the same thing. All this paper depreciated rapidly when used as a currency medium, so the tendency was to pay taxes with it, where it would bring its full face value. This was indeed a vicious circle.

The Customs Act, passed on December 20, 1836, and later amended, proved to be more fruitful, for the government could require payment in specie of the import and tonnage duties. The collection of imposts had already been attempted, without avail, by the Provisional Government; the act of the Republic divided the nation into districts and provided for the appointment of a collector in each district. A schedule of duties was established on various goods, and just in case the lawmakers overlooked anything, they levied a blanket 20 percent duty on any item not listed in the schedule. Later acts modified the list, required payment in gold or silver, and reshaped some of the districts. Galveston was the principal port of entry, and there Gail Borden, later the founder of the Borden Dairy Company, established the first customs house in 1837. Later, collectors were appointed at all other ports which might conceivably be used for foreign trade. Customs accounted for over 50 percent of the government's revenue during the first four years and over 80 percent the last five.

Congress, however, erroneously pinned its greatest hopes for financial relief on the "Five Million Dollar Loan." This was an act providing for the issuance of five million dollars worth of bonds bearing an interest rate of ten percent a year with an average maturity date of thirty years. To pay the interest on these bonds and to redeem them later, Congress pledged all the revenue from the sale of the public domain, together with all real property taxes collected after 1838. It was hoped that United States banks would purchase large amounts for investment purposes so, as an inducement, the bond act carried a provision offering to accept at face value the notes of any bank purchasing these Texas securities. A further inducement offered was the privilege allowing the owner of the bonds to exchange them directly for land at the minimum government price of fifty cents an acre. Two commissioners were appointed to proceed immediately to the United States to hawk the bonds to banks and investors. Unfortunately, by the time the Texas bonds were available, the United States was struck hard by the Panic of 1837. This produced bank failures in wholesale lots, frightened investors into hoarding their funds, and made anything that seemed the least bit like land speculation sound like a bad bargain. In short, the commissioners had no luck in selling the bonds, and it was not until the latter part of 1839, when the Pennsylvania Bank of the United States subscribed to half a million dollars' worth, that Texas was able to dispose of any of them.

Even before it was known that the bonds would be a failure, the pressing need for funds prompted the passage of two additional revenue measures. One authorized President Houston to sell $20,000 in land scrip, and the other authorized the Texas agent in New Orleans, Thomas Toby & Company, to sell $500,000 worth. This scrip was simply an open draft against the public domain in Texas providing for unsurveyed and unclaimed lands of the Republic to be sold at the rate of fifty cents an acre to the bearer. The purchaser of the land scrip had the right to locate whatever acreage he had acquired anywhere in the vacant land. To complete his title he had to have it surveyed and then submit a set of field notes to the general land office—an agency which did not become effectively open for several years. Sales of the land scrip were little more successful than the sale of the bonds.

These efforts signified the government's recognition of the fact that its only resource was the vast public domain, which it used not only to try to raise money, but also to attempt to induce immigration and to discharge its obligations to volunteers in the army and navy. The First Congress (and several of its successors) made donations of unlocated land to veterans of San Jacinto and of the siege of Bexar, to families of the martyrs of Goliad and the Alamo, and to all volunteers in the revolutionary army. These donations were usually referred to as "military bounties," and except for the special awards, became stabilized on a schedule of 320 acres for three months of service, 640 for six months, and 1,280 for nine months or longer. It was up to the owner of the bounty certificate to locate, survey, and patent his land. Naturally many soldiers sold their bounty certificates, which then passed into circulation, becoming one of the least fluctuating media of exchange in early Texas.

The granting of land to immigrants as a reward for migrating to Texas was one of the most vexing problems with which the men in the government had to deal—simply because they were nearly unanimously opposed to giving the government's land away free of charge. The reason for this reluctance to make homestead grants is easy to understand. Virtually every man who came to Texas before the Revolution had received a generous grant (for the most part a league and labor totalling over 4,600 acres) from the Mexican government. To correct any inequities that might have arisen after the outbreak of fighting in October 1835, the Convention of 1836 granted a league and labor to any family which was in Texas at the time of the Declaration of Independence and had not previously received that much land from Mexico. Here the founders of the nation wanted to draw the line on free land. The first draft of the constitution contained a provision that future governments of Texas would be prohibited from giving land away, but the prohibition was dropped before the document was completed. Since almost everyone in Texas in 1836 was a landowner and since privately owned land would have little or no monetary value so long as the government land was free, it was natural that the landowners, which is to say all Texans, desired to establish a minimum price on government lands, thereby automatically establishing a minimum price on their personal holdings.

It is to the great credit of these early Texans that in the end they put the needs of the country above their personal desires and private enrichment. It quickly became obvious that one of the fundamental necessities of the Republic was to attract stable families as immigrants. The one thing Texas had to offer a pioneer, which the United States did not, was free land. The government of the United States had fixed a minimum price of $1.25 per acre on public domain. Texas might sluice off some of the westward American migration by offering a better bargain. Consequently, the Congress of the Republic granted 1,280 acres to every family and 640 acres to every unmarried man who settled in the Republic after January 1, 1837. This act, which was later terminated in October 1837, was known as the Second Class Headright Act; First Class Headrights were those grants obtained by virtue of the constitutional provision offering a league and a labor to those in Texas before the Declaration of Independence.

Houston soon found that the greatest financial pressure came from trying to support the army and navy. Unfortunately circumstances at the time made it impossible either to disband or effectively reduce the military establishment, for Mexico continued to threaten invasion. By the close of 1836, Mexican forces on the Rio Grande were creditably estimated at five or six thousand men, while the Mexican government seemed to be growing increasingly hostile. At the same time, the Texas army had shrunk to less than fifteen hundred men, most of whom were without supplies or ammunition. Once, to obtain provisions to feed the troops, Houston had to pledge his personal credit. So destitute was the navy that one ship, the *Liberty*, had been sold in New Orleans because Texas could not pay the repair charges on it, and two others, the *Brutus* and the *Invincible*, were at that time awaiting a like fate in New York (from which they were narrowly averted when the bills were paid by a wealthy Texas sympathizer there). Since this left only the *Independence* available at the close of the year 1836, Texas was for all practical purposes without a navy of any kind.

Felix Huston then headed the army with the rank of brigadier general, having received the command when Rusk was named secretary of war. A good leader and a competent officer, Huston's greatest failing in Houston's eyes was the fact that he consistently and compellingly argued for an aggressive campaign against the Mexican forces at Matamoros. As a result of the Army Reorganization Act, the rank of major general was open; Houston decided to fill it with a more tractable officer. He offered the post to James Hamilton of South Carolina, a staunch supporter of Texas; but Hamilton was forced to decline it. Then Houston turned to one of the most capable officers ever trained at West Point—Albert Sidney Johnston. Johnston resigned his commission in the United States army in 1834 and entered the service of Texas in 1836 with the rank of colonel. With respect for his personality and capabilities, which were so amply proven by Johnston's later career, Houston appointed him to the vacant rank; thus placing him over the hot-tempered Huston.

Again a tornado of jealous ambition swept through the Texas camp. When Johnston arrived to assume command, Huston, miffed at having been passed over, found a pretext on which to claim an insult and challenged him to a duel. They met on the morning of January 5, 1837, exchanged several shots, and Johnston was severely wounded in the leg—a wound which was reopened nearly thirty years later when he led the victorious Confederate charge at Shiloh and from which he then bled to death. His critical condition after the duel with Huston, of course, made it impossible for him to take command. This left Huston in control of the army.

Once again the army was on the verge of civil disobedience. Houston himself visited the main camp to restore a semblance of order. While he undoubtedly remonstrated with Huston, he did not remove him from command. He needed the army to protect the settlements from invasion; he needed the support of the army "party" to retain an effectual control of the government. Houston attributed much of the lack of unity at the capital to men who were connected with the army or who had military ambitions. In this there may have been some justice for among others, the strongest anti-Houston men in Congress were Thomas J. Green and Moseley Baker, an inveterate enemy of the old chief since the retreat to San Jacinto. In describing his reaction, Houston later wrote: "We may yet save the country, but it will be a chance. Disorganization in the army heretofore has done all the evil. God avert the worst!"

Even the most optimistic Texans were forced to view the coming year with caution, if not outright alarm. The times were indeed critical and the future doubtful. Nevertheless, at the end of the year, the young nation could take much pride in the accomplishments of the preceding three months. A functioning government had been created and put into operation, and even though some of the departments were not yet organized, they were provided

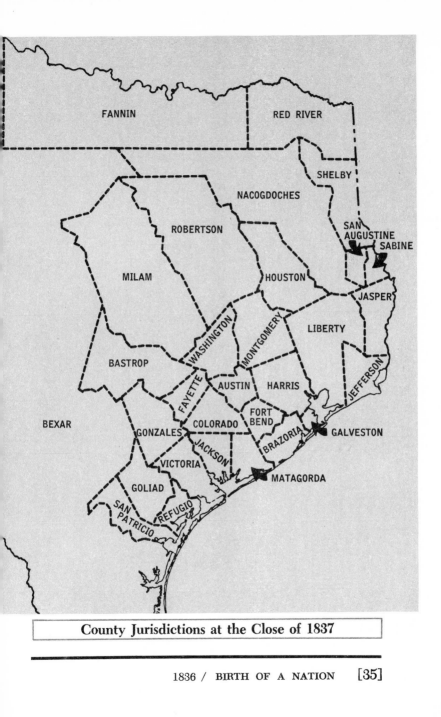

FANNIN

RED RIVER

SHELBY

NACOGDOCHES

ROBERTSON

SAN AUGUSTINE

SABINE

MILAM

HOUSTON

JASPER

LIBERTY

WASHINGTON

MONTGOMERY

BASTROP

FAYETTE

AUSTIN

HARRIS

JEFFERSON

BEXAR

COLORADO

FORT BEND

GONZALES

JACKSON

BRAZORIA

GALVESTON

VICTORIA

GOLIAD

MATAGORDA

SAN PATRICIO

REFUGIO

County Jurisdictions at the Close of 1837

for on paper. The great British legacy of self-government, expanded and enriched by two centuries on the American frontier, had yielded a monumental fruit in Texas. The achievements deserve applause.

The least noticed by historians, but probably the most significant of these, was the smooth transition of the local governments from feeble Mexican municipalities to vital American counties. Under the Mexican Constitution of 1824 and certain decrees of the state of Coahuila and Texas, the civil government of Texas had been divided into three departments, each headed by a political chief. Within and subordinate to the departments were the municipalities, with centers at such settlements as Liberty, San Felipe, and San Antonio de Bexar, each having vague and formless boundaries. The municipality was governed by an elected *alcalde* (or mayor) and *ayuntamiento* (or council). Provision existed for the election of a *síndico* (or attorney) and an *alguacil* (or sheriff), but there is no evidence that these offices functioned with any regularity. The Constitution of 1836 all but dissolved the governmental structure of the municipalities, which the First Congress replaced with the more familiar Anglo-American offices, each having fairly specific duties and responsibilities. The chief justice of each county (equivalent of modern county judge) sat with two of the justices of the peace elected from each precinct to form the county court at law. The commissioners court was formed by the chief justice sitting with all of the justices of the peace in the county. The offices of county sheriff and precinct constable were also established, as was the all-important post of county clerk. After the passage of the local government act little time was lost in putting the new structure into operation.

One of the most striking differences between the municipalities under Mexico and the counties under Texas was the establishment of well-defined boundaries. The municipalities, while covering a large area, were without fixed boundaries; among the first acts of the First Congress was one requiring each new chief justice to furnish the secretary of state with a description of his county's boundaries. As these descriptions came in, Congress made them legal by statutory enactment. Not unnaturally, there were conflicts between counties requiring surveys and redefinition of the boundaries. The process of fixing the boundaries of the local jurisdictions, therefore, took a number of years, but it was considered a vital necessity.

The regard for accurate boundaries was not confined to local subdivisions; another of the early acts of the First Congress was the famous Boundary Act of December 19, 1836, which established the limits of the territory claimed by the Republic of Texas. It was to prove highly controversial, first because of a conflict with the traditional boundaries of the old Spanish colonial provinces, and later in the twentieth century, because of the question of jurisdiction over offshore lands. The act acknowledged the treaty line of the Adams-Onís Treaty of 1819 between Spain and the United States to be the northern and eastern boundary of Texas. A line three leagues from shore along the Gulf was the southeast limit, and the center channel of the Rio Grande from its mouth to its source formed the western extent of the territory thus claimed. There was little problem over the justice or the location of the northern and eastern line between Texas and the United States, although a joint survey was made a few years later to fix the actual boundary between the Sabine and Red rivers. Controversy over the offshore lands did not arise for over a century, but the western boundary claimed by Texas evoked a storm of protest that has lasted to the present time.

A glance at the map on page 19 will reveal that the claim to the Rio Grande from mouth to source included the old Spanish settlements around Santa Fé and Taos in New Mexico. In fact, the Texas claim split the long-established province nearly down the middle. Even if the people of New Mexico had been desirous of becoming a part of the Republic—as many Texans believed them to be—it was preposterous to think that they would have acceded to such a disruptive split of the centuries-old jurisdiction. The Texas claim to the Rio Grande in its upper reaches was wholly unwarranted and untenable.

The claim to the lower Rio Grande, however, had much more validity. True, the traditional northern boundary of the old province of Nuevo Santander (modern Tamaulipas) was the Nueces River from its mouth to the intersection of the road from San Juan Bautista to Bexar, but Spanish and Mexican officials had largely ignored this division of the jurisdiction. For the most part, the region between the Nueces and the Rio Grande was a totally unpopulated desert. It proved more practical to administer the few settlements such as Dolores and Laredo on the Rio Grande, as well as the isolated ranches between Laredo and San Antonio, out of Coahuila rather than out of Tamaulipas. Indeed, in the 1830's, the *ayuntamiento* of Laredo considered itself a part of the political department headquartered at Bexar. Sparsely settled ranchos near the mouth of the Rio Grande, however, tended to look to Matamoros and the state of Tamaulipas; but it should be emphasized that fixed boundaries were trivial matters to Spanish and Mexican officialdom.

At the time of the Revolution, when the Texans became concerned with the question of jurisdiction, they not unnaturally fixed on the lower Rio Grande as the southern limit of Texas. This had become fairly well-accepted as the boundary between Coahuila and Texas, if not between Tamaulipas and Texas. From the time of Cós's formal surrender of Bexar in December 1835, the Rio Grande had been used by both Texans and Mexicans as the southern boundary. Thus, like Cós in 1835, Santa Anna agreed to withdraw his troops below the Rio Grande and acquiesced without question to the Rio Grande as the boundary in the Treaty of Velasco. As a matter of fact, it did not occur to Mexican officials to object seriously to the lower Rio Grande as the boundary of Texas until 1845. The only boundary claim Mexico ever pressed officially up to that time was that of the Sabine, for Mexico consistently ·refused to recognize the fact of Texas independence. Most of the controversy as to whether the Nueces or the lower Rio Grande was the boundary of Texas arose at the time of the Mexican War, and the claim that the Nueces was the boundary was advanced by American abolitionists and Whig politicians who opposed the war, rather than by Mexico. The validity of the Texas Boundary Act, therefore, must be reexamined later in connection with the causes of the Mexican War.

Subsequent to the passage of the Boundary Act, the question arose over whether the settlement at Laredo recognized that it was a part of Texas. No delegates from there had attended the Convention of 1836, nor had Laredo sent representatives to Congress, although Mexican troops from the vicinity had fought with the Texas armies against Santa Anna, and a number of these had reenlisted in Juan N. Seguin's volunteer company stationed at San Antonio. On orders from the secretary of war, Erastus (Deaf) Smith, in command of twenty-one mounted Rangers, left San Antonio on March 6 to raise the Lone Star flag in the plaza at Laredo. Unknown to the Texans, a detachment of Mexican cavalry was stationed there at the time. Smith and his men were discovered when they camped about five miles from the village, on the evening of March 16. The Mexicans rode to the attack the following morning, but they were observed by the Rangers about a mile before they reached the Texans' camp. There were apparently about forty Mexicans. Smith deployed his men in a mesquite thicket with orders to hold their fire until the Mexican charge had penetrated the lines sufficiently to permit the greatest damage to the enemy. The firing at close quarters lasted nearly an hour—the Mexicans suffered ten killed and ten wounded while the Texans had only two men wounded slightly. The scattered remnant of the Mexican cavalry retreated toward Laredo amidst the victorious shouts of the Rangers. Although his men were anxious to pursue the enemy and continue the fight, Smith learned from some of the wounded that there was a sizable force at Laredo, and he wisely decided to return to San Antonio. Jurisdiction over the disputed area thus remained unsettled; the Texans were able to range unmolested as far south as the Rio Grande, and the Mexicans were relatively secure in the possession of Laredo and the mouth of the river.

Smith's expedition went almost unnoticed by the citizens of Texas whose attention was riveted on the new United States Congress in Washington. The issue of recognition was coming to a head. Jackson's message of December 21, 1836, based on Morfit's report, had been ambiguous. In a word, he still intended to leave the decision to Congress, preferring not to embarrass his successor, Martin Van Buren. Many interpreted Jackson's words as unfavorable toward recognition of Texas; even so astute a politician as John Quincy Adams commented: "This message discourages any precipitate recognition of Texas, . . ." Houston, too, feared it would have an adverse effect on the United States Congress; but William H. Wharton, who had gone to Washington as the Texas agent in November, refused to be discouraged, optimistically predicting that "Congress will probably recommend a recognition in the course of a week."

To assist Wharton in Washington, Houston sent Memucan Hunt, with the hope that Hunt might be able to dispel some of the impressions given by the Morfit report. The two worked diligently—writing letters, making friends, coaxing congressmen, and taking such other measures as they thought would help the Texas cause. Santa Anna arrived in Washington after a leisurely trip up the Mississippi and Ohio rivers and had a friendly visit with Jackson. But the great expectations that he would be able to accomplish anything of value were quickly dashed. Jackson was determined to leave the matter to Congress, and Congress was determined to proceed at its own pace. Wharton's optimism, however, proved to be correct. On January 11, Senator Robert J. Walker of Mississippi introduced a resolution calling for the recognition of Texas, which passed the Senate on March 1. Meanwhile in the House a similar resolution was passed to the Foreign Affairs Committee which reported it out favorably, and linked to it an appropriation to pay the salary of a minister to Texas.

As his last official act, on March 3, 1837, Jackson appointed a brilliant young Louisianan, Alcée LaBranche, as United States *chargé d'affaires* in Texas. Houston delightedly responded by appointing Memucan Hunt (since Wharton was anxious to return home) as Texas minister to the United States. Recognition was an accomplished fact!

3

1837

AN ACCOMPLISHED FACT

On the afternoon of April 21, 1837, at three o'clock, exactly one year after the Battle of San Jacinto, a large crowd assembled outside a new but unpainted, two-story frame structure. From a tall, slender pole rising perhaps one hundred feet in the air, the Lone Star banner of the Republic of Texas rippled in the spring breeze. Below, a procession led by a tall, graceful man resplendent in a rich suit of velvet and wearing a hat with a fantastically broad brim, formed to enter the building.

The man was General Sam Houston; the building was the new capitol of the Republic; the place was the new city of Houston. Four short months earlier, the first town lots had been sold by promoters John K. and Augustus C. Allen. The town had been planned by the Allen brothers to replace the village of Harrisburg, which had been burned to the ground by Santa Anna's army. With a propitious name for their venture, the Allens had easily persuaded the government, which had found the village of Columbia inadequate, to locate the capital of Texas at least temporarily in Houston. Wild speculation and frantic construction had ensued, with lots selling as high as two to three thousand dollars each—on credit, not cash—and crude buildings bursting up on the once naked prairie site near Buffalo Bayou. Most were tents or log structures. By far the most pretentious was the building to be leased to the government for a capitol, which was one of the few frame buildings in town and was, at the time, the only one with a second floor. It was gracefully adorned with a two-story gallery running its entire width.

The ceremonial observance of the first anniversary of the Battle of San Jacinto took place in the new halls of Congress amidst a veritable torrent of impassioned oratory. The speaking was followed by a festive dinner and ball. Since men outnumbered women "disgracefully" throughout the Republic and particularly in the new city, ladies from miles around were invited to the ball. Amidst the rude frontier surroundings, the affair was impressively dignified. One observer commented that the nation was to be congratulated because its President had remained respectfully sober through the entire proceedings. Whether deserved or not, his reputation for heavy drinking was growing.

In addition, Houston had a natural love of flamboyance. He was undoubtedly aware of the publicity value of his appearances in Indian garb. The day following the ceremonies in the new capitol he wrapped himself in a colorful blanket and met with a council of Cherokee Indians. Not long afterwards, sitting cross-legged on a hand-hewn

Capitol at Houston

table in his two-room "White House" and naked from the waist up, he received John Audubon, the naturalist, who was then on a brief tour of the Texas prairies.

Yet in spite of his obvious plays for attention, Texans had to admit that San Jacinto had been his victory (despite the growls of protest from a number of his officers). And the brawling infant of a nation was his Republic (despite a growing dissatisfaction with his administration in and out of Congress). The stories of Houston's own escapades, however, are dimmed by the boisterous growth of the city which was his namesake.

On May 1, 1837, the second session of the First Congress assembled at the new capital city which at that time had an estimated population of six to seven hundred people, mostly male. Accommodations were wretched, the President's log home being one of the finest. Many of the congressmen were hard pressed to find a place to sleep at night, a number having to roll in blankets on the floor of the tavern which, incidentally, may have been the first building completed in Houston. One unhappy congressman wrote home that Houston was "the most miserable place in the world," and a visiting attorney described it as the "greatest sink of dissipation and vice that modern times have ever known." Drinking, gambling, and brawling must have been prevalent, but Houston was merely a frontier town in a frontier country. It was chiefly different from Columbia, the first capital, in the enthusiasm of its promoters.

As if to prove its kinship with Columbia, shortly before the capitol building was completed, it was christened by an "affray." A group of young men, some of them members of Congress, had begun to gather in the evenings within the unfinished legislative halls for the purpose of debating the politics of the day. One night, intemperance, combined with the vehemence of the argument, caused the building contractor, who feared for the safety of his structure, to order the group to leave. One of the disputants, apparently in the belief that he (or his sobriety) had been insulted, slapped the builder in the face. At dawn the following morning the two met, exchanged shots, and although neither was hurt, declared themselves "satisfied." Congress could now get down to business.

Houston's message to the opening session was thoughtful and, as usual, impressively delivered. The chief problems were to solve the financial crisis (a perpetual issue in the Republic), to settle the question of the land office and the public domain, and to arrive at a principle for direct taxation. Both houses thereupon organized fairly rapidly and addressed themselves to the affairs of the nation. One problem not mentioned in the presidential address was that connected with the state of matrimony in the Republic:

> Whereas, in many parts of Texas no person legally authorized to celebrate the rites of matrimony has existed; and whereas, from that cause many persons have resorted to the practice of marrying by bond, and others have been married by various officers of Justice not authorized to celebrate such marriages; and whereas, public policy and the interests of families require some legislative action on the subject . . . .

It was not that Texas was immoral; frontier conditions had just made conventional marriage ceremonies difficult. This act of Congress on June 5, 1837, legalized all such unsolemnized marriages and provided for the legitimatizing of the offspring involved.

Another social problem vastly more complicated and impossible of solution at that time was that of the free Negro in Texas. The Republic recognized slavery, and in common with most of the people of the United States, few Texans could conceive of a Negro's having the full rights of a citizen. Yet, there were a number of free Negroes in Texas at the time of the Declaration of Independence, many of whom had fought valorously in the Revolution. For the most part they had come to Texas from the nearby Southern states where free Negroes were generally unwelcome. It is noteworthy that this session of Congress, in an "Act for the Relief of Free Persons of Color," tried within the framework of the members' own prejudices to render justice to these people. The free Negro never attained the status of citizen, but he received land grants (and was assessed taxes) and was in the main treated more fairly in Texas than he would have been in almost any state in the

United States at that time. A harsh act in 1840 attempted to force the removal from Texas of all free Negroes, but its terms were not rigidly enforced and numerous relief acts exempted specific Negroes.

Although these excursions into social legislation were interesting, the main business of Congress was to provide revenue for the government. Additional import duties were scheduled, and highly unpopular direct taxes were levied; but there was little hope that these would produce the needed funds. To relieve the immediate pressure on the treasury and in imitation of Alexander Hamilton's solution to a similar problem faced by the infant United States in 1790, Congress passed an act for the consolidation and funding of the public debt. A stock fund was created against which interest-bearing certificates were to be issued to persons in return for other evidences of public indebtedness. In other words, persons having any legitimate claim against the government could submit it to be audited and receive in return a stock certificate which would not be redeemable until 1842, but which would draw interest in the meantime. Of course, in 1842 the maturity date of the certificates had to be extended, and most were not finally paid until 1852; but the funding act was evidence of the government's good intentions, and it did partially alleviate the constant drain on the few funds that Henry Smith was able to accumulate in the treasury.

Then, with the encouragement of Houston, Congress turned down the primrose path of paper money—a path which history has proved repeatedly to be one on which there is no turning around. Once a government has issued unbacked paper currency, be it in ever so small amounts, it is called on again and again to issue more and more and more until the paper bills cheapen to utter worthlessness. So it was to be with Texas, for Congress had not learned this universal truth of political economy and it believed that a small issue would be all that was needed to solve the financial crisis which bore so heavily on the government. On June 9, Congress authorized the printing of $500,000 in interest-bearing promissory notes. These were to circulate as currency for a year, at which time the government promised to redeem them—a promise which could be fulfilled then only by issuing more paper money. A redemption fund for these notes was provided, but it never developed. So destitute was the treasury that even the bill for printing the notes had to be paid in unbacked drafts.

While generally following Houston's leadership in attempting to resolve the financial emergency, Congress remained distinctly at odds with the President over the establishment of the general land office. Over his veto, the first session had passed an act requiring the chief executive to appoint a land commissioner and to open the land office. Although his veto had been overridden, he squelched the act simply by neglecting to execute it. His original veto had declared the act unfair to men still in military service; his excuse for inaction was principally based on the same motive.

The second session of Congress passed a supplementary act, again requiring the opening of the land office. Again Houston vetoed the measure, and again Congress passed it over his negative. To some, Houston's veto message was a masterpiece of statesmanship; to others it was just one more example of his willful arrogance. Houston averred that the importance of the land office was such that not only the "present and future prosperity, but even the salvation of the country," hinged on it. The act at hand, as well as the previous one, Houston considered to be inadequate. "It were far better . . . that no land law at all should be passed at the present, than that one should go forth to the world containing imperfections calculated at once to alarm and distress our friends, and inflict in the end irretrievable mischiefs and injuries to the community."

Right or wrong, willful or wise, it took courage for him to make such an unpopular stand in the face of the overwhelming support which the citizens and the members of Congress gave to the bill. A number of Houston's other actions during the spring and summer of 1837 were not calculated to win him public approbation. One of these was the virtual disbanding of the army, which was indeed a risky thing to do while Texas was still at war with Mexico. Three things may have persuaded Houston to take the gamble: (1) he was more alarmed by Felix Huston's talk of a Texas invasion of Mexico than he was by rumors of a Mexican invasion of Texas; (2) the United States' recognition of Texas' independence had opened up a variety of possibilities for the future, from annexation to protective alliances; and (3) there simply was not enough money available to continue paying and provisioning the troops.

In view of the previous difficulty when General Huston had rejected the appointment of Johnston as army commander, Houston reasoned that if he could not remove Huston from command, he could remove the command from Huston. In mid-May, while the out-spoken officer was attending the session of Congress, lobbying for support of his plan to invade Mexico, President Houston and his secretary slipped away to the army's main camp. On May 18 they issued furloughs to all but 600 of the men, furnishing them with transportation to New Orleans if they wished to leave Texas and offering them the conditional Second Class Headrights if they wished to remain as settlers. With his army gone and his hope of attacking Matamoros lost, Huston shortly thereafter resigned his commission and took up the private practice of law.

The President was much criticized for disbanding the army and thus imperilling the Republic; but his supporters argued that thus far the hostilities between Texas and Mexico had consisted of much blustering talk on both sides, with only very rarely an actual encounter such as that outside Laredo. Engagements at sea were as infrequent as those on land, but Houston's policy of public economy soon threw him into conflict with the navy and its adherents.

Early in 1837 the Mexican government had equipped several small ships as vessels of war and declared a blockade of the Texas coast. Feeble as the blockade was, the Texas navy was ill-prepared to prevent it. The *Independence* was then undergoing repairs at New Orleans. The *Brutus* and the *Invincible* lay in Galveston Bay without sufficient provisions to sail. Under these circumstances, the Mexican navy was able to capture two merchant ships which were bringing supplies to the Texas army, and this represented a rather considerable loss. The *Brutus* and *Invincible* were thereupon outfitted for action. On March 20, the *Invincible* blundered miserably by capturing the American merchant brig *Pocket*, which was believed to be carrying contraband to Mexico. Indemnities for the fiasco ultimately cost the Republic nearly $12,000. Houston tried to curb the little navy's aggressive tendencies, and a dispute over tactics arose with S. Rhoads Fisher, the naval secretary. Fisher wanted to cruise the Gulf, raiding the Mexican coast; Houston wanted the ships to patrol the Texas coast defensively. While this argument was being resolved, Texas sustained a major loss.

William H. Wharton had reached New Orleans on his return from Washington in April 1837. From there he decided to complete the trip to Texas aboard the *Independence* which, although undermanned, had been repaired and was attempting to return to Galveston. About thirty miles off the coast, two Mexican brigs-of-war intercepted her and, after a severe fight, forced her surrender. A Mexican crew boarded the *Independence*, claimed it as a prize, and sailed it into Brazos Santiago. From there the Texans were debarked and taken as prisoners into Matamoros. Among the prisoners was the doughty Wharton, who soon succeeded in escaping and returning to Texas. But the loss of the *Independence* reduced the Texas navy to two ships.

Fisher was adamant in his plan to take the *Brutus* and the *Invincible* on a hostile cruise into Mexican waters. The ships sailed from Galveston in June, and for two months they worked along the Mexican coast. They made several landings, took a few small prizes, and burned eight or nine villages. The *Invincible* captured the Mexican schooner *Alispa*, and the *Brutus* took another enemy ship. Under the misconception that it was loaded with war matériel, the *Invincible* then forced the surrender of an English merchant ship and brought it into Galveston where it was promptly released. The cost of the damages paid to the British roughly equaled the value of the other two prizes. The return to Galveston on August 26 brought the two Texan ships disaster. While lying outside the harbor, the *Invincible* was attacked by two Mexican ships, and the *Brutus*, in coming to her aid, ran aground on a sandbar. The crew of the *Invincible* successfully fought off the Mexican ships through the daylight hours, but then it also grounded on a sandbar while attempting to run for the harbor that evening. The ship was destroyed during the night but the *Brutus* was saved, only to be lost in a storm two months later.

Thus by the end of the summer, the Republic was left with no navy to guard its harbors and coastline and only a fragment of an army to fend off an invasion. The navy had proved little less amenable to direction than the army, and Houston suspended Fisher as secretary of the navy. This action was against the wishes of the Senate, and it rebelliously delayed confirming the appointment of his successor, William M. Shepherd, for several months. Adventurers and opportunists had marred the military defenses of the nation, and it was fortunate that the threat from across the river proved to be a hollow one.

A far more serious menace to the safety of the country was the mounting hostility of the Indians. Harassment along the frontier had been constant during the Revolution and throughout the months immediately following. It was in the spring of 1836 that John Charles Beales' colony at Dolores on the Rio Grande, succumbing to repeated Indian raids, was abandoned. A predatory Indian raid there on April 4 resulted in the tragic capture of the wives of two settlers and in the brutal murder of twelve colonists. A large band of four to five hundred Comanches formed in the wake of Santa Anna's army—raiding, plundering, and killing all who haplessly fell in their path. On March 4 a ferocious attack was made on a small settlement in present Lavaca County, where eight members of the Dougherty and Douglas families, early Irish settlers, were slaughtered. About the same time, all the members of the family of Laughlin McLennan (brother of Neil McLennan for whom McLennan County was named) were killed on the San Gabriel River.

Then, on May 19, a war party of Kiowas and Comanches, estimated at five hundred to seven hundred men,

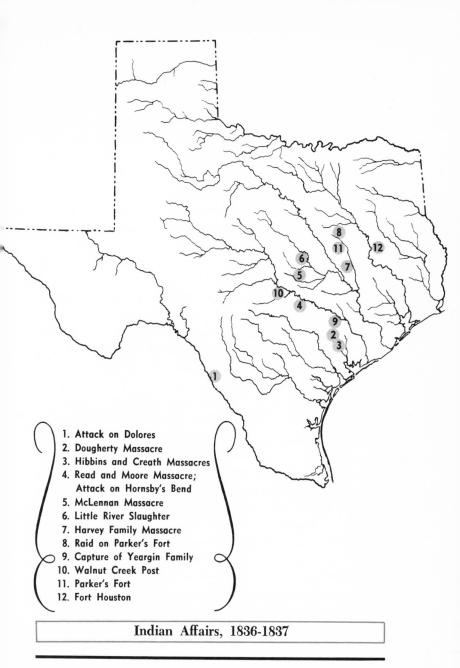

1. Attack on Dolores
2. Dougherty Massacre
3. Hibbins and Creath Massacres
4. Read and Moore Massacre;
   Attack on Hornsby's Bend
5. McLennan Massacre
6. Little River Slaughter
7. Harvey Family Massacre
8. Raid on Parker's Fort
9. Capture of Yeargin Family
10. Walnut Creek Post
11. Parker's Fort
12. Fort Houston

Indian Affairs, 1836-1837

treacherously using a white flag as a ruse, forced its way into Parker's Fort—a privately constructed blockhouse and stockade in present Limestone County—to commit one of the most memorable massacres in Texas history.

The hideous shrieks of the Comanches mingled with the anguished screams of ravished women and the tortured cries of brutally beaten children as the little community strived to repel the attack. Many of the settlers ultimately escaped with their lives, but John Parker, his sons Samuel and Benjamin, and a number of other pioneers were killed and scalped. Cynthia Ann Parker, a nine-year-old girl; her six-year-old brother; Mrs. Rachel Plummer and her son; and Mrs. Elizabeth Kellogg were all taken into captivity. Elizabeth Kellogg was ransomed about six months later; Rachel Plummer was purchased by a Santa Fé trader after a year and a half of horrible slavery; and her son was not redeemed until 1842, subsequent to her death. Cynthia Ann Parker was reared by the Comanches. She married Chief Nocona and became the mother of the famous Indian leader, Quanah Parker. In 1860, at the age of thirty-four, she was taken from the Indians; but she never became reconciled to living among her white kin and died in 1864.

Other depredations continued during the year 1836 all along the frontier from Red River to the Rio Grande. In Lavaca County, Comanches massacred the Hibbins and Creath families and took Mrs. Hibbins into captivity. In present Robertson County all the members of the Harvey family were scalped except a nine-year-old girl, who was enslaved. In Fayette County a Mrs. Yeargin and two small sons were captured. In Travis County, settlers Braman and Joseph Reed and Conrad Moore were murdered. In the same area, John Edwards met death by an Indian arrow, as did several settlers at Hornsby's Bend (near present Austin) on the Colorado. In present Bell County, on the Little River, virtually an entire settlement was wiped out.

The horrible massacres were paralleled by innumerable raids for livestock on the deserted farms and ranches. The various governments of Texas during 1836 were not unaware of the frontier conditions, but there was little in the way of an effective measure that they could take. As early as October 1835 a small company of Rangers had been placed under the command of Daniel Parker. The following month three companies were raised; one of these gained some prominence as Tumlinson's Rangers. In January 1836, the General Council of the Provisional Government appointed commissioners to attempt to treat with the Comanches. The Convention of 1836 discussed the problem, and the First Congress of the Republic created, on paper, a battalion of "mounted gunmen." Congress then instructed Houston to establish a line of blockhouse forts along the frontier, but the President had neither the time nor the funds to effect either plan.

In its second session in May 1837, Congress not only granted Houston a thirty-day leave to organize the corps of mounted gunmen, but it also provided that $100,000 of the promissory notes to be issued were to be allocated to the Rangers. Houston appointed an efficient cadre, and this group became the foundation of the famed Texas Rangers. Several blockhouse forts were built: one on Walnut Creek in present Travis County; another at the three forks of Little River; and still another, the well-known Fort Houston, located near present Palestine. Fort Houston developed from a former stockade post and was the site at which three men had lost their lives the previous winter. A company of over one hundred men under A. C. Horton was placed in the area of Parker's Fort. And a detachment of about twenty men built a small post at the headwaters of the Trinity, where on November 10, they defeated a raiding party of over 150 Indians.

Although depredations continued, the ranging companies were a strong deterrent force. Indeed, the Rangers proved to be the most effective method of dealing with the Indian problem and, in combination with the local militia, afforded a better basis for national defense than had the unruly army. Houston and his government were thus enabled to give fuller attention to foreign problems during the latter part of 1837.

To critics of the Houston administration, the diplomacy of 1837 was a failure—Texas had failed to achieve annexation to the United States. The optimistic hope that Santa Anna would be able to negotiate with President Jackson for the annexation of Texas was also dashed. Political animosity loomed large and Houston was blamed, but it was neither his fault nor that of his agents. Wharton had predicted in February that the United States would not consider annexation because of the dual objections of Mexico and the anti-slavery forces. In the light of the existing antagonism toward Texas, recognition alone was a victory, although it did seem to preclude immediate annexation. It is little wonder that the response in Texas was ambivalent. William Fairfax Gray, a distinguished attorney who migrated to Texas in 1837, wrote that "Texas, independent, and compelled to fight her own battles and pay her own debts, will necessarily have to impose heavy burdens on her citizens." Dr. John S. Ford, who was later to develop into one of Texas' most famed military leaders, commented: "The unsuccessful result of the diplomacy of 1837 was a powerful blow to the people of Texas."

Houston himself, in his address to Congress in May, had pointed out that recognition meant that Texas must struggle to deserve its place among the family of nations. He urged that an attempt be made to establish formal diplomatic relations with European countries. During April and May an unofficial representative of the British consular service had visited Texas and was so impressed with its future that he personally invested in a league of Texas land. Charles, the Count de Farnese, came to Texas in July with the vain idea of establishing Roman Catholicism as the state religion and of opening formal diplomatic relations with the Vatican. Although his proposition was impossible among people who cherished the principle of separation of church and state, he was received warmly; and his visit was interpreted to some extent as an enhancement of the status of the Republic. Before it adjourned, Congress, hoping to obtain British recognition, authorized the appointment of a Texas agent to England. Houston promptly selected James Pinckney Henderson for this important post.

Henderson, a wealthy member of an aristocratic family in North Carolina, was a man of culture and education. Trained as a lawyer, he moved to Mississippi in 1835 and the following year came to Texas, arriving in June 1836. Although he was but twenty-eight years of age, he had previously served as a colonel in the North Carolina militia; and Burnet, with the hope that the polished young man could influence some of the restless spirits then prevailing among the volunteers, quickly commissioned him a brigadier general in the Texas army. Henderson returned to North Carolina, raised a company of men, and brought them to Texas at his own expense. Upon the death of

Stephen F. Austin in December, Houston appointed Henderson to the vacant position of secretary of state in the cabinet. During the negotiations over recognition, Henderson showed so much finesse that there was little question that he was the best person in the Republic to send to England. He was to remain in Europe for three years, serving later in France. Thereafter he returned to his adopted country, where he aided in the final negotiations for annexation in 1844-1845, and subsequently became Texas' first governor in 1846.

In Europe, Henderson rendered invaluable service to the Republic. Arriving in London in October 1837, he found that there was already considerable interest in Texas being expressed by the British. He sensed a willingness to recognize Texas independence, and this could be attributed to two closely related factors: England was interested in expanding her commerce as well as in limiting any future expansion of the United States; the establishment of an independent nation to her southwest would certainly limit the growth of the United States. At the same time, an independent nation in this position would have open to it the possibility of fruitful trade relations with the undeveloped west. Yet, in England, Henderson also sensed a strong reluctance to recognize Texas from the same general source that instigated anti-Texas feeling in the United States—the abolitionists. Britain was staunchly anti-slavery. The slave trade had been abolished on British ships in 1807, and England, at the Congress of Vienna, had persuaded the rest of Europe to prohibit it. As a part of the great reforms of the early nineteenth century, Britain, in 1833, had emancipated all slaves in the Empire, with just compensation for their owners.

In Texas, the institution of slavery was established, and many Britons were afraid that the young Republic would condone the slave trade. Since this obnoxious commerce had been virtually stamped out throughout the civilized world (it having been illegal to import slaves to the United States since 1809) and since Britain was deeply committed to the total extermination of the slave trade, there would be created an impossible situation if Her Majesty's government officially recognized a new nation which might tolerate trading in, or an importation of, the unfortunate Negroes. Of course, British policy extended only to the international trade and not to the internal traffic in slaves, which was prevalent all over the southern United States.

Soon after Henderson's arrival in England, he obtained a lengthy interview with Viscount Palmerston, British foreign secretary. Henderson emphasized Texas' own opposition to the international slave trade and portrayed the future commerce of the Republic in glowing terms. Palmerston was duly impressed. A treaty of commerce, if accompanied by a treaty for the suppression of the slave trade, seemed possible. There remained one obstacle— England, like the United States, was having diplomatic difficulty with Mexico over the collection of indemnities to British citizens. Until the British claims question was settled, Palmerston feared antagonizing the Mexican government by premature recognition of Texas. Anti-slavery and the claims—the same hurdles that Texas had to jump in the United States!

While Henderson was fuming impatiently in London, Memucan Hunt was having trouble in Washington. In August he finally succeeded in submitting the annexation proposal to the United States state department, which informed him firmly and unequivocally that the United States would not consider the question of annexation. This rejection was a painful blow to Texas' fondest hopes, but neither Texans nor Texas' supporters in the United States gave up. In the meantime, Hunt was confronted with another major problem: the boundary between the United States and Texas.

Although this controversial boundary had been settled in the Treaty of 1819 between Spain and the United States, Mexico had repeatedly refused to recognize the treaty. Finally, in 1828, an agreement was negotiated with the shifting Mexican government to survey the line; but the Mexican Congress petulantly refused to ratify it until 1832. Shortly thereafter Santa Anna had overthrown the government and abrogated the constitution, with the result that the boundary remained unsettled at the time of Texas' independence. Meanwhile American settlers had spilled over into the Red River valley; and Miller County, under the jurisdiction of Arkansas, had been created south of Red River, taking in most of present Bowie County, Texas. Early settlers at such places as Jonesborough and Pecan Point were uncertain whether they lived in Mexican Texas or in Miller County, Arkansas, in the United States. The activities of Richard Ellis and his son at Pecan Point provide an example. At the same time that Ellis served as president of the Texas Convention of 1836, his son, who lived under the same roof, was serving in the Arkansas legislature! The following year Arkansas made it illegal for any of her citizens to hold an official position in Texas. But this was an empty threat because the claims to the area by Arkansas and Texas were still in conflict.

The problem hinged on the indefinite location of the treaty line and on vague claims by the United States to the Neches River rather than to the Sabine. The treaty actually specified as a boundary the Sabine River from its mouth to a point where it was crossed by the 32nd parallel and thence a line due north to Red River. Because of the relatively sharp westward bend of the Sabine, a small north or south variation in the location of the 32nd parallel would cause a wide east or west displacement of the line running north. Maps of the period exaggerated the bend of the Sabine and placed the 32nd parallel too far north, thus compounding the confusion. Until the 32nd parallel was accurately located and the north-south line carefully surveyed, the proper jurisdiction of the settlements in the Red River valley would remain in doubt. The United States was anxious to settle the issue; consequently as soon as the recognition of Texas was an accomplished fact, John Forsyth, the United States secretary of state, approached Hunt on the matter. Since Texas professed by its boundary statute of December 19, 1836, to accept the Treaty of 1819, Forsyth proposed that a joint surveying commission be set up to establish accurately the international boundary. Hunt, whose energies and thoughts had all been directed toward the questions of recognition and annexation, was unprepared to negotiate immediately. He communicated with Robert A. Irion, who had succeeded Henderson as Texas secretary of state, and Irion turned to Houston.

To Texas, an important ramification of the problem was that a number of headright and bounty lands had been located in the disputed area. Suppose a survey revealed that these lands were actually in Miller County, as Arkansas claimed. The Texans would then lose their lands. Houston, who was determined to circumvent the faulty land law which Congress had twice passed over his vetoes, took advantage of the situation to call a special session of Congress. The newly elected Second Congress was not due to meet until November; Houston hoped to find it more malleable than the First Congress had been toward the end of its term. His proclamation calling for Congress to convene in Houston on September 25, 1837, stated that the unsettled boundary prevented his execution of the land law (for which he had been given an October deadline) and necessitated the special attention of the legislators. Houston's opening message to the assembled Congress was cleverly based on the boundary problem but, in fact, he asked for a revision of the land law.

To some extent Congress complied. Its first official act was the suspension of the controversial land measure. Before long, however, it clashed with Houston again over the public domain. On October 24 the President vetoed a resolution concerned with the issuance of military land scrip on the grounds that it would not only cause a further depreciation of the promissory notes, but that it would also be in conflict with Congress' own suspension of the land law. Both houses promptly passed the resolution over his veto and soon proceeded to revise the general land law. The special session merged into the regular session so that Congress actually sat from September 25 to December 19. Early in December, after agonizing debates, Congress passed a massive revision of the land law intended to be equitable in every way and to satisfy all of Houston's previous objections.

"With great reluctance" Houston vetoed again; this time because the law neglected to carry out the constitutional injunction to sectionize the public domain, and because a provision of the new law dishonored certain obligations implied in the issue of the promissory notes. In a turmoil of criticism, both houses promptly overrode the negative. Why was Houston so recalcitrant? Did he have some special and hidden interest which he was trying to protect? His critics refused (then and later) to accept his statesmanlike messages at face value, and the overwhelming urge to establish the land office nearly swamped the chief executive in a tide of antagonism.

The work of the Second Congress was less vital than its predecessor's. Most of the three-month extended session was taken up with "private" bills for the relief of individual citizens, for the incorporation of cities, for the chartering of companies, and for the creation of counties. The routine business of government was attended to, and Congress did not fail to provide for the remuneration of its members. Although the ostensible reason for a special session had been the boundary dispute, no action was taken on it. Probably the most important general measures adopted, other than the land bill, were acts to augment the navy, to prohibit the future sale of land scrip, and to create a commission for the purpose of locating a permanent capital for the Republic.

The navy at this time was completely foundered. Houston had not executed an act of the First Congress calling for the purchase of four new ships. The primary reason was that the money was not available, and the secondary reason was that Houston wanted to avoid increasing his problems with military opportunists. The Second Congress now appropriated $280,000 (to be taken from the sale of the Texan bonds) for the acquisition of six new ships and provided for the appointment of a commissioner whose function would be to acquire and equip what was to become in another two years the "second" Texas navy.

No doubt the resentment against Houston, the man, augmented the feeling of dissatisfaction among legislators with Houston, the city. There were numerous reasons

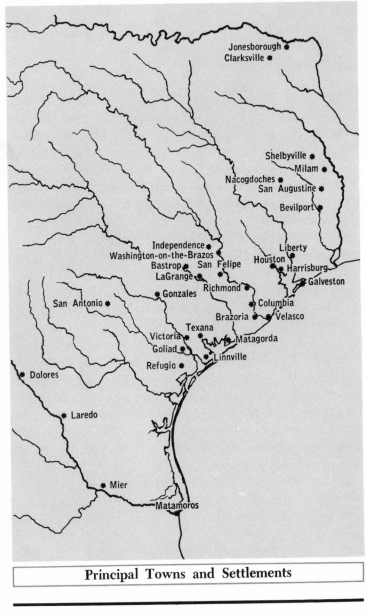

Principal Towns and Settlements

offered for proposing another location for the seat of government, and in the long run, the most lasting measure of the Second Congress was the creation of a five-man commission appointed to find a suitable location for the capital. Over the course of the next two years this group examined a number of sites and received innumerable petitions from aspiring towns. Its ultimate decision was for the creation of a new town on the western frontier—a decision that was strongly influenced by Houston's successor in office.

In the meantime, however, the Allen brothers' proud city thrived and remained the temporary capital for three more years. But Houston was not the only town experiencing the stimulating post-Revolution growth; the whole Republic was growing. Among the new (or relatively new) cities chartered by Congress were Houston itself, Shelbyville, Richmond, La Grange, Matagorda, Lexington, Milam, Bevilport, Texana, Columbus, Independence, and Clarksville. Older places which received corporate charters were San Antonio, Gonzales, Victoria, San Felipe, Brazoria, Columbia, Bastrop (or Mina), San Augustine, Velasco, Liberty, Nacogdoches, Goliad, Washington, Refugio, and Jonesborough. The increase in population—exaggerated though it was—occasioned the creation of the counties of Montgomery, Fayette, Fannin, Robertson, Fort Bend, and Houston.

No population figures are available, and contemporary estimates were unrealistically high or low, depending on the optimism or the gloom of the observer. It is safe to say that by the end of 1837 Texas had recovered the statistical losses incurred during 1836, and that new immigration to the Republic was beginning. It is also safe to say that the great tide of immigration which Texan boosters had so glibly predicted was thus far merely a vision.

4

1838

OPTIMISM AND GLOOM

In some respects the closing months of 1837 were as near to prosperity as the Republic was to come. The recently issued promissory notes, circulating then in New Orleans at about eighty cents on the dollar, had not yet lost their value. Recognition had given a boost to land values. A dozen business corporations were chartered by the Second Congress, and scores of unchartered, small businesses witnessed an increase in trade. Commerce appeared to be flourishing, and the value of imports, especially at M. B. Menard's new city of Galveston, rose to unexpected highs. Crops that year were generally good, the cotton harvest alone being estimated at two million dollars. Sad to relate, good times were largely a delusion. A money panic, beginning in Europe, hit the United States in May 1837, causing the most serious economic setback the country had yet seen—worse even than the Panic of 1819. A depression followed that was to last seven or eight years. Texas was seemingly prosperous only because the results of the Panic had not yet reached it. Conditions were soon to worsen; the bright future touted by New Year's Day orators dimmed perceptibly before the close of 1838.

Born in the optimism of the times was one of the most creditable agencies of the Republic—the consular service. Officially created by Congress in December 1837 as an office to handle certain commercial matters, the consular service had its roots in the earlier appointment of special agents such as Thomas Toby in New Orleans, David White in Mobile, and John Woodward in New York. The chief business of these early agents was to dispose of the bonds and promissory notes to interested investors, to buy governmental supplies, and to make the necessary exchanges of those bank notes drawn on United States banks which were received in Texas. The Consular Act of 1837 was not detailed, but it placed the supervision of the consular service under the state department. Appointments were made, usually upon application, of men who lived in the major cities. No salaries were paid, but the consuls derived some income from fees and commissions. Consulates were soon established at Baltimore, Philadelphia, Charleston, Vicksburg, Boston, and Natchitoches. In the next several years, offices were opened also in such unlikely places as Bangor, Detroit, and Key West, as well as in Cincinnati, St. Louis, and Richmond. During the last half of the Republic's existence, the consular service expanded to Europe—with agents in England at London, Liverpool, Plymouth, and a half-dozen smaller towns; in France at Paris, Bordeaux, Cette, Rouen, and Bayonne;

at Glasgow (Scotland); at Dublin (Ireland); at Antwerp (Belgium); at Bremen (Germany); and in the Netherlands at Amsterdam and Rotterdam.

In addition to conducting much of the foreign business affairs of the Republic, the consular agents were information centers about Texas where prospective immigrants could obtain at least a modicum of advice—as well as a good deal of encouragement. One contemporary observer noted caustically that "false representations are disseminated to lead people to Texas," and that he regretted the "disappointment and distress" which he saw among many newcomers. It probably was not so much the "false representations" that may have misled people as it was their own wishful thinking. On the other hand, many who came were not disappointed, as attested by hundreds of letters written by Texans to friends and families elsewhere and which were frequently printed in the home-town papers. The cynic branded these as cruel attempts of the miserable to secure company in their plight.

Although the depression was soon to strike with much severity, and although there was still much talk about the possibility of a Mexican invasion, the most formidable danger threatening the new settlers was the savagery of the bloody and restless Indians who, perhaps even then, were beginning to sense their inevitable destiny. Hardly a place in Texas was really safe from the possibility of attack, and no family ever knew at what instant the terrible war whoop of a horde of leaping, painted wild men might break the peace of the night; or at what moment they might awaken to find that, with unbelievable stealth, these same Indians might have driven off their livestock and set fire to their barns and houses.

Hard pressed from the north by the tribes which the United States had crowded to the Indian Territory in its "removal" program, and themselves harassed like the settlers by the fury of the fierce Comanche and Kiowa on the west, the Indians along the Texas frontier grew desperate as the prongs of white settlement extended into their traditional hunting grounds. An investigating committee assessed the problem in the fall of 1837 with much gravity. The small group of Alabama and Coushatta Indians, recently arrived in Texas and roaming in Liberty County, were not considered dangerous. The ancient Caddoan bands around Nacogdoches were "thought to be the greatest rogues and the most treacherous Indians on our frontiers." The Keechi, Tawakoni, Waco, and Pawnee of the central prairie region were well mounted, and they considered themselves at war with the Republic. These Indians were labelled as fiends by the investigators because of the outrages perpetrated on prisoners, especially female captives. The Lipan, the Tonkawa, and the remnant of the Karankawa in the southwest were believed to be so dominated by Mexican agents that they should be considered "as a part of the Mexican nation." About 500 Kickapoo, Shawnee, Delaware, and related Indians, recently crowded into Texas by the Indian policies of the United States, roamed freely in the northern prairies between the Trinity and Red rivers. To the east of these bands of wilder Indians resided the Cherokees, a complete enigma to the investigating committee, which noted the civilized state of these Indians' settlements and commented that the Cherokees would feel the horrors of a savage attack almost equally with the whites.

The Cherokees presented a dilemma. Whether the ultimate solution reached by Texas in 1839 is a dark disgrace to the otherwise honorable history of the Republic is a

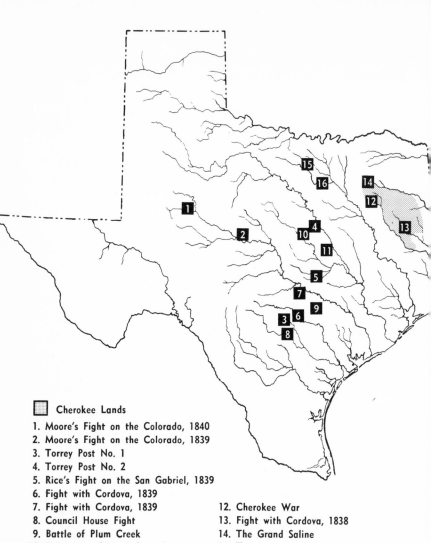

Cherokee Lands
1. Moore's Fight on the Colorado, 1840
2. Moore's Fight on the Colorado, 1839
3. Torrey Post No. 1
4. Torrey Post No. 2
5. Rice's Fight on the San Gabriel, 1839
6. Fight with Cordova, 1839
7. Fight with Cordova, 1839
8. Council House Fight
9. Battle of Plum Creek
10. Tehuacana Council Ground
11. Falls of the Brazos

12. Cherokee War
13. Fight with Cordova, 1838
14. The Grand Saline
15. Temporary Post on Headwaters of Trinity
16. Bird's Fort

Indian Affairs, 1838-1849

moot question which even today every person must decide for himself. Most of the facts are plain. Driven from their native countryside in the southern Appalachians, a branch of the Cherokee tribe had migrated to Texas in 1819 and 1820, settling first along the upper Trinity. Pressure from the aggressive Indians of that area caused them to move southeast to the region of present Smith, Rusk, Cherokee, and Van Zandt counties. Their astute leader, Chief Bowles, at once began negotiations with the Mexican government to obtain legal sanction of their settlement. Bowles even hoped to secure a title to the land so occupied. His efforts were to little avail, despite the fact that the Cherokees not only lived in peace but also cooperated with the Mexican government in helping to put down the Fredonian uprising around Nacogdoches in 1826. Yet Mexico did recognize the existence of this civilized tribe within her boundaries, and when an empresario contract was made in their area, the lands occupied by the Cherokees were specifically exempt from settlement.

At the outbreak of the Texas Revolution, the Cherokees remained, to some extent at least, as intruders on a foreign soil. If they chose to side with Texas against Mexico, they would make an imposing ally; if they sided with Mexico and attacked the Texas army from the rear, or raided the settlements while the Texans faced Santa Anna to the south, they would make a terrifying enemy. Reports had reached various members of the Consultation in 1835 that Mexican agents were circulating among the Indians trying to arouse them against the Texans. Sam Houston, an adopted member of the Cherokee tribe, who had lived for several years among the Cherokees in the Indian Territory, took the lead in seeking to conciliate the Indians. As chairman of a special committee he drafted a resolution which the Consultation adopted on November 13, 1835—a "solemn decree" professing the friendship of the Texans toward the Cherokees and stating that "we will guarantee to them the peaceable enjoyment of their rights to their land . . . ." To this declaration, as a pledge of the public faith, the members of the Consultation affixed their personal signatures.

On December 28, 1835, after the split between Provisional Governor Henry Smith and the Council, Smith appointed Houston, John Forbes, and John Cameron as commissioners to execute a treaty with the Cherokees in keeping with the wishes of the Consultation. This Houston did on February 23, 1836, overstepping perhaps the letter but not the spirit of the "solemn decree." Essentially, the treaty committed the Indians to a policy of friendship and committed Texas to a guarantee of the Cherokee land claims.

Two questions were to arise in regard to the treaty: Was it a legal and binding instrument on Texas? Did the Cherokees keep their promise of friendship? From the beginning, substantial doubt surrounded the treaty's status. Although authorized by the Consultation, the government which executed the treaty was virtually defunct at the time it was made. Houston had actually acted on orders from Henry Smith, whose powers had been revoked by the General Council which presumed itself to be governing Texas. But more important, no treaty made by an agent could be binding until ratified by the government responsible for it. Houston's Cherokee treaty was never ratified by Texas! Houston, who felt that his own honor was at stake, bent every effort to gain official sanction for his negotiations, but on October 24, 1837, the Texas Senate refused to ratify the treaty.

The Senate's refusal was based on two counts: (1) the treaty was not a legal contract, and (2) the Cherokees themselves had violated it. The Senate reasoned that both signatories to the treaty ("the Provisional Government of Texas on the one part and the Cherokee and their associate bands . . . on the other part") were illegal and fictitious creations, neither of which was capable of making a valid treaty. The Provisional Government could not claim to represent either Texas or Mexico, nor did it own or control any land which it could give to the Indians. On the other side, there was no such organization, group, or Indian community such as "the Cherokee and their associate bands." The Senate report stated further that it had been a deliberate and malicious misrepresentation for the Cherokee chiefs to claim that they represented the twelve bands listed in the treaty. These included such distinct Indian groups as the Delaware, Shawnee, Kickapoo, Alabama, Caddo, and Choctaw.

Having established to its own satisfaction that the treaty was illegal to begin with, the Senate went on to state that there was "*notorious* evidence that part at least of the tribes . . . have been the most savage and ruthless of our frontier enemies ever since and even at the very date of the signing of this Treaty. It is also *notorious* that no part of said tribes have ever been our friends in war." These points were well taken. The Cherokees seem to have remained neutral during the Revolution, but they certainly were neither friends nor allies; and several of the bands specifically listed in the treaty had been violent enemies of the settlers. The Senate therefore resolved to "disapprove of and utterly refuse to ratify the Treaty or any articles thereof."

It has been frequently alleged that the real, but unstated, reason for the nullification of the treaty was the intense desire of the Texans to obtain the lands that had been promised to the Indians. That men coveted the Indian lands, there can be little doubt; but considering the uncounted thousands of acres at their disposal, a contention that the members of the Texas Senate utterly disregarded their sacred honors and were motivated entirely by greed may be seriously questioned. Whether they were right or wrong in what they did, the historian who fails to credit the honest sincerity of the Texans' own statements does himself and posterity a disservice.

In any event, the failure of the treaty of October 1837 had the inevitable result of antagonizing the Cherokees. Houston held several conferences with Chief Bowles, attempting to reassure him; but the Indians grew impatient for confirmation of their land title. The Cherokees influenced, if they did not actually control, other tribes in the region. Their hostility toward the whites spread like a contagion among the red men. By the opening of 1838 virtually all of the bands in East Texas were ready to fight. Into this caldron of dissatisfaction was injected the venom of the war between Mexico and Texas.

As early as the spring of 1837 a party of Mexicans had been detected attempting to induce the frontier tribes to align with them against the Texans. The savages were promised arms and ammunition and were to be permitted to keep all the plunder and prisoners that they might take. Enslavement of white women and children was encouraged. Furthermore, the Mexicans promised the Indians a perpetual title to the lands which they then roamed. It was not known for a certainty that these *provocateurs* were agents of the Mexican nation; they may have been mere brigands intent on plunder, or disaffected Mexicans living within the borders of Texas. Evidence does exist, however, that the government of Mexico once contemplated such a sanguinary scheme to stir up the Indians from the Rio Grande to the Red River against the Texans.

For months persistent rumors reached the Texas government to the effect that Mexican agents were working among the Indians. As the bitterness of the Cherokees and their friends mounted, the task of fomenting warfare on the frontier undoubtedly became easier. With the aid of the Cherokees, the hit-and-run raids might be turned into organized rebellion. At Nacogdoches in the summer of 1838, Vicente Cordova, a cunning Mexican, who had patiently hidden his enmity toward Texas, decided that the time was ripe to strike.

Cordova had lived all, or most, of his life at Nacogdoches. He was thirty-eight years old at the time of the Texas Revolution and a man of intelligence and respectability. He had served Nacogdoches as a member of the *ayuntamiento* and as *alcalde,* and in 1836 he was elected primary judge of the county under the Provisional Government. Even then, while holding the full confidence of the Anglo-American population, he was planning rebellion. At the outbreak of the Texas Revolution in the fall of 1835, he had held a secret meeting of the Mexican population of Nacogdoches in his home and had perfected a small militia organization to attack the Texan volunteers then laying siege to Bexar. In December he reached an agreement with Chief Bowles of the Cherokees to furnish him 1,200 Indians. Before they could march from Nacogdoches, however, he learned of the surrender of General Martín Perfecto de Cós, and temporarily abandoned his plan for uprising. In March of 1836, following the Texas Declaration of Independence, Cordova apparently renewed his alliance with the Cherokees and informed Mexican authorities at Matamoros of his readiness to spring at the Texans' backs. Again before his plans matured, Santa Anna surrendered at San Jacinto, and the Mexican leader again was forced to bide his time. Sometime in the spring of 1838 he received a commission from General Vicente Filisola to enlist the East Texas Indians as auxiliaries to the Mexican army, and he entered into a secret correspondence with Manuel Flores who, it later became evident, was acting as Filisola's special agent to the Texas Indians.

Renewing his alliance with Bowles and the Cherokees, Cordova continued to nurture his plans for rebellion. In August 1838, an uncontrolled outbreak of thefts and murders attributed to his Cherokee allies forced him to reveal his plans. With a combined force of nearly six hundred Indians and Mexicans, he established headquarters on an island in the Angelina River; and in a letter to Houston, he announced the rebellion, promising not to molest the families of the settlers if Texas would not harm the families of his men. While Cordova's behavior throughout the affair seems to have been that of a high-minded Mexican patriot, the Texans were aghast to learn of the perfidy of Chief Bowles who appeared to have been a party to the rebellion during the entire time he was pledged to a treaty of alliance with Texas.

The government lost no time in calling out the militia; the insurgents broke up almost immediately, Cordova fleeing at the head of about one hundred men, and the Indians dispersing onto the prairies. Henry W. Augustine, with about one hundred fifty Texans, pursued Cordova but failed to snare him; Thomas J. Rusk, with the remainder of the Texas army, moved against the Cherokee village. The anticipated battle did not occur. Most of the warriors were gone, but Bowles himself was there. The chief vigorously denied any connection with Cordova or the uprising and claimed that when Cordova came to the village he was unable to secure any assistance except from a few "bad" Indians. According to historian John Henry Brown,

Cordova then went to the Kickapoo village where he successfully enlisted that band in his cause.

An inhuman attack on the Killough family by a force of Mexicans and Kickapoos led to a battle on October 12 between Texans and the motley group then commanded by Flores. The renegades escaped, but meanwhile Rusk had called out the militia again and on October 16, under his command, the Texans fell on an encampment of about nine hundred Indians and Mexicans. Cordova was believed to be in command. After a furious battle of about an hour's duration in which the Mexican-Indian coalition sustained heavy losses, the enemy fled. Cordova and a number of his followers withdrew to Mexico.

The peace was temporary, and the victory a hollow one. The Cordova Rebellion of 1838 was but a prelude to bloodier events of the next year in which the same actors again were to play the leading roles. Indeed, for the next several months, despite the break-up of Cordova's organization, the tempo of Indian attacks in East Texas quickened. Desperately seeking to avoid an all-out war against his friends the Cherokees, whom he believed in the main to be innocent, Houston tried to contain the Indians on the one hand and restrain the settlers on the other by effective use of the Rangers. For the remainder of his term in office, he sought to minimize the conflict. Hoping that time would ease the situation, he delayed taking action.

The year 1838 which had opened so propitiously for Texas was to run a ragged course and close in a fury of dissension. Other than in East Texas, where the Cordova Rebellion had been followed by a rash of depredations, Houston's Indian policy, combined with the alacrity of the Texas Rangers, appeared to meet with some success. Treaties were made and ratified with the Tonkawa, Lipan, Comanche, Keechi, Tawakoni, Waco, and Tawehash Indians. Domestic affairs moved relatively smoothly, though the economy entered a decline which was the natural consequence of the economic panic. The adjourned session of the Second Congress, meeting from April 9 to May 24, produced no vital legislation. But in the area of foreign affairs, the ship of state struggled against alternate waves of success and failure.

In London, a charming but persistent J. Pinckney Henderson continued to press the Texas case for recognition. Before his arrival in October 1837, Parliament had discussed the Texas question; during November and December the Texas minister had paid several calls on Lord Palmerston, the British foreign secretary. Palmerston, won over to at least a partial support of Texas, had presented the matter to the cabinet, and finally, on December 27, the cabinet had denied the Texas petition. Somewhat discouraged, the indefatigable Henderson began making plans to try his success in France; but before leaving England he hit upon an unusual diplomatic tactic.

Once again approaching Palmerston, he suggested an opening of trade between Texas and Great Britain by agreement, not treaty. Such an agreement would be tantamount to recognition, but it would not commit England officially. The details, as worked out, provided that Britain would open her ports to Texas vessels and give ships flying the Lone Star flag the customary clearance at the customs houses, although England would still officially consider Texas as a Mexican province. British port officials would "shut their eyes to the circumstances of [ships'] having Texian papers" according to Henderson. In return, of course, the anxious Texas ports would be opened to the Union Jack and the thriving commerce which it portended. Henderson believed that such trade relations would both bolster the Texas economy and develop a respect for Texas in England. Palmerston approved the rather unusual idea, presenting it to the Board of Trade which finally gave approval in April. Submitted to the Texas government, it was officially proclaimed by President Houston on July 4, 1838. It was a small triumph for Texan diplomacy.

Stimulated by this success, Henderson turned to storm the citadel of France. At first the difficulties were even greater than in England. The French foreign minister, Count Molé, refused even to confer with him as a diplomatic agent for fear the meeting would be interpreted as recognition. France, too, was involved in a claims dispute with Mexico and was at that time pressing hard to force the reluctant Mexican government to settle. With the support of the Earl of Granville, the British minister to France, Henderson arranged an unofficial, social meeting with Molé. The meeting was something of a farce, since Molé spoke no English and Henderson did not yet speak any French. Henderson resorted to a lengthy written explanation of the Texas case which he had translated and sent to Molé shortly thereafter. Several months passed before he could learn whether Molé had read it or not, and he meanwhile observed with interest the development of France's difficulties with Mexico.

Diplomatic relations between the two were suspended in April; in May, France established a blockade of the Mexican coast; and in October, a French fleet entered the harbor at Vera Cruz to present a French ultimatum. Mexico dilly-dallied for a month, but finally refused to negotiate, whereupon, on November 27, the French fleet bombarded and destroyed the supposedly invincible fortress guarding the harbor. Mexico then quickly reopened the discussion, but again refused to come to a settlement; French troops occupied Vera Cruz, and in the ensuing skirmish, Santa Anna, who rushed to lead the people's defense (and to restore his waning prestige), lost a leg. This injury, incidentally, helped him to recapture the popular imagination; and stumping about on a polished wooden leg, he once more became a "hero" and won a second chance to dominate Mexico.

The shooting at Vera Cruz ended the "Pastry War," which derived its name from the fact that one of the French claims was on behalf of a French baker in Vera Cruz whose shop had been looted by Santa Anna's troops. Britain stepped in to mediate the dispute, and Mexico finally agreed to a payment of $600,000 damages to French citizens.

France's negotiations with Mexico had drawn a curtain between Henderson and French officials; the curtain was opened with the advent of the Pastry War. The Texan learned in October that Molé had read his dispatches and had sent a secretary from the French embassy in Washington on an inspection trip to Texas. The inspector was none other than the Count Alphonse de Saligny, who was eventually to become the French ambassador to Texas. A month later, Molé consented to the drafting of a commercial agreement similar to that which Henderson had made with Britain.

While Henderson had impatiently bombarded officials in London and Paris, Memucan Hunt, in Washington, had faithfully danced attendance on the United States state department, and Alcée LaBranche had approached the Texas government on the matter of the brig *Pocket*. LaBranche succeeded in persuading Texas to accept responsibility for the capture of the *Pocket*, which the first Texas navy had overzealously mistaken for a Mexican prize. By written convention, Texas agreed to pay $11,750 to the claimants in the United States.

A second convention between Texas and the United States, relative to the surveying of the northeastern boundary, was negotiated by Hunt in April 1838. It provided for recognition of each nation's land grants in the disputed territory and for the establishment of a joint surveying commission to locate the line. Both conventions were ratified in May and proclaimed by Houston on November 6, 1838. The boundary was surveyed the following year.

Hunt's major efforts suffered a crushing blow when Forsyth refused to discuss the annexation question. In January of 1838, hopelessly discouraged, he had asked to be replaced in Washington; but Texas Secretary of State Robert A. Irion persuaded him to remain at the post. Hunt then suggested that Texas "appear indifferent" to the annexation question, with the hope that the United States would make the next advance. In April the Texas Senate discussed at length the advisability of withdrawing the petition for annexation but, by a slim vote, decided not to disturb the *status quo*. In June, however, a resolution introduced in the United States Congress by Southern members, calling for immediate annexation, was defeated. From June 16 through July 7, during the morning hours of each day's session, John Quincy Adams filibustered against Texas; and Congress ultimately adjourned without action.

Hunt would no longer remain in Washington, and Houston determined to save the dignity of Texas by the "formal and absolute withdrawal" of the annexation petition. Giving Anson Jones these instructions, Houston appointed him as Hunt's successor. From this time on, Jones became one of the central figures in the diplomacy of

Texas, later styling himself in his own memoirs as "The Architect of Annexation."

A native of Massachusetts, Dr. Anson Jones had arrived in Texas in 1833 at the age of thirty-five with a medical degree from Jefferson College in Pennsylvania. His practice thrived in Brazoria and he soon was considered one of the leading citizens of Texas. During the Revolution he enlisted as an infantry private and, although he also served as a surgeon, he fought valorously as an infantryman at the Battle of San Jacinto. In the Senate of the Second Congress it was Jones who had championed the withdrawal of the annexation proposition; so it was not surprising that Houston chose him to succeed Hunt. Jones was a serious, thoughtful man; warmhearted yet austere. His sincerity won him respect and some success in public life; his vanity and a wounded ego were to leave him embittered in his later years.

Upon arriving in Washington in October 1838, Jones made the formal announcement of the withdrawal of the petitions for annexation. Texas was to stand alone as an independent nation. It was a grand gesture, and it gave Texas increased stature in the eyes of many—both detractors and supporters. It certainly facilitated Henderson's negotiations in Europe. But at home in Texas it was viewed with feelings of alarm, suspicion, and regret. Yet most Texans were forced to agree with Hunt that "it would be derogatory to ourselves to insist upon it any longer."

Thus, on this staunch note of pride, Houston's term in office began drawing to a close. The constitution, which assigned a two-year term to the first President (with three-year terms to all subsequent chief executives), also prohibited a President from succeeding himself in office. Houston therefore could not be a candidate in the forthcoming election. With his towering personality out of the race, the high honor was within the reach of many who aspired to it. The election of 1838 promised to be hotly contested, but ended in a macabre runaway.

There were no real issues and, in the long run, only a few candidates. It was to be a contest of personalities, the public and the candidates themselves soon dividing into pro-Houston and anti-Houston forces. Mirabeau B. Lamar, the mercurial Vice-President, placed himself at the head of the opposition to Houston, but for some time carefully avoided an outright announcement of his candidacy. His name had been boomed by friends as early as May of 1837, but Lamar felt that Thomas Jefferson Rusk, should he choose to run, could defeat him, so he waited, watchfully and anxiously.

In the words of John S. Ford, "Rusk was the only man in Texas who could show the shadow of a claim as the peer of Gen. Houston in the esteem, admiration, and love of the people." Rusk was indeed popular. He had the support of the army; he was a hero of the Revolution; and he had won renown as an Indian fighter. Quiet, soft-spoken, and judicious, Rusk was also known as a supporter of Houston.

In December 1837, Lamar finally swallowed his pride and approached Rusk directly to inquire whether he would run. Rusk wrote to Lamar saying that he would not enter the race and added graciously that he would be "pleased, dear sir, to see your name before the people for the office of Chief Magistrate." Whereupon, in January 1838, Lamar formally announced his candidacy—the first hat thrown in the ring.

Houston supporters, led by Francis R. Lubbock, held a meeting in May. Lubbock had come to Texas in 1836 following the Revolution and, after serving as clerk of the House of Representatives, was appointed comptroller at the age of twenty-two. In and out of politics all of his life, Lubbock later served as a Civil War governor of the state, as aide-de-camp to Jefferson Davis, and as state treasurer. Too young himself to be a candidate in the election of 1838, he urged the nomination of Rusk as the spearhead of the pro-Houston party. Houston himself favored Rusk, as did many of the leading men of the Republic.

Urged to run by numerous groups, Rusk steadfastly refused to allow his name to be used. His reasons were that he would not be thirty-five, the age required by the constitution, until after the election; that he was financially embarrassed and could not afford either to run or to serve; and that he had already given his promise to Lamar. His declining of the honor forced the Houston men to cast about hastily for a candidate strong enough to defeat Lamar, whose campaign was gathering strength daily.

Who could it be? Suggestion followed suggestion only to be cast aside. This man was unpolished, that one unlettered, the next unknown. Austin was dead, Wharton was unavailable, and Henderson was in Europe. Henry Smith was too old and too controversial, and Hunt was recovering from ill health. The Houston men turned to Peter W. Grayson.

Grayson, known as one of the old Texans, was a wealthy man who had immigrated to Austin's colony in 1830. An attorney, he had gone with Patrick Jack to secure Austin's release from prison in Mexico in 1834. He had served as Austin's aide-de-camp during the early days of the Revolution but had not actually participated in any of the fighting. He had held the post of attorney general in the *Ad-*

Interim cabinet. Following a fruitless diplomatic mission to the United States with James Collinsworth in the summer of 1836, he had been appointed attorney general of the Republic. When Hunt resigned, Houston had offered the Washington position to Grayson but he had declined, only to accept the job of Texas naval agent in the United States.

Grayson proved to be a poor choice as a candidate. Lamar attacked him as a land speculator and besmirched his reputation for not having fought in the Revolution. Tales of the escapades of a black sheep cousin in Kentucky who bore the same name were circulated as if Grayson were the man involved. Although he was in the United States when the campaign reached the peak of intensity, he may have been disturbed by the attacks. On July 9 he removed himself from the race by committing suicide. He had stopped at Bean's Station in eastern Tennesssee, where he left a note to the innkeeper complaining of melancholia. No other motive for suicide was ever uncovered, although romantics mentioned an unrequited love affair.

When the news reached Texas, the Houston party hastily chose another candidate—James W. Collinsworth. He, too, was an unfortunate choice. The chaos in the Houston camp was evident—Collinsworth was only thirty-two years old and could not have served, even had he won. True, he seemed to be older than he was and he had already had a full career in Texas. Indeed, he was chief justice of the Texas Supreme Court at the time, and probably no one stopped in the headlong rush of finding a candidate to consider that this distinguished jurist was such a youth. In the end, it was not his age but his disposition that barred him from the office. Described by the historian Henderson Yoakum as the victim of a "false habit," Collinsworth appears to have become an alcoholic. A few weeks after his nomination he committed suicide by jumping from a steamboat into Galveston Bay. According to friends he had been under the influence of alcohol for nearly a week prior to his death.

Frantically, but now with little hope of success, the Houston men nominated Robert Wilson, a prominent businessman who had represented Liberty and Harris counties in the First and Second Senates. But Wilson's entry in the race was far too late for an effective campaign; and besides, he was an unpopular candidate. Lamar won by a vote of 6,995 to 252. Lamar's running-mate, Burnet, narrowly defeated two opposing candidates for the vice-presidency.

Because of the circumstances of the election, it may be considered dubious whether Lamar's landslide really represented a repudiation of Houston's policies by the voters. Nevertheless, Lamar chose to interpret the results in this light. His aggressive leadership in the next three years often left Congress and the people trailing far behind. At the next election the voters turned their backs on his administration. But those three years, December 1838 to December 1841, were eventful and exciting and perhaps the most important ones in the Republic's history.

5

1839

LEADERSHIP
BY LAMAR

In MANY RESPECTS the Republic of Texas was like a
dream come true—a romantic utopia developing on the
frontier, heavily endowed with all the natural blessings of
vast amounts of land, fertile soil, beautiful rivers, and good
climate. It beckoned to men of spirit everywhere. The
siren call of danger and opportunity and excitement
reached out and plucked the heartstrings of adventure-
loving men in all walks of life. Rich and poor, erudite
and illiterate, cultured and uncouth—they all responded;
mingling together they created one of the most stimulating
societies the world has ever known.

There was Sam Houston, who epitomized it all. There
was Lamar, the dreamer-poet-soldier. There was Ashbel
Smith, Yale-educated physician, incongruously forced into

[87]

an "affair of honor" by the *code duello*. Even the polished Henderson, at home in the courts of Europe, turned killer in Texas: "I regret that the beast forced me to do that which some ruffian ought to have done, but I shall never regret that I killed him as I am sure he then would have killed me if I had not slain him . . . ." Frontier Texas made subtle distinction between a shooting affray and a killing and between a killing and a murder.

There was Felix Huston seeking military glory, and Thomas Jefferson Green seeking whatever opportunity he could. There was Taylor White, a poverty-stricken illiterate who became Texas's first cattle king and built one of the first Texas-sized fortunes—a sharp contrast to mild mannered James Shaw, heir to an immense estate in Ireland. And there was young Jack Hays and his intrepid, fearless band of Texas Rangers—Tom Lubbock, Ben McCulloch, George Howard, and a score of other bold and reckless souls.

Women, too, found Texas irresistible. Jane Long, the "Mother of Texas"; Angelina Eberly, who defied Sam Houston and resisted an army in the "Archives War" of 1842; and Jane McManus Storm Cazneau, a remarkably independent female whose startling life has almost faded into oblivion. Before coming to Texas for the first time, she was involved in a scandal in the East. Jane came to Texas in 1832—to speculate in land—at the head of a group of German immigrants whom she had rounded up in Europe! Her enterprise and initiative are almost too fantastic to believe. After the failure of her attempt to colonize she returned to the East and became one of the best-known ladies in Washington society. She mingled with the great of the land, and joined a circle of New York-Boston writers. She published occasional pieces in the New York *Sun*, and later became an assistant editor of that paper.

She returned to Texas in 1838 and stayed for about a year, following up this visit with a book, published in 1845, about the Presidents of the Republic of Texas. Lamar dedicated a book of poems to her; a duel was narrowly averted in Matagorda when several of the proper ladies in town refused to invite her to a ball; United States Secretary of State James Buchanan sent her on a secret mission to Mexico in 1847; she was involved in filibustering expeditions to Cuba and Nicaragua; and one man wrote that she had more to do with starting and ending the Mexican War than any other person.

A zestful breed, these bold spirits; they liked to fight, to play, to drink, to gamble, to quarrel, and to court. They loved life and treated it carelessly. The most prosperous businesses in Texas were the grog shops (known euphemistically as "groceries"). The national pastime was gambling—on anything from tossing silver dollars to poker, horse racing, and land speculation. The favorite hobby (besides whittling) was talking—hour-long orations on every possible occasion and wonderful, tall tales which earmarked Texas forever. The men roared with boisterous laughter at themselves, at each other, and especially at timid newcomers; and they filled their leisure hours with skillfully plotted (if somewhat unrefined) practical jokes.

The riotous essence of all this marked President Lamar's inauguration on December 1, 1838. A day of drinking and gambling, a shooting affray, and uncounted street brawls were climaxed by a grand ball that night. "To the ladies, God bless them, they expect us at a ball tonight, and require every man to keep himself in condition for duty." The inaugural ceremony itself was turned into one of the greatest practical jokes of the time. Sam Houston knew that the incoming President had labored long to make his inaugural address a literary masterpiece. He determined to steal the show from him. Dressed in knee breeches and a powdered wig, the very picture of George Washington and the only person at the ceremony in costume, Houston interrupted the proceedings to make a "few" farewell remarks before Lamar was introduced. It was a parody on the famous "Farewell Address." Houston talked for three hours. Tall stories, gross innuendoes, and bucolic jokes were intermingled with an elaborately exaggerated defense of his own administration. The delighted audience grinned and smiled and roared with laughter. Lamar squirmed discomfitedly on the platform, exasperation growing as the minutes turned to an hour and the hours

Sam Houston

Mirabeau B. Lamar

stretched to three. By the time Houston finished, Lamar was literally too sick with frustration and nervousness to deliver his own address. He passed it to a friend who, never having seen it before, read it in a dull monotone. The old chief and half the audience were gone before he finished.

Houston had won the day—but Lamar still had the presidency. His message to Congress on December 21 set the tone for three years of tumultuous government. He challenged the legislators to be vigorous—the key word of his administration despite his personal illness. (Lamar's health was failing when he came to Texas; he was sick on several occasions while in the presidency, once being incapacitated for nearly three months.) The initial message was long and Lamar touched on many aspects of the Republic's future. He spoke of frontier defense, the Cherokee Indians, the army, the navy, and the eternal problem of finance. He dwelt at length on the creation of a National Bank of Texas to be modelled somewhat after the old Bank of the United States. Foreign policy and domestic problems were surveyed, and it was in this message that he urged the establishment of a system of public education crowned with a university. A portion of these words has become immortal: "It is admitted by all, that a cultivated mind is the guardian genius of Democracy, and while guided and controlled by virtue, the noblest attribute of man. It is the only dictator that freemen acknowledge, and the only security which freemen desire."

Congress responded to the challenge with some of the most significant legislation of the Republic period. This was the Third Congress, newly seated by the general elections of the previous fall, although most were old members. Highlighting Lamar's program was the education bill which granted three leagues of land to each county in the Republic to be used in support of the public schools and endowed two future universities with fifty leagues, all of which was to be located and surveyed in the vacant public domain. The county school land might or might not be located in the county to which it belonged. The university land was located in Central Texas, but the pressure of settlement there later caused the state legislature to substitute acreage in West Texas, where the discovery of oil in the twentieth century resulted in the enrichment of the University Fund. The original provision calling for two universities was subsequently abandoned, and the endowment went to the school later established at Austin.

This act, signed by Lamar on January 26, 1839, is the foundation of all state-supported education in Texas, its effectiveness having been multiplied and implemented by additional legislation in the years that followed.

Of almost equal social significance was the Homestead Act, passed on the same day. It provided that every head of a family could hold, free from any financial judgment or execution, his homestead (fifty acres or one town lot with certain improvements thereon), his beasts of burden, his basic household goods, and the tools of his profession. This meant, of course, that no matter how indebted a man might become, no court could enforce the foreclosure of such minimum property; it protected, especially, those persons who had suffered in the Panic of 1837. This humane legislation was largely the creation of the Third Congress, although it had roots in an earlier decree of Coahuila and Texas and in a suggestion made by Stephen F. Austin. The law, through extensions and modifications, continues in force to the present time.

Other domestic legislation of Lamar's Congress included the establishment of a state library, the creation of a patent office, a naval survey of the bays and harbors of the coast, and the construction of a military road to run along the frontier from Red River to the Rio Grande.

Such measures as these and others similar to them were expensive. In the area of finances, Lamar proved to be an extravagant spender before his administration closed. At the outset, however, he and Congress concerned themselves with the problem of revenue. One of the most far-reaching acts, unbeknown to its framers at the time, pledged the revenue of the customs houses to support the payment of the bond issue, few of which had yet been sold. It was this that provided a basis for the future Texas claims declaring that since the United States took over the collection of customs after annexation, it also must assume the bonded obligation.

The poor sale of the bonds, the rapid decrease in acceptance of the promissory notes, and the almost complete lack of money of any kind, all persuaded Congress to take another disastrous step into the inferno of paper money. By acts of November 16, 1838, and January 19, 1839, the President was authorized to issue a new form of non-interest bearing promissory notes, at first limited to a total issue of $100,000 but later extended whenever specific appropriations were made. Between January 1839 and September 1840 Lamar's administration issued the fantastic amount of $2,780,361 in denominations of one, five, ten, twenty, one hundred, and five hundred dollars. Within a few months after their issue the notes began circulating for as low as fifteen and twenty cents on the dollar, and by the end of 1840 their value utterly collapsed. These bills were engraved (not printed as formerly) and, like their predecessors, had to be signed by the President. The earlier notes, or "old issue," were called Star Money because of a small star imprinted on the face; those of Lamar's administration, the "new issue," quickly became known as Redbacks for the logical reason that the back side was engraved in red ink. A third type of paper money, introduced by Houston's government and proliferated by Lamar's, was called 'Change Notes because the issue was in denominations of one, two, and three dollars; and these could be exchanged at the Treasury for the large denominations of Star Money and Redbacks. Houston had issued $10,000 in 'Change Notes; Lamar was to issue $150,000.

The Third Congress also incorporated a number of cities; chartered several businesses and another private university; passed a score or more relief laws for individuals (including the legitimatizing of certain children born before the matrimonial legislation of 1836); created new counties; revised the judicial system; improved the postal service; and, in the last act of the session, provided the death sentence for horse thieves and their accomplices.

In the area of frontier defense Congress was so anxious to act that no less than a dozen acts were passed for the same purpose. Eight companies of volunteers were authorized and three companies of militia were activated. Edward Burleson, an old Texan, Indian fighter, and hero of the siege of Bexar, was enjoined to raise a regiment of cavalry. One million dollars was appropriated to pay for a grand scheme of protection against the raiding Indians. A cordon of eight military posts was to be established along the frontier from the Red River to the Nueces, and detachments of mounted men were to be stationed at each. Settlers around these posts were to be given quarter-section homesteads, and the law optimistically authorized the erection of sixteen trading posts for the Indians. The whole structure came practically to naught. Perhaps the main reason was the fact that there were not enough men willing to volunteer for the Indian service to fill out the elaborate organization. It was not that Texans were unwilling to fight the Indians—they simply were unwilling to "join up" to do it. The three militia companies were put in the field, but only one of the eight volunteer companies completed organization. Burleson was able to recruit but a slim cadre of officers. Once again, the most effective frontier defense came from the Rangers, a company of fifty-six men being authorized by Congress.

In February, less than one month after Congress adjourned, the illustrious Indian fighter John Henry Moore led three companies on a major campaign against marauding Comanches on the upper Colorado. Then forty years old, Moore was perhaps the most experienced man in Texas in Indian warfare. He had settled in Texas in 1821 and had led expeditions into the Indian country in 1823 and 1824. At the site of present La Grange he had built a blockhouse fort, known as Moore's Fort, for the protection of settlers in the area. He had commanded attacks on the Waco in 1834 and the Tawakoni in 1835. It was he who assumed command of the Texan volunteers at Gonzales in the first battle of the Texas Revolution, and he is credited with designing the famous banner: "Come and Take It."

Moore, with his vast experience, was the type of leader whom men were willing to follow. Comanche raids of the previous months had convinced the settlers of the necessity for a punitive expedition against a principal village believed to be located on the upper Colorado. Moore and his men reached the encampment on February 14 and crept within a few hundred yards of the sleeping Indians under the cover of darkness. The Indians' horse herd was stampeded, and at daybreak Moore ordered a charge. Furious fighting at close range lasted for several hours. The Texan force of eighty men, including sixteen Lipan scouts, was hopelessly outnumbered by an estimated five to six hundred Comanches. After the advantage of surprise was dissipated, Moore decided to withdraw. The Indian losses were heavy, while the Texans had but one killed and six wounded.

Such expeditions as these had the principal effect of convincing the savages that the settlers were able and willing to strike back. The expeditions also eased the mounting, hopeless fury of the settler who lived in constant dread that his homestead might be the next to be cruelly ravished by the Indians. Of course, the sword cut both ways; after one of these raids the Indians talked for weeks about revenge, and there frequently followed a new rash of depredations.

Of greater consequence, perhaps, than Moore's fight on the Colorado was the campaign which began in March against a combined force of Indians and Mexicans and ended in May with the defeat of Vicente Cordova and Manuel Flores. Cordova, whose uprising near Nacogdoches had been dispersed, had taken refuge in the prairies of the upper Trinity. In March 1839, he decided to contact personally the Mexican leaders at Matamoros—principally Flores, the Indian agent, and General Valentin Canalizo, the commander. With a small force of seventy-five, including Mexicans, Negroes, and Indians, he moved south, hugging the outer fringe of the frontier line. On March 27, his camp in the hills near present Austin was discovered by scouts of General Burleson's command at Bastrop. Gathering about eighty volunteers, Burleson raced to catch the refugee, overtaking him two days later near present Seguin. Cordova offered a disciplined resistance which, after several hours, Burleson penetrated by a furious charge. Cordova lost approximately twenty-five men but fled safely with the remainder of his force.

Captain Matthew Caldwell, in command of a company of Rangers at Gonzales, learned of the fight and rushed to the scene in time to lead a pursuit of the Mexicans. It was a wild chase, Cordova having gained nearly twenty miles before Caldwell got on the trail. Across the Guadalupe, through the hills west of San Antonio, over the brush country to the old Rio Grande road they raced, Caldwell unable to gain. Men and horses grew hungry and fatigued. Finally the short rest stops grew longer, and a temporary camp was made. Both pursuer and pursued suffered. A hundred odd miles southwest of San Antonio, Caldwell, who had started without provisions, gave up. Cordova ultimately reached Matamoros but was to return to fight in Texas again in 1842.

Meanwhile, Manuel Flores, with whom Cordova had been in correspondence, had set out from Matamoros to contact him. Unaware of the fight on the Guadalupe and Cordova's flight, Flores, with a mixed band of Indians and Mexicans, proceeded north toward the Trinity. On the Colorado, not far from present Austin, the band was sighted by Lieutenant James O. Rice and a detachment of Rangers. Rice followed Flores for two days, waiting for a propitious time to attack. Finally, on the North San Gabriel, he charged the enemy camp, killing Flores in the first fire. The Mexican's party scattered, abandoning their bags and equipment. Among the baggage was found the correspondence between Cordova and the Mexican leaders, as well as instructions to both Flores and Cordova.

In the documents, the whole plot from the beginning of the Cordova Rebellion in the summer of 1838 was brought to light. One of the letters was addressed to the Cherokee Indians, reassuring them of the peaceful possession of their lands if they would cooperate with the Mexican agents. To Texans at the time, this correspondence was positive proof of the Cherokee duplicity; to an unprejudiced eye looking for the truth, the documents are ambiguous; to a majority of twentieth century romantics, the probability of Cherokee treachery is lightly dismissed. But frontier Texans were neither romantic nor unprejudiced where the Indians were concerned. Lamar determined to act.

Even before the revealing correspondence was discovered, Lamar had taken a firm stand. In his message to Congress he had adhered to the reasoning of the 1837 Senate, over which he had presided. He also pointed out the utter impossibility of the continued existence of the Cherokee tribe as a separate and independent government within the boundaries of Texas. With pretensions of sovereignty, Bowles and the other Cherokee leaders referred to their people as the Cherokee Nation. The question of land titles was one thing, but that an independent and alien nation should exist within the Republic, Lamar announced, was a "monstrous political anomaly." Even had the Cherokee treaty been legally introduced and ratified, Lamar believed that "this government is now wholly absolved from the performance of its conditions, by the notorious and habitual violation of its principal stipulations by the Indians."

Albert Sidney Johnston, secretary of war, informed Chief Bowles on April 10 that the government was convinced of his duplicity. Cherokee Indians and their allies were definitely known to be fighting with Cordova, and General Johnston believed that Bowles' assertion that he had driven Cordova from the Cherokee village was merely a ruse to gain time for Cordova to get to Mexico. Shortly thereafter, Johnston ordered Major B. C. Waters to erect a military post on Grand Saline Creek within the territory claimed by the Cherokees. Trouble followed immediately.

Bowles called out his warriors, surrounded Major Waters and his small detachment, and forced the Texans to leave. Lamar reprimanded the Indians severely, charging Bowles with fomenting much of the unrest. "You and your people have held repeated correspondence with our enemies; have received and cherished their emissaries among you; and have entered into belligerent compacts with them; and have given countenance to an insurrection raised in your own vicinity . . . . Professing friendship yet in constant collusion with our foes, you cry peace, peace, when every action betrays a secret disposition to hostility. Your village has been the chief point where our enemies have met. . . ."

About the end of May, the documents found on the Flores party reached Johnston and Lamar. They decided upon the immediate removal of the Cherokees from East Texas. Supported by a force of about five hundred militiamen under General Kelsey Douglas, Johnston and Vice-President Burnet went to the Cherokee village on July 12 with an offer to buy the Indians' crops and livestock and to pay the costs of their move to the Indian Territory of the United States.

According to the Texas commissioners, Bowles agreed that the Cherokees were interlopers and agreed to rejoin the main body of the Cherokee tribes in the United States. On first one pretext and then another, however, he delayed concluding the removal agreement. Meantime he secretly mobilized his forces. Fighting broke out on July 15, and that afternoon the Indians were defeated in a hard fight on the Neches. The Cherokee War, which was to end disastrously for the Indians, had begun.

Bowles and his men retreated. The following day, near

the headwaters of the Neches River, another battle ensued in which Bowles himself was killed. A third skirmish occurred near present Grand Saline, before the Cherokee power was totally broken. Most of the Indians scurried across Red River; a small band under John Bowles, son of the old chieftain, attempted to reach Mexico but it was intercepted by General Burleson on December 25, 1839.

Thus, with hatred and misunderstanding, bloodshed and death, the Cherokee problem was resolved. Recently there has been a tendency to defend the Indians and to belittle actions of the settlers. This tendency has resulted in a warped and unfair portrayal of the role of the Texas government, whose actions, whether just or merely justified, were at least sincere.

Even while the frontier was ablaze with bloodshed and destruction, a bold plan to build Texas' capital city on the westward edge of civilization reached fruition. The original commission, invested with the responsibility of locating the seat of government, had selected a site near La Grange; but its action was rejected by Houston and Congress in 1838. Another five-man commission was created by the Third Congress on June 14, 1839, with instructions to locate a site, to be named for Stephen F. Austin, somewhere in the western part of the Republic.

Strongly influenced by Lamar, the commission almost precipitately chose a location on the Colorado just above the little frontier settlement of Waterloo. According to well-founded tradition, Lamar himself had picked this site when on a buffalo hunt the year before. Judge A. W. Terrell wrote that Lamar then stood on the very hill where the present capitol now stands and "while looking from that hill on the valley covered with wild rye,—the moun-

Double Log Cabin

tains up the river, and the charming view to the south, remarked, 'This should be the seat of future Empire.'"

Within weeks after the commissioners had designated the site, surveyors laid out a town facing the Colorado River between Waller and Shoal creeks. Early in May Edwin Waller arrived with a gang of workmen to begin the construction of the government buildings. For use through the summer, a tent camp was pitched west of present Congress Avenue near a beautiful spring. Much haste was necessary to get the buildings completed in time for Congress to assemble in November.

Most of the buildings in town were made of hewn logs cut from a post oak forest a few miles north of the river, but a saw mill in the "Lost Pines" near Bastrop provided the planks and dimension lumber needed for the more elaborate structures such as the President's mansion and the temporary capitol. The temporary capitol was located west of Congress Avenue, facing east. It had a simple floor plan: Senate room on the north, House on the south, broad entrance hall and committee rooms between. To the east, on Congress Avenue, was a separate building for the Supreme Court. Also on the avenue, a double log house was built to serve as an office for the President. At its rear, a story and a half high, stood the Land Office Building. Three double log houses on the next block were built for the war department and the adjutant general. Across the street, similar structures were erected for the state and navy departments. The treasury department was to be housed in a large frame building south of these. On a rise of ground one block east, the President's mansion, a two-story plank edifice, seemed more pretentious than it was.

Austin was the most exposed settlement in the Republic—an insane place to build a capital, said Lamar's enemies. But despite the Indian danger, scores of immigrants flocked in during the summer. On August 1, the government held an auction of town lots and almost all were immediately sold. Log cabins began to dot the hillsides; and in the heart of town, on Congress Avenue, a large two-story hotel (Bullock's) was erected, the first floor of which was built of logs, the second of cottonwood planks.

The log houses of the first residents, like log houses all over Texas, were of two standard forms: one room with a lean-to; or the double cabin style. Actually, a double log house was simply two single log cabins standing side by side and covered with the same roof. Frequently called dog-runs, these double log houses had an unusual natural grace, especially in the wooded hills of Austin. The broad, roofed passage between the two houses was always the coolest place to escape the heat of the summer and not unnaturally, it was there that the family dogs collected— hence the name. The amount of work involved in building such structures varied greatly, depending on how carefully the corner notches were cut and whether the logs were hewn for a good straight fit. Although unhewn pine was used in many parts of Texas, most of the houses in Austin were of post oak, hewn on all four sides to a square shape. Because of the haste to complete the buildings, the logs were not allowed to season through the winter, and the result was considerable shrinkage and warpage. The cracks between logs were filled with mud or plaster, frequently mixed with straw. Shakes riven from white oak made the best roofs, but many of the Austin houses were covered with cedar shakes and some with pine and post oak.

Rising as it did in such a beautiful natural setting in the wilderness, Austin must have been an impressive and inspiring sight. It was the result of a dream rather than a speculative promotion—built by the government, rather than by private enterprise. By the fall of 1839, the town was ready to receive the government; the population was then estimated at seven hundred. On October 17, President Lamar arrived with an official cavalcade. At its head rode Albert Sidney Johnston, followed by the rest of the cabinet and the government clerks. Forty wagon loads of furniture, books, paper, and the archives and records of the government trailed behind. That night a gala celebration, complete with toasts and oratory, was held at Bullock's Hotel. Austin was a proud city!

The year 1839 not only witnessed the impressive legislative program, the solution of the Cherokee problem (for better or for worse), and the creation of a capital city; it also saw the Republic achieve increased status abroad. In June, Lamar appointed James Hamilton of South Carolina as a special commissioner to sell the so far unsuccessful five million dollar bond issue in Europe. Little luck attended his efforts, but in pursuit of the goal, he was able to coax further recognition of the Republic of Texas from among the nations of Europe.

Hamilton was a prominent man of affairs. Educated in New England as a lawyer, he was elected governor of South Carolina in 1830 and was a principal leader in the nullification controversy there. A growing interest in Texas led him to give financial support to the Texas Revolution, and it was to him that Houston offered the command of the Texas army in 1837. Personal affairs—and perhaps a wise foresight—forced him to decline; but after Lamar's election, he agreed to help Texas secure the elusive "Five Million Dollar Loan," as the Texans called their bond issue. Hamilton and Lamar had long been friends; the older man, fifty-three at the time of Lamar's inauguration, exerted considerable influence on the Texas President. It was Hamilton's suggestion, actually, that precipitated the effort to sell the bonds to European governments.

His approach had much logic: the withdrawal of the annexation petition signalled Texas' determination to stand alone; it would be to the benefit of most of Europe to develop a strong independent state in North America as something of a counterbalance to growing United States power; and furthermore, the prospects of trade with an independent Texas should prove alluring. If the governments of Europe would buy the Texas bonds, reasoned Hamilton, then they would make a sound investment and at the same time assist in guaranteeing the future of a new Republic.

There was good reason for Lamar and Congress to be optimistic of Hamilton's success. Not only was the argument reasonable, but Hamilton himself had previously negotiated a similar foreign loan for his native South Carolina. As one-time president and director of the Bank of South Carolina, Hamilton's experience in financial matters probably exceeded that of any one person then in

Texas. He met with Lamar and Congress in the spring of 1839, when the details of his part in the loan were framed. He was allowed ten percent commission, which would yield him a gross profit of one-half million dollars if all the bonds were sold. He was to work in conjunction with A. T. Burnley, a Virginian, who had been appointed by Houston. By 1850, Texas' indebtedness to Hamilton had reached $210,000 in gold, the larger part of this representing money which he had laid out of his own purse in order to advance the Texas cause. Texas' failure to settle promptly caused him financial embarrassment and finally indirectly brought about his death in 1857 when, on his way to make an adjustment of the debt, his ship sank in the Gulf of Mexico. It is a reflection of the man's character that, when the ship was going down, he gave his life preserver to save a woman and child.

It was this man—aristocratic, suave, and experienced—who became the chief Texas representative in Europe. On his way to Europe he stopped in Philadelphia to visit his old friend Nicholas Biddle. Biddle was president of the Bank of the United States which, although it had lost its charter in 1836, was still the most powerful financial institution in the country. Despite the fact that the earlier loan commissioners had failed completely to interest United States investors, Hamilton hoped that Biddle at least would support his forthcoming negotiations on the European money markets. And he resolved to do his best to persuade Biddle to make a loan to Texas himself. Somewhat to his surprise, he was successful in both.

Biddle respected Hamilton and could see the logic in his approach to European investors. After difficult and involved arrangements were completed, Hamilton exchanged $400,000 in Texas bonds for bank notes (not specie). The notes had to be discounted seven and one-half percent at New Orleans, but it was a great boost to Texas. For Hamilton it was a major triumph; and for Biddle a risky speculation, since it remained questionable whether Texas would ever be able to refund the bonds. Elated by this success, Hamilton continued to Europe, stopping a few weeks in London to renew old acquaintances before going on to Paris.

The previous month the new French foreign minister, the Duke of Dalmatia, had invited Henderson to a dinner and had reopened the discussion of formal recognition of Texas. Saligny's report on Texas had been received by the foreign office and was decidedly favorable. (Close observers said that Saligny recommended Texas because he wanted the job of minister there in order to advance his own fortune while in the diplomatic corps of France—the allegation was probably true.) In the ensuing weeks, Henderson labored to work out a treaty which would be acceptable to France and favorable to Texas. Just when action was expected, word reached the French that Hamilton was coming with instructions to make greater concessions than Henderson was willing to grant. Negotiations virtually halted until Hamilton arrived.

Since the South Carolinian was interested in selling the bonds to the French government, he advised Henderson to make the concessions which France desired—especially in regard to the cotton trade—in order to expedite the treaty. Negotiations were concluded in September, and on September 25 the Treaty of Amity, Navigation and Commerce Between France and Texas was signed by the diplomats. Ratification by both governments followed promptly, and thus France became the first European nation to recognize Texas, the treaty being the first formal, fully ratified one that Texas was a party to. Most of the terms of the treaty dealt with commerce, granting certain values to the goods of each country. France made an exceptional concession in her acceptance of Texas merchant ships, which were neither built in Texas nor predominantly manned by Texas citizens. To Hamilton, as well as to most Texans, the significant aspect was recognition and the exchange of ministers.

Henderson, whose private life in France had been touched by romance, resigned his post to marry Frances Cox, a Philadelphia girl whom he had met in Paris. The wedding ceremony was held in London in October and, after a short honeymoon, he and his bride left for Texas, reaching there in January 1840. Hamilton, too, returned to Texas to secure from Congress a modification of the bond issue, which he deemed essential to its success in the depressed money markets in Europe. Both Henderson and Hamilton were given warm welcomes. Henderson proceeded to San Augustine to establish a law practice; Hamilton went to the new capital of Austin where he found the Fourth Congress in session. His victory in Philadelphia, together with Congress' pressing need for funds, guaranteed the enthusiastic passage of the changes he desired.

Meanwhile, somewhat more interesting affairs were afoot south of the Rio Grande. Stripped to the barest essentials, the fate of the Republic largely depended upon securing from Mexico the recognition of its independence. This one matter was the key to further recognition in Europe, the successful sale of the bonds and consequent financing of the government, and the ultimate annexation of Texas to the United States. The efforts to achieve Mexican recognition entangled the Republic in the confused hodge-podge of Mexican politics for several years, beginning shortly after Lamar took office. During the imbroglio between Mexico and France, Lamar had sensed that the time might be opportune to open negotiations with the Mexican government. As the affair of the Pastry War reached its climax in the disgrace at Vera Cruz, the Bustamante party in Mexico crashed from the zenith to which it had climbed following Santa Anna's capture at San Jacinto. Now returned to popularity as the hero of Vera Cruz, and stumping about proudly on his wooden leg, Santa Anna rose rapidly back to power. In March 1839, he was again vested with the chief executive authority of the nation.

Believing the situation favorable, Lamar appointed Barnard E. Bee as special agent to Mexico, with instructions to attempt to secure recognition and to make a treaty of peace. He was supplied with two official commissions: one as special agent and the other as diplomatic envoy, should Mexico formally receive him. At the same time, the Texan *chargé d'affaires* in Washington was instructed to urge the United States to mediate the negotiations.

Bee, who was Lamar's secretary of state at the time, was a native of South Carolina. He had joined the Texas Revolution in time to serve in the *Ad Interim* cabinet and later he became Houston's secretary of war. It was Bee who had accompanied Santa Anna on the Mexican's leisurely trip from Texas to Washington to intervene on Texas' behalf with Andrew Jackson. Certainly, Bee was a logical choice to remind Santa Anna of his promise to recognize Texas.

Bee was to demand unconditional recognition, but if Santa Anna demurred on the Rio Grande boundary, Bee was authorized to offer up to five million dollars to purchase the land. Richard Dunlap, in charge of the Washington negotiations, was given similar instructions. He broached the matter to John Forsyth who, after consulting the Mexican minister to the United States, agreed that Powhatan Ellis could act as mediator. Ellis had returned to Mexico in the spring of 1839 to re-open the United States embassy. Bee discovered on his way through New Orleans that the British might also be enlisted to aid in the negotiations.

Since Texas was willing to pay five million dollars to establish the boundary, the wily British saw a chance to redeem the worthless Mexican bonds which they held. The proposition was that British bondholders would accept territory in Texas worth five million dollars and at the same time Mexico would accept the Texas money. By this imaginative solution, Mexico would gain the Texas money and rid herself of the British problem; Britain would solve the claims question; and Texas would gain its recognition and its boundary (although it would ultimately cost her ten instead of five million dollars—five million in land and five million in bonds). The details of this happy arrangement may have been worked out by James Hamilton who was with Bee in New Orleans and from whom intricate ideas seemed to flow unceasingly.

In any event, Colonel Bee began his mission with every hope of success, arriving at Vera Cruz on May 8, 1839. He was received courteously by the post commandant—but as an individual, not as a foreign envoy. A statement of the purpose of his visit was requested; and when it was made known, the government absolutely refused to meet with him. Bee could not believe that Santa Anna would so utterly reject his pledge to Texas. He wrote home: "We must give him more time—at this moment he does not dare take a move openly in favor of Texas. He is playing a great game." Recognition from Santa Anna could be anticipated when once again he was "firmly seated as Emperor," Bee added.

Bee's opinion was strengthened by the appearance in Vera Cruz of an Italian named John Vitalpa, who claimed to be a secret agent of Santa Anna. Vitalpa's proposal involved great secrecy as well as the transfer of money directly to Santa Anna. Bee was not so fatuous as to agree, although he felt that this brightened the prospect of future negotiation. On June 1, believing he could accomplish no more, Bee returned to New Orleans accompanied by Vitalpa, who continued to importune him.

Intrigue piled upon intrigue. Vitalpa had been in correspondence with James Treat, a soldier of fortune who had lived much of his life in South America and who had spent seven years in Mexico City during Santa Anna's first rise to power. Treat was also associated with a group of land speculators in New York who had invested in Texas property, and he was in correspondence with James Morgan, one of the promoters of Galveston.

Through Morgan, Treat proposed that he could take up the Texas mission where Bee had left it, acting in secret as an old friend of Santa Anna. Treat was certain that his scheme would meet with success. In New York, in June 1839, Treat met James Hamilton, who was on his way to Europe. Hamilton was impressed with Treat as a person of high moral character, and with his plan. Hamilton wrote to Lamar, urging that Treat be made a secret agent and an assistant to Bee. With this encouragement, Treat headed for New Orleans where he met Bee and Vitalpa upon their arrival from Vera Cruz.

Treat made as strong and as favorable an impression on Bee as he had on Hamilton, and Bee quickly fell in with the plan, adding his own recommendation that the negotiations be handled as Treat suggested. Of course, the basis of Treat's idea was that a secret agent with good contacts in Mexico such as he enjoyed could succeed—through the discreet use of the traditional *mordido,* the well-established Mexican custom of oiling the machinery of government by making a gift to certain officials. The process would cost between a half-million and a million dollars, but this could be deducted from the five million dollars which Texas was already prepared to pay.

With Bee's enthusiastic endorsement, Treat went to Austin in July. Lamar, like the other Texans, was charmed by Treat's manner and was quickly sold on the scheme. Treat, after being appointed secret agent on August 9, headed for Vera Cruz via Philadelphia and New York. To support his plan he had to have cash, obtainable by Texas only through the Philadelphia bank from which Hamilton had negotiated the loan. It was not until October that he sailed from New York, arriving in Mexico in late November. There he found that the kaleidoscope of Mexican politics had taken another spin: Santa Anna had relinquished his position to Bustamante—and a major federalist uprising against the centralists was blossoming in northern Mexico.

This movement had started a year earlier with the development of a federalist army under Antonio Canales. Canales had appealed to Lamar for support, even sending a quasi-envoy in the person of General Juan Pablo Anaya to the Texas capital. Texans were certainly sympathetic to the federalist movement because it was this group that supported the Mexican Constitution of 1824 and had fought against the centralist dictatorship since before the Texas Revolution. In fact, the uprising in Texas had the same origin as the one which now burgeoned in the northern provinces. Lamar was friendly, but officially neutral. It was something of a dilemma. If the federalists were able to return to power in Mexico, an alliance with them now would insure recognition; but if they failed, such an alliance would render useless the Bee-Treat mission and would postpone indefinitely the hope of Mexican recognition.

Although the government was neutral, General Canales himself crossed over into Texas during the summer to urge the Texans to join him. He enlisted nearly two hundred adventurous men in his army. These Texans, under Samuel W. Jordan and Reuben Ross, fought at Matamoros and at Mier. Ross and about fifty men then returned to Texas, but Jordan and the remainder plunged on into the interior to continue fighting with Canales. Jordan was a daredevil adventurer whose persistent loyalty to the federalist cause during the ensuing year may have been motivated largely by a hope for plunder. (In 1841 he was to attempt to join a centralist expedition to put down a federalist uprising in Yucatan.) On October 3, he and his men distinguished themselves at the Battle of Alcantra by overwhelmingly defeating a centralist army. Flushed with success, Canales and his Texan allies invaded Monterrey, which they nearly succeeded in taking during heavy fighting from December 23 through December 27. Like wildfire, the rumor spread through Mexico that Texas was allied with the federalist insurgents and that the Texans were invading Mexico. Centralist generals responded bombastically by proposing a campaign for the reconquest of Texas. Entreated by letters from Hamilton and alarmed that the Treat mission might suffer, Lamar issued a formal proclamation of neutrality on December 12, 1839.

Thus matters hung at the end of the year. It had been a busy twelve months which encompassed the Cherokee War, the building of a new capital, the treaty with France, and the negotiations with Mexico. The Fourth Congress, which assembled in November 1839, could only view with abject dismay the economic chaos left by Lamar's first year in office. Civil expenses had jumped from $192,000 in 1838 to $555,000 in 1839; and military expense from $881,000 to $1,523,445. Furthermore, Lamar and the Third Congress had blithely issued paper money (Redbacks) totalling nearly twice the face amount of the appropriations. The excess amount was due to the rapid depreciation of the Redbacks. The nation looked to the next year with an optimism born of desperation, but the hope for better times was unfulfilled—the year ahead was to be one of the hardest in the Republic's history.

6

1840

HOPE UNFULFILLED

A TRUER PERSPECTIVE of Lamar's landslide in the election of 1838 unfolded in the congressional elections of 1839. The Lamar victory had not been due so much to a rejection of Sam Houston or even to a fondness for Lamar as to the utter disintegration of the opposition party caused by the disastrous demise of their candidates. The Houston party had only been dormant; it rose from the grave to which Lamar's friends had so volubly consigned it to smite the administration a mighty blow. Ample fuel for the campaign of 1839 was found in the extravagance of the government during the past year, but in Houston's opinion, the major issue should have been Lamar's treatment of the Cherokees. On this question, however, most of the nation stood with Lamar. After all, rejection of the pact which Houston made with his Indian brothers had begun much earlier, and almost the entire citizenry now was indignant over the late Chief Bowles' complicity with Cordova, Flores, and others. Lamar's friends believed this would "knock old Sam out of the next Presidency"; Houston's supporters believed that "there exists no difference between the people of this County and Gen H. except the Cherokee question. . . ."

The General himself was absent from Texas at election time, courting Margaret Lea and visiting his old advisor Andrew Jackson. He was nevertheless sent to the Fourth Congress by his neighbors in San Augustine County. Into the House with Houston went thirty new members, most of them anti-Lamar. Fewer than a dozen of the strong Lamar faction were returned by their constituents to Congress. Friction between the executive and legislative branches was easy to predict.

Riding to Austin for the opening of Congress, Houston followed a route from San Augustine to Nacogdoches and then through the former lands of the Cherokees. He viewed with anger and sorrow the devastation of the Cherokee villages and the destruction of their fields. In a speech at Nacogdoches he bitterly denounced the war. Shortly after Congress assembled he grimly castigated the government for treating the Cherokees with "duplicity and fraud" and for driving them from Texas "unjustifiably," making an able defense of the Cherokees' position. Subsequently (whether in respect or in irony is not known), Houston was presented with Chief Bowles' black hat, rent by the bullet which had killed the old Indian leader. Houston exploded in indignant wrath. For an hour and a half he verbally flailed the Congress, the administration, the land-hungry speculators, and especially Vice-President Burnet, whom he accused of having private interests which would benefit from the expulsion of the Cherokees. Houston's behavior, according to a contemporary editorial, "excited the grief and shame of his friends, and the just reproach and scorn of his enemies."

There was little question of the former President's animosity toward the administration. What had been a jocular attack to save political face in 1838 was transformed into a determined and embittered personal battle in 1839. At every opportunity Houston now leaped to his feet to oppose the administration or to heap contempt and ridicule—his most effective weapon—on Lamar and Burnet. With consummate political skill, he introduced the famous Cherokee Land Bill, which provided for the survey and sale of the desirable Cherokee lands. Revenue from the sale would go far to alleviate the distressed treasury department, and the prompt disposal of the lands would please those who supported the extermination of the Indians, whether from avaricious motives or not.

Thus Houston's bill adroitly derived support from the followers of administration policy and was, on the surface, a seeming capitulation to the inevitable. It passed both houses and was approved by Lamar himself on February 1, 1840. Beneath the surface, however, the bill was a scathing condemnation of the Cherokee affair because implicit in its terms was a subtle admission that the Republic had obtained its rights and title to the disputed Indian lands by force, in the Cherokee War. The point dealt with the ownership of those lands for the years between 1821 and 1839. If the Cherokees did not own them—as the government of Texas had claimed—then the lands had been a part of the public domain during that time, and the government would have to recognize the legality of a number of headright and bounty locations which had been made in the area. But, if the Cherokees' title was valid, then those locations would have been illegally made; the Republic would have acquired the Cherokee lands intact in 1839 and could rightfully dispose of them as provided for in the law. In other words, to sectionize and sell the lands as proposed in Houston's bill, ignoring the locations made by settlers, was tantamount to an admission that Texas was basing its own title to the land upon the validity of the Cherokee claim and the fact that this had been nullified by war.

The passage of the bill branded the administrators as two-faced hypocrites. Houston had, at one masterful stroke, vindicated his own policy and the actions of his Indian friends and blasted the integrity of his enemies. Lamar and his cabinet belatedly realized the untenable position into which they had been duped, and the act was never executed. The hidden meaning of it soon became clear to all, and another session of Congress revoked it, substituting a land bill consistent with the policy of the government and legitimatizing the prior titles of settlers in the area.

The ingenious tactics of the Cherokee Bill merged with pure obstructionism by the Houston party on other elements of Lamar's policy. What sport they made of the new capital! With overdone humor, they professed to fear an Indian attack, pretending to stand alertly on guard at the windows of the House chamber to watch for the expected hordes of savages. A Houston newspaper reported: "The way the married ladies in Austin attend balls and parties is . . . they always take their children with them—put them in the next room, and dance with fear and trembling—otherwise they might return and find their sucklings minus a scalp." Sam wrote: "This is the most unfortunate site upon earth for a Seat of Government," and in one of his earliest speeches to Congress he lampooned the locating commission for its work.

The barrage against Austin continued throughout Lamar's term in office; in the Fourth Congress Houston men also found other means of harassment. The administration was especially vulnerable for its handling of financial matters. "I do not visit 'court,'" Houston wrote to a friend, referring to receptions at the President's mansion. "It is said to be rather fine—so it should be from what appears on our financial records." But underneath the rivalry of personality, Congress managed to achieve a moderately successful program of legislation. The common law of England (and the United States), which was already followed in the Texas courts, was officially adopted. A lengthy revision of the postal service was made, detailing the duties of postmasters and the routes which the mail was to follow through the Republic. An act to suppress dueling was passed, and another law provided for the erection of lighthouses at the important ports. Justice was rendered the innocuous Alabama and Coushatta Indians by granting them a reservation in Texas and by appointing an Indian agent for their benefit. In a contrary vein, a particularly harsh law was enacted to drive the free Negroes out of Texas. A similar law had been introduced in the Third Congress but had failed to muster sufficient support. Opinion in Texas was clearly divided on the subject of the free Negro, and there is no evidence that the terms of the extreme law of 1839 were rigidly enforced. Indeed, a number of relief bills were passed by subsequent Congresses for the benefit of individual Negroes, and in 1842 Sam Houston was to render the Fourth Congress law inoperative.

Congress revised the tariff and taxation laws and created a sinking fund (requested by James Hamilton, the bond commissioner) to support the "Five Million Dollar Loan." A new bond issue for $1,500,000 was authorized, at eight percent interest, which forthwith became known as the "Eight Percent Fund." These efforts to provide revenue proved useless; the government was to operate with Redbacks again—and drive still lower the value of Texas's credit. Twenty thousand dollars, to ransom captives held by the plains Indians, was appropriated, and the legislative agenda was completed with the passage of the usual number of special laws for the relief of individuals, for the creation and definition of counties, for chartering cities, and for incorporating businesses. The Fourth Congress, like its immediate predecessor, held only one session, adjourning on February 5, 1840. Before adjourning it approved Lamar's appointment of James Treat and looked favorably—even hopefully—on the negotiations. A Senate resolution enthusiastically endorsed the peace efforts, and Congress, like Lamar, officially scorned the federalist uprising in northern Mexico.

The Texas attitude, designed to conciliate the centralist government in Mexico, was disheartening to both the insurgents and their Texas volunteer allies, then encamped outside of Monterrey. Discouraged by the hard fighting and the determined resistance of the regular troops, General Antonio Canales' army began to melt away from him. Because of wholesale desertions at the end of the year, Canales was forced to flee Mexico, crossing the Rio Grande, despite Lamar's proclamation of neutrality, on January 7, 1840. At this point forty or fifty of the Texans who had been with him left to return to the settlements, and Canales moved the pitiful remnant of his army up river to Laredo, where he sent forth a call for a convention of representatives from the towns of northern Mexico. On January 18, the convention met and organized the provisional government of the Republic of the Rio Grande. The movement emulated the Texas Revolution, and it is only natural that its leaders continued to hope for support from that quarter. Jesús Cárdenas, the provisional president, attempted to open diplomatic correspondence during February 1840. He offered José Antonio Navarro, then living in San Antonio, the post of official emissary to Texas. Navarro declined but expressed his sympathy with the effort.

Meantime, Colonel Sam Jordan and sixty or seventy Texans who still remained with the federalists, after vainly urging Canales to withdraw to the Nueces to recruit volunteers, finally abandoned the effort. Shortly thereafter Canales was soundly defeated at the Battle of Morales, barely escaping with his life. He fled to Texas in company with Cárdenas, where the two, going separate paths, tried to arouse support for the now virtually nonexistent Republic of the Rio Grande. Obtaining letters of introduction, Canales personally called on President Lamar in Austin. No official support was forthcoming, but perhaps Lamar encouraged him informally; for again Canales was able to enlist volunteers—and again Jordan joined him, with over one hundred men. William S. Fisher, with two hundred men, Juan N. Seguin, with a hundred men, along with approximately three hundred Mexican *rancheros,* restored Canales' army. He reentered Mexico in the summer, with great hopes that additional volunteers would flock to the new federalist banner.

Jordan and his Texans filibustered through Coahuila during August and September, raiding and plundering small villages in the area; Canales and the main army moved south along the coast. Turning to join Canales, Jordan was betrayed near Saltillo in October 1840 and was surrounded by an army numbering over six hundred centralists. Remarkably, in the ensuing fight, about one hundred Texans disposed of a reported 408 centralist soldiers before the Mexicans turned and fled. *Los diablos Tejanos!* They had lost only three men! Jordan and his command then fought their way back across the Rio Grande. Canales, meanwhile, moved toward Tamaulipas, but about this same time Jordan was struggling for his life at Saltillo—he surrendered to the centralists at Camargo with hardly a battle. To his credit, he provided in the terms of the surrender for the safe return of the Texans who accompanied him. Thus ended the unofficial support of the Republic of the Rio Grande—and thus did it die in November 1840.

The Texans who went to Mexico in search of a fight lost out on the biggest Indian raid of Texas history. Indeed, the raid, which swept across southwest Texas into Victoria and Linnville, was devastatingly destructive—partially because of the absence of the several hundred men who had been recruited in and around Victoria by Canales. The affair began with the famous Council House Fight at San Antonio early in the year.

Three Comanche chiefs rode into that ancient city in January 1840 and boldly confronted Colonel Henry W. Karnes of the militia force with demands for a treaty. They claimed that they represented a general council of all the Comanche Indians, and that the wiser heads in the tribe favored peace with the white men. The punitive raids, such as Moore's on the upper Colorado, had alarmed the Indians. Karnes told them that no peace treaty could be considered unless the Comanches released their white prisoners. The emissaries so quickly agreed to this that Karnes grew suspicious. Nevertheless, he made arrangements for a meeting under a flag of truce with the head chiefs of the bands, in March, to work out the terms of the treaty. At this time the Indians were to bring with them all of their captives. The peace council was ill-starred at the outset, for it seems likely that neither Karnes nor the Indians were completely frank. Karnes, rightly, did not believe that the Indians would bring in the captives, and he was prepared to violate the flag of truce should the Indians fail to keep their promise. In reporting to Secretary of War Albert Sidney Johnston, Karnes wrote that he had persuaded the Indians to send enough of their prominent men to the council "to justify our seizing and retaining those who may come in, as hostages for the delivery of such American captives as may at this time be among them." He advised Johnston to send sufficient troops to the council to handle such a maneuver. But, in case the Indians were in earnest, a properly empowered commission should also be sent to negotiate a treaty.

Johnston readily agreed to the meeting. Any measure that promised the slightest chance of releasing white captives had to be tried. Hugh McLeod and William G. Cooke were named commissioners, and William S. Fisher (who, a few months later, went off with Canales) was sent with three companies of infantry. On March 19 the disastrous conference occurred; a group of sixty-five Comanches, led by Chief Muguara, rode into San Antonio. With them came their squaws and children, who fell to playing in the yard outside the Council House, while old Muguara and a dozen younger chiefs went in to palaver with the commissioners. The Indians seemed unalarmed at the presence of the troops, as if they had nothing to hide. However, they brought with them only one captive, fifteen-year-old Matilda Lockhart.

This duplicity of the Indians was alone enough to infuriate the Texans, but the sight of the girl and the tragic recital of her treatment at the Comanche camp enraged the white men almost beyond control. Her poor little body, frail from near starvation, was covered with bruises and sores. The flesh from her nose had been burned away to the bone, with both nostrils gaping open and devoid of flesh. According to Mrs. Mary A. Maverick, who took the girl into her home until her family arrived, "She told a piteous tale of how dreadfully the Indians had beaten her, and how they would wake her from sleep by sticking a chunk of fire to her flesh, especially to her nose, and how they would shout and laugh like fiends, when she cried."

Her story was sobbed forth in the presence of the Indians and the Texas commissioners, and she reported that there were at least fifteen other captives still being held at the Indians' camp in the hills west of town. She said that the Indians planned to get as high a ransom as possible for her; then they would bring in the others, one at a time, and repeat the bargaining.

The tension in the Council House could almost be felt. "Where are the other prisoners you promised to bring in to this talk?" asked one of the commissioners angrily.

"We have only one prisoner," Muguara is reported to have replied. "The others belong to other tribes." Aghast at the bald-faced lie, the commissioners stood silent for a moment.

One young brave stepped forward in the stunned silence and brashly asked, "How you like that answer?"

Before replying, McLeod ordered a company of infantry, commanded by Captain George Thomas Howard, to enter the building. While the commissioners continued the talk, Howard posted guards at the doors and formed his men in a line in the back of the room. During this talk, the Indians acknowledged that they had violated all previous treaties, including the agreement for the present meeting, but insolently demanded that they be given the opportunity to ransom the prisoners. When Howard had stationed his men, the Texans informed the chiefs that they were now prisoners, that they would be held as hostages, and that they must send for the other white captives to be brought in.

Nothing could be more terrifying than a dozen proud Comanche chiefs suddenly being told that they were to be locked in prison. One of the strongest sprang upon Captain Howard with a knife, stabbing him in the side. Another almost simultaneously leaped on a guard at the main entrance. Sheer bedlam broke loose. Screeching war cries mingled with the roar of firearms, made louder by the close quarters. The Indians fought like wild animals caught in a trap. But they were outnumbered and could not win against the rifles and pistols. In moments Muguara and his chiefs lay dead.

As soon as the fighting commenced, the warriors outside the Council House leaped on the infantry company stationed in the yard. Again fierce hand-to-hand fighting ensued. Rarely, if ever, had the superbly mounted Comanches fought at such close quarters. Their ferocity was terrifying, but again they were no match for the better armed infantry. Even the squaws entered into the fighting. In the confused melee, the soldiers fired on the women as well as on the braves. When the tumult died, a few surviving Indians dashed for their horses, but some mounted men, commanded by Lysander Wells, ran them down and killed them before they could escape. A lone brave was left, barricaded inside a stone-walled room. Soldiers smoked him out and riddled his body with bullets. One renegade Mexican escaped; all the Indian men except two aged ones were killed, as were three women and one child. Twenty-seven wailing squaws and their children were taken prisoners. Seven soldiers were killed and eight were wounded.

McLeod later sent one of the squaws back to the Indian camp to demand that the white captives be brought in. She never returned nor, of course, did the Indians bring in their prisoners. According to later reports, the Comanches, enraged at the loss of their people, tortured more than a dozen white prisoners to agonized deaths. But their revenge was to be more fierce than this cruelty. They withdrew to the west, where they contacted other bands, and brooded and plotted during the spring and early summer. Knives and lances were sharpened, bows were restrung and tested, quivers were filled with new-made arrows; while night after night the braves danced around the campfire, leaping and shouting to the blood-tingling rhythms of the war dance. By July, the most spectacular Indian raid of Texas was organized. It seemed to have been more carefully planned than most.

Later evidence revealed that there had been some communication between the Comanches and Mexican agents. It is a strange coincidence that the Indians knew just when and where to seek retaliation. In June, Canales had recruited nearly five hundred Texans in the general vicinities of San Antonio, Gonzales, and Victoria. In July, like wolves ravishing an unguarded lamb fold, combined bands of Comanches, estimated to total one thousand warriors, raced into Southwest Texas. A Mexican letter, taken later from the body of a dead Indian, had suggested that such an attack in that area would be profitable. The Indians skirted the major settlements and struck southeastward in a great sweeping arc toward Victoria, hardly stopping to murder and plunder on the way. On the afternoon of August 6 this blood-thirsty army struck the town of Victoria. The people were utterly unprepared. Death and destruction visited nearly every home. Fiendish, painted red men raced their ponies through the streets, howling savagely. Pathetically frightened, the citizens rushed to the strongest houses in town and put up a determined resistance. It was of little avail, but it did save some lives. The Indians appeared to be more interested in plunder than murder. They rounded up between two and three thousand head of livestock and made camp that night outside of town.

The following afternoon the main body of warriors headed toward the coast to the town of Linnville, then a thriving merchant village. On the morning of August 8, throwing themselves to the sides of their horses, the Indians moved into the town. To the unsuspecting inhabitants it appeared that an immense *caballada* of Mexican ponies was being driven in for trade. Suddenly the red men, with spine-tingling shrieks, reared up and straddled their animals. Fury and terror reigned. Thoughtless of defense, the villagers fled in panic to the water side. There they rushed aboard boats and paddled out into the bay, trembling with fear, but safe. Some Indians plunged their horses into the water and caught a few of the stragglers on their lances. A barrage of arrows drove the boats further from shore. All those who failed to reach the boats were killed or made captive.

While the citizens looked across the water in helpless terror, the savages butchered and scalped the men and tortured the screaming women. Every house and store in town was sacked. Near-naked braves festooned them-

selves in ribbons and calico and paraded gaily along the
dock. While the whites continued to watch the pillage,
the Indians loaded their mules and horses with all the
provisions that they could carry, set fire to the town, and
rode off in triumphant derision.

News of the attack on Victoria and the sack of Linnville spread through the settlements. Almost immediately
volunteers from other communities rushed to the scene.
At La Grange the old Indian fighter, Ed Burleson, set
out at once to raise a force to follow the Indians. As he
was organizing his men, a messenger from that intrepid
Ranger, Ben McCulloch, arrived: "We made a draw fight
with them at Casa Blanca. Could not stop them. We
want to fight them before they get to the mountains."

Burleson fell in with the plan and determined to in-
tercept the enemy at Plum Creek, twenty-seven miles below Austin, near present Lockhart. The Indians, encum-
bered by several thousand horses and mules and hundreds
of pounds of looted provisions, moved more slowly than
their wont. Time permitted a rendezvous of Texan forces
before the Indians reached the area. When Burleson arrived with his forces, he found the indomitable Felix Huston there, at the head of another group of men. Ahead of
Huston, McCulloch and his Rangers had chosen the site
of the battle; Matthew Caldwell, Thomas W. Ward, and
Jonathan Bird, each with a company of volunteers, had
also raced to the Texan camp. In all, approximately two
hundred enraged Texans placed themselves under the
general command of Felix Huston.

On the morning of August 12 the Indian entourage
appeared. While some of the Indians attempted to save
their prizes, others performed remarkable feats of bravery;
dashing furiously toward the Texan lines to discharge
bows and muskets, then flinging themselves to the side

of their horses' protective bodies, racing away. Z. N. Mor-
rell described one of the most daring chiefs, who attracted
the admiration of everyone: "He was riding a very fine
horse, held by a fine American bridle, with a red ribbon
eight or ten feet long, tied to the tail of the horse. He
was dressed in elegant style, from the goods stolen at
Linnville, with a high top silk hat, fine pair of boots and
leather gloves, an elegant broadcloth coat, hind part before, with brass buttons shining brightly up and down
his back. When he first made his appearance he was carrying a large umbrella stretched."

Waiting until the Indian party was close in, the Texans
burst upon them furiously. A running fight, extending

over twelve to fifteen miles, ensued. Between seventy and eighty Indians were killed, and several hundred horses and pack mules were recovered.

Plans for a great punitive raid into Comanche country were immediately made. John H. Moore, who had attacked a Comanche camp on the Colorado in the spring of 1839, was chosen to lead the expedition. Under his command, a hundred determined men pushed out of Austin early in October. For days they followed the trail into the west. An estimated 275 miles up river (probably near present Colorado City) they spied a large Comanche village. That-night some of Moore's men crept to the top of a bluff overlooking the Indian wigwams while he and the remainder of the Texans sneaked across the river.

He nearly took the Indians by surprise, and as the Texans' charge was made, under cover of heavy supporting fire from the bluffs, the enemy were thrown into panic. In the tremulous light of dawn, hot and bloody fighting at close quarters broke out. The Indians were neatly trapped between the charging Texans and the bluff. Over 130 perished, without the loss of a single Texan life. Again, several battling squaws went down with their braves, but most of the women and children were taken prisoner. Much of the Linnville plunder was recovered, as were another several hundred head of stock.

From 1840 until their final defeat in 1876, the Comanches remained implacable enemies of the white settlers. The sweeping raid on Linnville has been customarily interpreted as the retaliation for the Council House Fight; but the curious circumstances of its careful organization, its perfect choice of time and place, the discovery of the letter from a Mexican agent, and the fact that the Indians were more interested in plunder than murder and rapine, all indicate that the attack was more than mere revenge.

The Indian raid had alarmed the entire nation, and to the citizens of the frontier capital of Austin, the menace of further depredations loomed frighteningly large. The Lamar government, however, was more concerned with its complex diplomatic negotiations—all of which were directed toward expediting the success of James Hamilton's efforts to sell the Texas bonds in Europe. This goal had dictated most of the government policy decisions during 1840.

In Europe, Hamilton had his troubles. After having persuaded Congress to establish a sinking fund for the bonds, he returned to England with his co-worker, Albert Burnley, where he found that even the best United States securities were selling far under their face value, and selling slowly at that. The Texas bonds did not have a chance, at least not until the news from Texas was more promising. "Every false rumor of Mexican and Indian invasion brings us to a standstill," he wrote in April 1840. The need to present Texas in a more favorable light led Hamilton to continue Henderson's negotiations with Lord Palmerston for official British recognition of Texas. Although the British foreign secretary put him off with repeated delays, Hamilton was not discouraged, for he knew that Britain desired to sustain Texas independence if she could do so without disrupting trade with Mexico. But he warned: "A premature invasion of Mexico would dash our well-digested schemes to the ground, and subvert, in one hour, my incessant and irksome labor for the last eighteen months." No wonder Lamar and Congress were constrained to adopt a friendly attitude toward the Mexican government!

While Palmerston delayed, Hamilton crossed to the continent and successfully concluded a treaty of recognition and trade with Holland. By September 15, 1840, the drafting of the treaty was completed; the following day Hamilton was officially presented to the king; on September 18, the document was signed. The Netherlands became the third nation to recognize Texas—the second in Europe. The treaty, like the one with France, guaranteed political friendship and reciprocal trade privileges. Its importance to Texas, however, was overshadowed by the impending treaty with Great Britain.

Before Hamilton returned to London, he paid a call on the Belgian foreign minister at Brussels, where he picked up the threads of earlier negotiations with Belgian ministers. He found Belgium quite well-disposed toward Texas, but it was to take him many months to arrange a treaty, because Belgium demanded certain trade concessions which Hamilton was not prepared to relinquish. For over a year, the Belgian ministers continued to haggle, and it was not until late in 1841 that the government finally recognized Texas officially.

After opening the question at Brussels, Hamilton had the Belgian discussion transferred to London so that he could pursue the all-important work on the British treaty. In October, Hamilton submitted a rough draft for the treaty to Palmerston. Revisions and more delays followed, but finally, on November 13, 1840, the first of three treaties with England was signed. The first was a treaty of commerce and navigation. The following day a treaty stipulating British mediation with Mexico was consummated. Two days later, Palmerston forced Hamilton reluctantly to sign a third treaty providing for the suppression of the slave trade which, pursuant to British policy with other nations, permitted her to search Texan vessels for slaves in certain waters and in certain specified ports.

The first treaty was the one which Hamilton and Texas wanted; the other two were necessary concessions to

British objections regarding Texas. Palmerston made it clear that they could not have one without the others. Hamilton feared (erroneously as it later proved) that the third treaty for the suppression of the slave trade would not be well received in Texas. Consequently he sent only the first two to Austin for Senate ratification by a special English agent, Arthur Ikin; the third was carried personally by Albert Burnley, with a long letter of explanation. It did not arrive until after Congress had adjourned and consequently was not ratified until January 1842. The other two, however, were promptly approved. Britain delayed ratification until all three had been accepted in Texas, and the formal exchange of ministers did not take place until 1842. But Hamilton's purposes were served in the resultant publicity. He could now push the sale of the bonds.

Just as he felt success within his grasp, news of the failure of James Treat's negotiations for recognition in Mexico was to reach Europe and stymie his efforts once again. Hamilton had banked heavily on Treat's success. Earlier he had written optimistically: "If Holland . . . recognizes, and Treat succeeds, our loan will go like a locomotive over a rail." But the ubiquitous secret agent faced more problems in Mexico than did Hamilton in Europe. Treat had reached his destination in November of 1839, with instructions to negotiate Mexican recognition of Texas by almost any means he could find. Almost immediately his efforts were swept into the mill race of Mexican politics, which swirled around the fight between federalists and centralists. The whole affair of the Republic of the Rio Grande, and Colonel Jordan's raid through Coahuila, had done little to facilitate Treat's delicate negotiations.

Shortly after his arrival in Mexico, he began complaining that the exaggerated accounts of the activities of the Texans with Canales greatly excited his Mexican friends. Nonetheless, he moved into the game of intrigue with a sureness born of experience. He soon became acquainted with a number of the more influential members of Congress and began to feel assured of the ultimate success of his mission. It would be a slow, tedious business, he admitted; because, even though most of the Mexican leaders would frankly admit in private that Mexico had lost Texas, they dared not say so publicly. "They are too *weak,* too *imbecile,* too much divided *among themselves* and *afraid* of *each other to act straight forward, boldly* and *openly,*" he explained to Lamar.

Among others in Mexico, Treat won the warm support of Richard Pakenham, the British minister, who, cool at first, soon decided that Treat was one of the best qualified men he had ever known. It was Pakenham who persuaded the Mexican secretary of state to meet with Treat, and it was Pakenham who continued to support the Texan agent in every way possible. The mission was destined to fail, however, for the very reasons Treat noted on his arrival. The officials, willing enough to concede privately, were unable to act publicly.

After interminable delays, Treat was finally officially accepted as a Texan agent on April 25, 1840; in May he succeeded in presenting the Texas proposition to the Executive Council; and in July, the matter was submitted, without recommendation, to Congress. Then, a revolution of federalists broke out in the capital, and it was not until mid-August that the government recovered itself. By then, however, Bustamante and the cabinet were afraid to take up anything as controversial as the Texas question, for fear of losing the tenuous support which they had.

Treat urged Lamar not to despair, but Lamar had ideas of his own. Another federalist uprising was developing into a full-fledged revolution on the peninsula of Yucatan. Perhaps Texas had erred in not supporting the federalists of northern Mexico; perhaps neutrality had gained less than a threat of joining forces with the insurgents might have. If so, the Yucatan rebellion offered another opportunity. Lamar thus resolved to press the centralist government by making common cause with the Yucatan federalists. Circumstances conspired to make an aggressive policy possible—not by land, but by sea. For, by this time, Texas had another navy, impatient to sail and anxious to fight!

The "first" Texas navy had virtually ceased to exist after the battle off the Galveston coast in June 1837; the "second" Texas navy had its origins in appropriation bills of 1837 and 1838. As naval commissioner, Samuel May Williams had been authorized to expend $280,000 on the construction of six ships for Texas. The Baltimore ship builder, Frederick Dawson, received the contract; and in June 1839, the first vessel of this new fleet arrived. It was a 170-ton schooner, christened the *Viper* but soon renamed the *San Jacinto*. Meantime, the navy had acquired the brig *Potomac*, which was used as a receiving ship, and a steam packet, which was renamed the *Zavala*.

The remainder of the new ships were delivered in the following year: two 170-ton schooners, the *San Antonio* and the *San Bernard;* two 400-ton brigs, the *Wharton* and the *Archer;* and a 600-ton sloop of war, the *Austin*. Delivery was completed in April 1840. The Texas navy, at that

The *San Antonio*

time, comprised six new sailing ships, a steamship, and a wharf-bound schooner. It made a very creditable appearance in the harbor at Galveston. The sight of the handsome vessels floating at anchor, like mastiffs on a chain, gave definite feelings of security, pride, and dignity to citizens and government officials alike.

Handsome, well-outfitted ships alone did not make a navy—a reliable corps of officers and crews of competent seamen were even more important. Among the appointments that Lamar laid before the Fourth Congress in November 1839, was that of Edwin Ward Moore, who was made "post captain" of the new navy. There is evidence that arrangements for Moore to take command had been made several months earlier for, even before he resigned his commission as lieutenant in the United States navy in July 1839, Moore was accused of recruiting men for Texas.

Then twenty-nine years old, Moore had a charming personality, coupled with what many of his colleagues considered a brilliant mind. He was definitely a seaman's seaman, having enlisted in the navy at the age of fourteen and having passed through the midshipmen's training course which, at that time (before the establishment of the Naval Academy), was the principal means of procuring officers for the United States navy. Of an adventurous disposition, he was undoubtedly persuaded to abandon his promising career in the United States navy—then notoriously slow in promotions—for the greater opportunities which the Texas navy offered.

Almost immediately after his appointment, Moore provisioned the *Wharton* and took her on a snappy cruise to New York, nearly setting a record for the run from New Orleans. A handsome new ship, a sharp-looking crew, and bright new uniforms made recruiting easy in New York— if slightly illegal. The United States charged that Texas violated neutrality, but Moore had seen a lawyer first. All the men whom he enlisted signed statements to the effect that they were "sailormen hailing from Texas and calling themselves Texians." With good ships, and the exciting possibility of prize money in the conflict with Mexico, Moore got good men—in some respects the cream of the younger men in the United States navy. Commodore Moore and the Texas navy were soon ready to sweep the Gulf and take control of the waters off the Mexican coast.

If Lamar could not *Treat* with Mexico—as a contemporary pun on special agent James Treat's name had it— then he could use the new navy to force recognition. In July 1840 Moore and his fleet sailed for Vera Cruz. They bore instructions for Treat and carried an implied threat to the Mexican government; but they were ordered not to fire on any ships or take any prizes unless fired upon first, or until the wheels of diplomacy ground to a halt. Moore was also directed to establish friendly communications with General Anaya, who was then leading the federalist uprising on Yucatan. Anaya, anxious for allies, gave the Texas navy the freedom of Yucatan ports, a helpful convenience for the cruise in Mexican waters. Even more helpful were the accessible Arcas Islands, lying between the peninsula and the mainland, where Moore established his base of operations.

Because of a mix-up in orders, some of which were not delivered until too late to be effective, communications between Moore and Treat nearly broke down. Moore occupied the navy during the summer with a telling demonstration which proved that Texas could control the Gulf in case of a renewal of hostilities. He believed that if the navy were only permitted to do so, it could force the recognition of Texas. In frequent dispatches to Lamar and others, he urged action: "With all due deference, I cannot refrain from the expression of the opinion that we have temporized too long already . . . . You might, without the least prospect of being molested by [the Mexicans] on the Frontier, dictate to, and no longer *ask* at their hands . . . . In my humble opinion they will never acknowledge [Texas independence] until they are made to *feel* it. . . . Every Mexican Vessel can be captured that dares put to sea, and their whole Sea coast be kept in a perfect state of fear and trembling . . . . Now is the time to push them for they were never so prostrate!"

In his assessment of the situation, Moore was probably right. Treat's negotiations were at an impasse; the centralist government apparently was merely using him to forestall an alliance between Texas and the federalists, first those in the north and now those on Yucatan. Had Texas supported the Republic of the Rio Grande, openly and with strength, it is possible that recognition might have been forced in the spring. Had the navy turned hostile in September 1840, it is not unlikely that, in the resultant demoralization in Mexico, the entire centralist power structure might have been upset. But belligerency would have been risky. Britain, opposed to any interruption of trade, was against it. Hamilton, too, pleaded with Lamar not to imperil the bond sales by war. Thus, the uneasy truce continued into the fall of the year.

By mid-October, in frustrated exasperation, Treat himself gave up hope of making any progress with Mexican officials. Even Pakenham, the patient British minister, wrote that Mexico's behavior was unreasonable, and even preposterous, under the circumstances. The armistice, which Britain hoped to mediate as a substitute for recognition, was impossible. Treat, whose health was failing him, boarded the Texan ship *San Antonio*, where he died on November 30, while the sloop was anchored off Tampico awaiting a rendezvous with Moore and the rest of the navy.

October had found Moore even more frustrated than Treat; indeed, the whole navy was impatient for action. It came somewhat unexpectedly on October 20 when a shore battery opened fire on the Texans. Moore promptly informed Treat that hostilities were commenced, forwarded dispatches to that effect to Texas, and prepared to execute the blockade which he was so sure would bring Mexico to her knees. But bad luck immediately began to plague him. The captain and most of the crew of the *San Bernard* were laid up at the Arcas, desperately ill; the *Austin* was hopelessly short of coal and had been on half rations for weeks; the *San Jacinto* was sunk in the shoals at Arcas while trying to aid the crew of the *San Bernard* and was lying half under water; and the *Zavala*, which had made for a Yucatan port to reprovision, was seriously damaged in a storm.

Moore needed money to supply his ships, salvage the

San Jacinto, and repair the *Zavala.* Any attempt to impose the blockade had to be deferred to the more immediate necessity—cash. Hastily, the commodore bargained with General Anaya. Eighty miles up the big Tabasco River, in the heart of Yucatan, was the important city of San Juan Bautista, firmly held by a strong force of centralists. Anaya had been unable to drive them out. If the Texas navy could effect the capture of the town, what would Yucatan pay? Twenty-five thousand dollars, said Anaya, $10,000 in cash and a $15,000 reduction of the navy's debt to the federalist government on Yucatan for supplies and provisions which had been furnished Moore on credit.

Up the broad river limped the *Zavala,* the *Austin,* and the *San Bernard.* A day after the navy turned its guns on the garrison, the centralists capitulated, surrendering the city, the presidio, and the troops. Moore had won his first naval victory—eighty miles inland!

But plans to besiege the Mexican coast were cancelled in favor of returning to Galveston when the news arrived that the *San Jacinto* had finally been broken up on the shoals. Moore himself had come down with the fever, as had over half the officers. On the flagship *Austin* alone, between August 1840 and January 1841, twenty-five men had died. Losses on the other ships had been as great. Continued operations were impossible; the fleet joined the *San Antonio* off Tampico, where it had captured a Mexican prize worth $7,000 in cash, and the navy reluctantly headed home. Little did Moore dream that all but two of his ships were to be decommissioned and that these two would be set to making a coastal survey.

But 1841 was to be a tough year for everyone in Texas.

7

1841

A TOUGH YEAR
FOR EVERYONE

"Times are terribly severe," observed the astute Dr.
Ashbel Smith of the utter collapse of the boom spirit in
Texas during the autumn and winter of 1840. "The ter-
rible pecuniary depression . . . is everywhere felt."

Citizens in all walks of life felt the want of funds;
some of the most prominent names in Texas were listed
on delinquent tax rolls; sheriffs considered it useless to
attempt to collect even the current taxes; and merchants
throughout Texas despaired of receiving anything but
worthless Redbacks on overdue bills. The proprietor of
a hotel who asked a guest to make a small payment on
his delinquent account was met with the rebuff: "If you
come to insult me again, sir, by God, I'll shoot you, sir."

Joseph Plummer, customs collector at Aransas Pass,

wrote expressively of the severity of the times on December 12, 1840: "We labor under many privations here. . . . the population are nearly all removed. . . . I have been compelled to assume payment for rent [on the customs house] and would be pleased to receive the money, for it is all I can do to keep body and soul together. . . . How long such a state of things will exist I know not."

Lamar's staunchest supporters wrote him in the vein of this letter from J. D. Andrews: "Our money is very scarce here, indeed, so much so, that . . . I have never witnessed anything like it before. Nevertheless, it is still passing at 6 for one."

Even Lamar's government, which had long tried to keep up an optimistic front, was forced to admit the seriousness of the economic situation. Secretary of the Treasury John G. Chalmers wrote that Texas promissory notes and other securities of the government were worth but one-sixth of their face value—an embarrassing statement for an official to have to make. Lamar had not created the depression, but his reckless expenditures had certainly augmented it. At election time, naturally, the Lamar party was mercilessly scored by Houston and his followers, and few of the Lamar men were returned to their seats in Congress.

The Fifth Congress was not only composed of many new faces, it was also largely dominated by Houston. Assembling in Austin on November 2, 1840, it faced the future dourly. The treasury was bankrupt; the frontier was collapsing; the nation was becoming depopulated. Indian depredations and threats of a Mexican invasion menaced the country. There were few people and no money, and land values gave little indication of rising. Lamar's glowing address, emphasizing the achievements of the previous year, failed to stir the members. Introduced by a Lamar man on the second day of the session, a bill to take the census of the Republic was voted down on its first reading—on the grounds that it would probably do Texas more harm than good if the true number of people in the Republic were known.

A spirit of economy and retrenchment pervaded Congress from the beginning of its session. Bills for reducing the civil list, for cutting salaries, for decommissioning the fleet, and even for abolishing the army were promptly introduced. Other bills suggested the consolidation of the government departments into fewer buildings and the renting of those thus vacated for revenue. As is inevitable, however, in any legislative body, some members eventually brought forward pet schemes requiring expenditures and appropriations. On January 2, James Shaw, a veteran of San Jacinto and one of the Houston men in the House, called his colleagues' attention to the fact that they were deviating from their announced purposes, with the following resolution:

> Resolved, that each member of this House be requested to wear crepe on his left arm until the adjournment of the present Congress, in sad remembrance of the unexpected and lamented deaths of our two worthy and respected brethren, 'Retrenchment and Reform,' who stood so conspicuous in our minds at the commencement of the present session, but have unfortunately sickened and died for the want of faithful and sober physicians.

Houston clearly controlled the House—at least for the first month or six weeks. Lamar, wrapped in his dream of empire, failed completely to gauge the temper of the legislators. He was sick in spirit from the refusal of his contemporaries to see his grand vision, and wasted in body from the pressures of office on his consumption-ridden frame. Soon after Congress met, Lamar took to his bed with an intestinal disorder, and on December 12, he was voted a leave of absence to seek medical care and rest. Burnet was made acting President, although a bill to increase his salary commensurate with his new responsibilities was quickly squelched.

But another request from Lamar (before he left Austin) stirred the parsimonious Congress to the deepest agonies of indecision. Treat's failure to obtain recognition from Mexico, coupled with the arrogance of the centralist government and the firing upon the Texas navy at Tampico, had exhausted Lamar's patience. He urged that Texas use the army and navy to force Mexico to recognize Texas independence. On December 15, in his first message to Congress, Burnet delivered a fiery message which taunted the pride and patriotism of the members. A joint committee was promptly appointed to consider a declaration of war on Mexico. Burnet forwarded to this committee a proposal by the glory-seeking Felix Huston for a grand invasion below the Rio Grande.

In the radiant heat of the jingoistic fire which Burnet and Huston had kindled, Houston temporarily lost his grip on the House. The joint committee reported back with a staunch endorsement of Burnet's message and resolutions of war against the enemy. "Let the sword do its proper work," Burnet had cried, and an eager Congress answered the call:

> For the last four years, continually renewed talk of invasion has entailed upon the Republic all the evils of actual war, without affording the opportunity which national valor has always improved, of reaping a harvest of glory from every battlefield. The injury to our interests which this state of things has produced, is only surpassed by the indignity which it offers to our national honor.

All thought of economy was forgotten, and there was even some talk of immediate adjournment so that the members could rush home to raise volunteer companies. With great difficulty, Houston mustered sufficient strength to table the resolution, but on December 21 another resolution declaring war was introduced by James S. Mayfield, which passed its first reading that day. Despite repeated efforts to call it up for a second reading, the Houston machine managed to keep it off the floor until December 30, when Burnet sent in another war message. The two war resolutions now before the House, and Burnet's second message, were adroitly sent back to the original joint committee.

Less precipitate this time, the Joint War Committee held the resolutions until January 12, and then, in a lengthy analysis of Texas's situation, reported in favor of defensive measures. For one thing, the committee seriously doubted whether Mexico actually intended to attack Texas; for another thing, Texas flatly could not afford to finance an offensive war. The committee's report voiced Houston's ideas. In fact, Houston was so pleased that he jumped to his feet and put forth a resolution that the entire report of the committee be printed. The next day the bill for disbanding the army, which had been cast aside during the war talk, was called up for a second reading and passed. Burnet was exasperated; on January 13 he sent a sour message to the House: "Retrenchment is not necessarily economy. . . . I trust the honorable Congress will not, at a crisis like the present, yield their judgment to hasty impulse. . . ."

But Burnet and the war faction had lost—Houston, pacifism, and economy were back at the helm again. Military expenditures could hardly have been slashed more than they were. All the ships of the navy except two were decommissioned, and Moore lost most of his officers and men. These two ships were ordered to carry out the harbor survey that Lamar had promoted through the last Congress. The army was completely disbanded, through failure to make an appropriation for it. The office of secretary of the navy was amalgamated with that of the army. The ranging force was reduced to three spy companies of fifteen men each, but a corps of volunteers was authorized to carry out a three-month campaign to dislodge the Indians on the upper Brazos. An ingenious device, to protect the frontier without cost, was passed. It permitted the organization of volunteer ranging companies in each county. The men serving in these companies would be exempt from taxes (which they were not paying anyway), from militia service, and from work on the county roads.

Although he normally commanded the Fifth Congress, Houston had difficulty preventing the passage of a bill to correct the allegations concerning the Cherokee lands, which Lamar and others had choked on in the previous session. During the vehement debate of the revised Cherokee Land Bill, Colonel Samuel Jordan, who had just returned to Austin from his grand filibuster into northern Mexico, became so incensed that he attacked Houston with a hand ax. Adolphus Sterne, a long-time German resident of Nacogdoches, who was in Austin testifying before the Committee on Public Lands, saw the blow coming and diverted it.

History is silent on the immediate aftermath of this attack, which apparently occurred at Bullock's Hotel on the evening of December 10. Jordan remained in Austin until the end of the session and then went to New Orleans to raise a company of volunteers to fight with the centralists against the federalists in Yucatan. By a quirk of fate, he missed the boat which was to take him to the fighting in Mexico and, in a fit of despair, committed suicide.

Congress remained in session until February 5, 1841. Its other efforts in the area of finance included an act to trade land scrip for the worthless promissory notes of the Third Congress, an act granting an extension of time to those persons who still owed money to the government for lots purchased in the Austin town site, an act authorizing the mercantile and banking firm of McKinney, Williams, and Company to issue private bank notes (in the hope that this would bolster the economy), and an act (the most hotly contested of the session) to establish "a system of bankruptcy" (procedures for declaring bankruptcy).

In the field of social legislation, Congress authorized several individuals, who desired to do so, to emancipate their slaves; it exempted a number of the Negroes from the act of the previous Congress; it wrote a statute for divorce and alimony; it legalized certain marriages; it tried once again to suppress gaming, and it even discussed a bill to prevent "tippling," which would have limited the amount of liquor a man was allowed to drink to one gallon. (There was much hilarious debate on the question of how much intoxicant should be considered the legal limit—the gallon specified was beyond the capacity of all but the most ardent tipplers.)

The most significant work of the Fifth Congress concerned the attempt to establish settlers on the frontier. Once again, Congress resorted to land donations as a means to induce immigration. No one then in Texas really favored a free-land policy; but from the very beginning, Texas governments had been pushed to granting free land as a temporary expedient. The Convention of 1836 had granted a league and a labor, later known as First Class Headrights; the First Congress had granted Second Class Headrights of 1,280 acres to each family who migrated to Texas between January 1 and October 1, 1837. The Second Congress provided 640 acres, as Third Class Headrights, to those who came between October 1, 1837, and January 1, 1840. The Fifth Congress extended the time to January 1, 1841, which ended the headright program.

The reluctance of the government to give land away is obvious; each of the headright acts had a terminal date and each was hoped to be the last. During the five years prior to 1841, it was generally believed that Texas would soon begin to sell its lands to increasing hordes of frontiersmen. The give-away lands were to be used only to prime the pump of immigration, so to speak. The realistic Fifth Congress sought a more effective solution.

Increased immigration was a stark necessity. Immigrants would push the frontier westward, would crowd the Indians back, and would protect the older settlements from raids. Immigrants would bring money into Texas and make capital improvements on these lands. Immigrants would raise land values all over the Republic; they would fight in the militia, pay taxes, work on the roads, and so on, *ad infinitum*. To induce immigration seemed to be the most direct route to peace and prosperity.

Since direct donations of land had failed to bring the rush of settlers, the congressional mind began to revert to the old Mexican empresario system, with the creation of colonies promoted by some active leader. Burnet advised Congress to establish "a colony of brave and active yeomanry upon the inland frontier. . . ." Before the end of the session, three bills for such colonies were introduced: (1) the Franco-Texienne Bill, (2) the Ben Fort Smith Bill, and (3) the Peters Colony Bill.

The Franco-Texienne proposal called for the introduction, into the unoccupied parts of Texas, of some eight thousand Frenchmen as combination soldiers and colonists. This quasi-military force was to be stationed at twenty posts along the frontier, under the supervision of a French company, which would allocate lands to its soldier-colonists, supply them with provisions and ammunition, and build and maintain the forts. In return for this service to the Republic, the company was to receive three million acres of land and be given the privileges of working all mines in the company's territory for twenty years, of bringing goods into the Republic duty free, and of trading with Mexican settlements at Santa Fé and Chihuahua.

The bill had strong support from Houston and his party. It should have passed easily, but it faced strong opposition and increasingly violent protest. It was argued that it was dangerous to give a European nation such a foothold in the Republic. "And in this grand scheme of conquest, where would Texas be found?" asked Francis Moore, editor of the *Telegraph and Texas Register* and vituperative opponent of Houston. Texas needed no such protection on its frontier, he stoutly declared. In two years the "handful of naked, half-starved, unarmed savages" would be scattered by "hosts of hardy pioneers" coming into Texas.

Editorial fantasy, perhaps; yet, it was such a dream, of hosts of Anglo-American settlers (rather than foreigners), that brought about the defeat of the Franco-Texienne project in the Senate even after it had passed through the House. Congress dropped the French proposal, partially because of the opposition and partially because of an alternate scheme more pleasing to all, which called for the introduction of settlers from the United States. The curiously timely proposal came from a group of twenty men, eleven from England and nine from Louisville, Kentucky, none of whom knew much about Texas or were known in the Republic.

Their leader was a musician named William S. Peters. Three of his sons, all music teachers, and several other musicians in Louisville had concocted the plan. Peters, who had migrated to the United States from England, enlisted some of his friends in London to join in the project. On this preposterous foundation—little more than an idle dream of men wholly unsuited either for business ventures or for the frontier—the Fifth Congress was to build the entire immigration and land policy of the Republic's last five years.

The bill for the Peters Colony was introduced on January 17, 1841; it quickly passed through both houses within two weeks and was signed by Burnet on February 4, 1841. Its only opposition was a far more practical proposal from Benjamin Fort Smith which called for the establishment of a similar colony; but Smith's bill was tabled after the second reading. There is no clear explanation for the smooth passage of the Peters Colony Bill through the turbulent waters of Congress—except that the session was drawing to a close, and congressmen were growing desperate. Even Houston swung from the Franco-Texienne scheme to the support of the Peters Colony.

This law of February 4, 1841, authorized the twenty petitioners to establish a colony of 600 families between the Trinity and Red rivers, on the northwest frontier. Each settler was to receive a free grant of 640 acres and the contractors were to get a premium of 60 such sections for their services. Thus, only within the bounds of the colony could an immigrant get land without cost. All other free land programs were stopped. Although the colony, from its inception to its final death throes in 1852, was a nightmare of ineptness, misunderstanding, and controversy, it was responsible for the largest immigration Texas received from any single stimulus.

The defeat of the Franco-Texienne Bill was an uncomfortable shock to one of its most enthusiastic supporters, the Count Alphonse de Saligny, French *chargé d'affaires* in Texas. Saligny, a pompous, peppery man who despised the frontier conditions of the Texas capital, had a personal interest in the scheme. During the debates, he had tried unsuccessfully to lobby for it by inviting congressmen to his home—the French Embassy—for formal dinners and soirees. His gold-plated table service, six- and eight-course meals, and fancy manners were not popular. Wrote Isaac Van Zandt in disgust: "We sat at the table four hours—I was wearied to death, but had to stand it with the company—We had plates changed fifteen times."

More shocking to the dapper count than the defeat of the bill was the "democratic" attitude of the citizens of Austin, who did not show him proper respect. Continued affronts to his dignity were climaxed by a quarrel which he had with Richard Bullock. That ridiculous, yet significant, episode began with Saligny's arrival in Austin. He stayed at Bullock's Hotel, but refused to pay his bill because he thought the charges exorbitant. Bullock responded by numerous frontier expressions of contempt which circulated freely around Austin. Saligny moved out of the hotel and demanded that the government punish the innkeeper for his insults to a foreign diplomat. Congress passed a special law punishing anyone guilty of "slanderous words" against any foreign minister—for Saligny's benefit.

The quarrel between Bullock and the French *chargé d'affaires* continued, however. Near the hotel, Saligny kept his stable of fine horses and some corn stored to feed them. Bullock's pigs (like those of most of the inhabitants) were unrestrained in their search for provender. When they discovered the corn in the French stables, Saligny's servant attempted to drive them away. Bullock charged that he killed ("most maliciously and wantonly") between fifteen and twenty-five pigs. He attacked the servant, beating him with a stick. Saligny promptly caused Bullock's arrest for assault. The count claimed that he had made repeated efforts to keep the pigs out of his stables; that he had, innumerable times, repaired the fences which the pigs had trampled down; that on another occasion the pigs had entered his study and eaten some of his papers; and that only five pigs were killed.

Bullock was freed on bail supplied by the secretary of the treasury; and he immediately renewed his verbal attack on the Frenchman's character, his disposition, and his ancestry. Now Saligny demanded his arrest under the law forbidding the slander of a foreign minister. While he and the Texas state department exchanged lengthy notes on the matter, affairs reached a climax. Saligny went to call on the United States *chargé d'affaires*, George Flood, who was a resident of Bullock's hotel. Bullock barred his entrance and ordered him off the property.

Indignantly, Saligny demanded either prompt redress from the government or the return of his passports. After several futile attempts to pacify him, the exasperated state department gave him his papers, and Saligny left his post early in April 1841. Although the whole town sympathized with Bullock, the comical dispute had serious repercussions. Saligny had powerful connections in France, and through his influence, Texas was dealt a heavy blow—the Five Million Dollar Loan, finally arranged by James Hamilton after painstaking negotiations, was cancelled!

In mid-February, Hamilton had concluded a contract

with the extensive French banking houses of Lafitte and Company. They had agreed to take the Texas bonds if the French government would guarantee them. To the French minister of finance, he argued that Texas was willing to put up as security for such a guarantee "a Territory as large as the Kingdom of France and the good faith of law-abiding and debt-paying people." The loan would put Texas on a sound financial basis and at the same time permit the development of a healthy sinking fund for the redemption of the bonds. The government of France appeared agreeable and, early in March, Hamilton wrote to the Texas state department that formal consent would be forthcoming in about a month. Then, it would take about one more month for Lafitte and Company to make the money available to Texas.

To protect holders of Texas securities against the ravages of speculation, in case the great news of Texas' coming solvency leaked out, Hamilton made a public announcement of his contract with the French banking firm. These happy tidings were greeted with great relief in Texas—and by Texas' creditors. Treasury notes and bonds, which had been as low as twelve cents on the dollar, suddenly rose to 25 and 50 cents. There were even some rumors that Texas might pay off its notes at face value.

Five Million Dollars! Why, Texas could pay all its debts and have money to spare. Disposition of the money became the topic of the day in Texas. Politicians and newspapers jumped into the act with scores of plans for spending it: Pay off the debt—Develop the agricultural resources—Cancel all taxes—Establish a national bank—Print more Redbacks—Refloat the navy—and so on.

Then, as excitement mounted, Saligny's angry influence began to make itself felt in Paris. Hamilton had received both written and verbal assurances from the French prime minister that France would support the loan. On March 31, 1841, Guizot coolly informed the Texas agent that such a proposal must be submitted to the Chamber of Deputies, and he doubted whether it would pass. Next the official organ of the French government came out with an editorial against Texas. The French minister of finance was Saligny's brother-in-law! When the attitude of the government changed, Lafitte and Guizot withdrew from the arrangements. After tedious months of deliberations, the loan came crashing down about Hamilton's ears. But Hamilton was no more disappointed than the Lamar government or hundreds of other Texans.

Indefatigable, Hamilton turned to England, where he arranged a series of conferences with cabinet officials, trying to get British backing for the bonds. For six months he bombarded the British ministry with various ideas which might interest them. On October 4, 1841, Britain made a final refusal.

Still undefeated, Hamilton reopened the negotiations with Belgium, which had been pending for over a year. He offered that nation favorable trade rates and security in the public lands of Texas. He suggested, since he had to return to Texas, that Belgium send its own agent to the new Republic to investigate conditions. To this Belgium agreed, appointing Captain Victor Pirson. Together, Pirson and Hamilton were to reach Texas in January 1842. To his consternation, Hamilton was to find that the Sixth Congress had cancelled the bond issue. Between the time of his French arrangements and his arrival in Texas, events had occurred which were to discredit entirely the Lamar administration and bring Houston back to office; whereupon, the bond law was repealed as another of Lamar's wild schemes. It had actually been passed during Houston's first administration, but it was Lamar and his friend Hamilton who had pursued it.

Undoubtedly the most damaging fiasco of the Lamar administration—the disastrous Texas-Santa Fé expedition—took place during that interim. Unquestionably, its failure did more than anything else to blast the election hopes of Lamar's followers. Lamar embarked on this project without the legal consent of the Houston-dominated Fifth Congress. But it must be said in his behalf that he fully believed he had congressional approval, despite the fact that Congress failed to authorize the expedition. To understand Lamar's reasoning, it is necessary to review the complex situation.

Mexico was divided between the centralist and federalist factions. All over that nation, where the centralists had overthrown the republican Constitution of 1824, there had been a continual series of uprisings and revolts against the dictatorships—first of Santa Anna, then of Bustamante. Since Texas' own revolution began as a rebellion against the centralists, Texans could not help feeling some sympathy for the insurgents of northern Mexico, of Yucatan, of California (which in 1841 was virtually independent of centralist control), and of other areas. With good reason, it was generally believed in Texas that the bulk of the population of Santa Fé and New Mexico were likewise opposed to the centralist dictatorship and would welcome the chance to throw off that yoke of oppression.

In this light, the inclusion of the Santa Fé settlements within the statutory limits of Texas does not appear so preposterous. It is evident that no thinking Texan took seriously the idea that Texas' traditional limits extended to the western Rio Grande, but it is fairly clear that many Texans thought that such an inclusion would be welcomed. Lamar's principal plan was to establish trade and friendly communication with the inhabitants of those regions and invite them to participate in the newly formed republican government of Texas. To this end, the Third Congress, on January 26, 1839, had authorized the President to open a trade with "the Mexicans on the Rio Grande." Though this resolution was directed at northern Mexico and the ranches which lay between the Nueces and the Rio Grande, its spirit comprehended the settlements on the upper Rio Grande in New Mexico. At that time Lamar began advocating an expedition to Santa Fé, pointing to the trade (much of it contraband) which ran from Arkansas and Missouri to Chihuahua and Santa Fé. In 1839, for example, one Henry Connelly, a merchant-trader, passed through Texas with a reported third of a million dollars in specie, which he had netted in trade at Chihuahua City. The value of the commerce on the Santa Fé Trail, from Independence, Missouri, to Santa Fé, was also well known among Texans.

It took but a glance at a map for even the dullest to realize that an overland route, from the Texas ports into Santa Fé, would enable Texas merchants to compete advantageously for the New Mexican market. Lamar believed that Texas should establish contact with Santa Fé, and open a trade route to New Mexico. A visit to the Texas capital by William G. Dryden, a citizen of Santa Fé, convinced him that the people there would welcome the liberal laws of the Republic of Texas. On April 14, 1840, he wrote a public letter to the citizens of that region, describing the Texas Revolution and the republican form of government in Texas, and inviting them to participate in it. He announced that he intended to dispatch commissioners, with an armed escort for protection against the Indians, to open "a safe and convenient route of communications between the two sections of country, which . . . we hope to see united in friendship and consolidated under a common government."

When Congress assembled that November, he asked for official sanction for such an expedition. One bill passed the House; another passed the Senate. But neither cleared all legislative obstacles to become law. Lamar returned to the capital from his sick leave to find that Congress had adjourned without action on the Santa Fé expedition. However, because both houses had approved separate bills for the same purpose, he assumed that the legislative branch approved.

In April 1841 he issued a call for volunteers. The dual purpose of the expedition was well known—to open trade and to induce New Mexico to become an integral part of Texas. The expedition would have to be of a quasi-military nature because it would cross the hostile Comanche country. Merchants, adventurers, and soldiers flocked to the banner. William G. Cooke, José Antonio Navarro, Richard Brenham, and George Van Ness were named civil commissioners. Their duties were to effect the extension of Texas government in Santa Fé if the people there desired it. Hugh McLeod was placed in command of the military escort, with George Thomas Howard as his assistant. George Wilkins Kendall, editor of the New Orleans *Picayune,* and Thomas Falconer, an English journalist-tourist, went along for the adventure. In all—merchants, teamsters, tourists, and officials—the expedition totalled 321. Twenty-one wagons carried trade goods with a value of approximately $200,000.

The whole force was organized into five military companies and placed under military discipline. A general air of excitement prevailed as the caravan made ready to depart. Kendall later wrote: "It was looked upon as nothing more than a pleasant hunting excursion" along that portion of the route that was known, and as for the unexplored Indian land, "all were eager to partake of the excitement of being among the first to explore it."

Starting from Brushy Creek, outside of Austin, on June 19, 1841, the Santa Fé Pioneers, as they called themselves, headed into the wilderness—and ultimate disgrace and captivity. The route carried them generally north to the Brazos River, from which they turned northwest across the unknown badlands, and up onto the seemingly limitless plains. Harassed by Indians and suffering from lack of water and a shortage of provisions, the expedition was divided at the foot of the Caprock into two separate sections.

Near present Tucumcari, armed detachments of Governor Manuel Armijo of New Mexico encountered the first of the advance party. Instead of being welcomed, the Texans were met by a hostile army. Captain William G. Lewis, one of the advance party, turned traitor and persuaded the first section of the expedition to lay down its arms and surrender. On October 5, Armijo used this Judas again to capture the main body of the Texans. Without firing a shot the Mexicans made prisoners of the entire Texas expedition.

Ignominiously defeated by the hardships of the arid plains and disgracefully captured by a ruse, the dejected Texans quickly discovered that a worse fate was ahead of them. Armijo ordered them delivered overland to Mexico City. Walking the entire distance on foot, under the vigilant prodding of Mexican bayonets, the "Pioneers" were subjected to numerous bullying indignities. To add insult to injury, Armijo confiscated their trade goods. Try

as they might, they could not convince the authorities of the peaceable intent of the expedition.

A heated controversy arose between the United States and Mexico over the purposes of the expedition, as well as over the manner in which the prisoners were handled—and between political factions in Texas over the wisdom of sending the expedition in the first place. Most of the men were held prisoner in Perote Castle, outside Mexico City, until their general release in 1842. A few, however, released themselves by effecting miraculous escapes from the formidable Mexican prisons; others found release by death from smallpox, starvation, exposure, yellow fever, and even leprosy.

Mexico's harsh treatment of the prisoners was denounced by most of the foreign diplomats in Mexico City; indeed, the unreasonable intensity of feeling toward *los*

Tejanos, prevalent among many Mexican officials as well as the citizenry in general, is difficult to understand. Certainly a factor in the centralists' attitude, however, was an alliance between Texas and the Yucatan rebels, which began to blossom even as the doomed Pioneers sloughed their dusty way toward Santa Fé in the summer of 1841. By the time they were captured, the Texas bond with the federalist insurgents was consummated, and the Texas navy was making preparations once again to blockade the Mexican coast.

These developments, occurring quite apart from the Santa Fé expedition (though linked because of the belief that there was strong federalist sentiment in New Mexico), began with Lamar's decision in February 1841 to make one more effort at a peaceful settlement with Mexico. This decision was based largely on the second British treaty, which affirmed England's intent to mediate with Mexico on Texas' behalf. James Webb, then secretary of state, was named special agent and given full instructions on March 22. They were substantially the same as Treat's and Bee's had been: he was to obtain peace, gain recognition, and not give up the Rio Grande boundary. Perhaps Lamar entertained some deluded hope that the proposed juncture of the people of Santa Fé with Texas would reinforce the Republic's position in Mexican eyes.

Webb sailed to Vera Cruz, where he was refused permission to land. He then requested Pakenham, the friendly British minister, to come to his aid. Pakenham got the same blunt refusal from the Mexican foreign secretary. Mediation was hopeless, and the peace mission impossible in view of the Mexican government's stubborn and irrational behavior. Webb turned to go to Yucatan to negotiate the alliance with the federalists there, but his ship was caught in a storm and he was forced back to Galveston.

In Texas, Webb urged Lamar to recognize the independence of Yucatan and, with this ally, make war on Mexico. Texas could furnish the navy; Yucatan and Tabasco, the troops. Lamar agreed and, on July 20, invited Yucatan to send an agent to Texas. The rebels there responded with alacrity, sending Martin F. Peraza, who brought with him a plan of alliance. After several conferences and minor alterations, this plan was adopted on September 17, 1841.

It pledged the services of the Texas navy to Yucatan for both defensive and aggressive purposes. Any prizes captured were to belong to Texas, but other war revenue would be split between the two nations. On its part,

Yucatan was to advance $8,000 to get the navy back afloat, and pay an additional $8,000 per month as long as three or more ships were in her service.

Here again, Lamar went contrary to Congress, which not only decommissioned the fleet, but also tabled the war resolutions. Nevertheless, it was too good a deal to pass up. Since it would not cost Texas any money, there was reason to believe that the tight-fisted congressmen might approve. It was to take Commodore Moore several months to re-outfit his ships. Not until December 13 was he ready to sail, bearing orders from Lamar to carry out the Yucatan agreement. But by then, Lamar was no longer President, and his successor was mightily chagrined at the naval arrangements. Retribution could wait until Moore returned; President Houston was patient—if somewhat vindictive.

The fall election of 1841 was the bitterest in the history of the Republic's politics. Lamar's aggressive policies, whether successes or failures, had created strong animosities which provided the Houston party with great campaign ammunition. It was still a battle of personalities, however, and the criticisms of Lamar's government were slanted in that vein. As a matter of fact, for a year and a half or longer before the election, many of the public denouncements of Lamar's policies were made with an eye on the election.

The Houston men had no problem finding a candidate. Houston was constitutionally eligible and was willing (indeed, anxious) to run. Lamar's party had more difficulty. Since their leader could not succeed himself in office, they had to find a man who could beat Houston. To make matters worse, Burnet and Lamar were at odds toward the end of the term, and Lamar was reluctant to support Burnet. The Lamar party approached both Albert Sidney Johnston and Thomas J. Rusk, but these men refused to run. The Lamar party was in almost the same shape that the Houston party had been in for the previous presidential race. Ultimately the supporters of Lamar had to rally around David Burnet.

Immediately the Houston party began a personal attack on Burnet. He "lacks tact and judgment," wrote Anson Jones, "and is always too much under the influences of his prejudices." In retaliation, Burnet's supporters found much to say about Houston's drinking. James Morgan castigated Houston's habits, doubting whether he could survive until election time. Edward Fontaine noted: "The people are becoming more and more afraid of trusting the *righting* of the Ship of State into the hands of a hero who can't *stand upright* himself." In the *Telegraph and Texas Register,* Francis Moore editorialized disgustedly: "A few days past he *was brought* to this City in such a state of brutal intoxication, that his own friends were filled with shame and disgust."

Houston's penchant for ardent spirits was well known and was as much a part of his personality as were his humor and flamboyance. By 1838, he began to make vows of temperance, and after his marriage to Margaret Lea, his heavy drinking tapered off. Because his political opponents made such capital out of his earlier disgraces, it is difficult to ascertain the true extent of his alcoholism, if such it really was.

The bitterness of this campaign of 1841 was doubled by Burnet's violent personal hatred for Houston, which developed into a passion with him that year. Houston, using the familiar weapon of ridicule, had frequently poked fun at Burnet and, on one occasion, had called him a hog thief. Enraged, Burnet challenged him to a duel. (Houston was not a duelist, but even his worst enemies could not accuse him of cowardice.) According to one contemporary, Houston lightly passed it off, saying that Burnet would have to get in line as there were twenty-four ahead of him. Another source stated that Houston sent him a note saying that he never fought "downhill." Whatever the reply, Burnet was further infuriated.

Edward Hall, in a letter to John G. Chalmers on July 21, 1841, commented caustically on the possibility that "Falstaff Sam Houston" might be elected. "I with many of the friends of Judge Burnet almost despaired of obtaining even a showing for his election, but hopes are brightening every day, and I now begin to think that we shall get a very respectable vote if not a majority . . . . Among the stories conjured up by the Houston Clique is the Vile & Outrageous lie that Judge Burnet is a drunkard & this from Houston's party *shows* that their cause is getting rather interesting if not desperate."

As the campaign drew to an end, however, it was Houston's friends who grew confident, while the Lamar-Burnet faction waxed more heatedly into personal insult and invective. The vote was 7,915 for Houston; 3,619 for Burnet. General Ed Burleson, Houston's choice for Vice-President, won easily over Memucan Hunt. The great majority of Texans agreed with another contemporary observation that Houston, "drunk in a ditch, is worth a thousand of Lamar and Burnet."

8

1842

IN A DITCH

FATE DEALT SAM HOUSTON a tricky hand of cards in 1842. He played them inscrutably, willfully, and sometimes malignantly. If he did not win, at least he got a draw—to the consternation of his enemies and the bewilderment of his friends. In the words of Ashbel Smith, he "exhibited a propensity . . . to make enemies" of his supporters. His enemies saw him as a frightened, vacillating coward, and as James Welsh put it, a "dam blackguard Indian drunk." To a relatively impartial observer, Charles Elliot, the new British *chargé d'affaires* in Texas, he was "the fittest man in this Country for his present station." Elliot noted that although he said and wrote what seemed "to be capricious and contradictory," he only did it for appearance's sake, to prevent a rupture in his party or a break with Congress.

Thus, a dramatic enigma to all, Houston coped as he could with the rapid turn of events during the first year of his second administration.

A candid picture of the President at this time, human if unflattering, was drawn in the reminiscences of friends with whom he stayed while his wife was on a visit to Alabama. His constant whittling scattered splinters of wood all over Mrs. John Lockhart's house. His habit of spitting soiled her clean porch. "By exerting no undue energy and exercising a bit of consideration, he could have expectorated over the rail," she complained. But worse, the temptation of a good jug overcame the frowning image of his absent wife one night, and he began to indulge. Long after others had retired, he called a Negro slave to bring him an ax and with it energetically chopped off one of the beautiful, hand-carved wooden posts of a fine old four-poster bed. The disturbance, of course, brought his host, Judge Lockhart, rushing into the room. With unwavering dignity and inebriated logic, the President explained that the post had interfered with his breathing and had thus kept him awake. The judge quietly withdrew, leaving Houston to his slumbers. This was his last reported fall from the virtue of moderation.

Indeed, his election was celebrated at a "cold water *doin's*," where Houston refused to take even the "smallest drop of the ardent." The inauguration, too, was coldly sober. Josiah Gregg, the well-known Santa Fé trader, was disappointed in the affair and in Houston's labored address. He had anticipated a fiercer speech, but he found Houston's costume sufficiently flamboyant: "a linsey-woolsey hunting shirt, and pantaloons, and an old wide brimmed white fur hat."

Houston had worked for days on the written message, intending it to be impressive. His first message to Con-

Sam Houston

gress was blunter: "There is not a dollar in the treasury. The nation is involved from ten to fifteen millions. The precise amount of its liabilities has not been ascertained . . . . We are not only without money, but without credit, and for want of punctuality, without honor." The chief points of his message were rigid economy; no involvement in costly offensive wars or expeditions; and a pacific Indian policy, based on the establishment of trading posts, which would reduce to one-fourth the amount spent by Lamar on frontier defense.

To show his sincerity in this program of retrenchment, he refused to occupy the two-story President's mansion (where Lamar gave a gala farewell ball) and roomed instead at Bullock's Hotel, then being operated by Mrs. Angelina Eberly. The Sixth Congress received his message enthusiastically and set about eagerly to reduce expenses. Robert Potter, congressman from East Texas, commented that "there was an idea in vogue that this was a two-horse government, and he thought they would soon have it regulated so as to work with one mule." True to the prediction, the civil list was cut from $173,000 to $32,800 by abolishing certain positions and reducing all other salaries. Congress even cut its own members from five dollars per day to three dollars, and Houston unflinchingly took an annual reduction from $10,000 to $5,000.

On the grounds that neither man nor nation can improve its fortune by additional borrowing, all the outstanding bond issues were cancelled, as Hamilton was to find to his surprise when he reached Austin that spring. A more drastic step was the suspension of the entire public debt until the government should become able to meet its obligations. "We have no money," said Houston. "We cannot redeem our liabilities. These facts are known, and we had as well avow them by our legislation. . . . We have now no other remedy left. The evil is upon us."

Suspension was not repudiation. Both Houston and Congress believed that a frank admission of the situation, with a promise to pay when it was possible, would raise the nation in the public's estimation—and perhaps give some support to the wild emissions of Lamar's printing presses. Since some appropriations were necessary, Congress resorted to a new type of paper money—exchequer bills—of which some $350,000 were authorized.

Houston thought these drastic measures would sufficiently restore the nation's credit to permit a $300,000 loan by public subscription. In its zeal for the economy program, Congress denied the President the chance to try. In fact, the legislative thriftiness may have gone too far. Some of the regular government routine had to be handled by Congress itself because the departments were destitute of clerks. Mail service was drastically (and injuriously) curtailed; the state department was unable to secure "indispensable necessities"; and Houston had to plead with Congress to restore sufficient funds to the budget to permit the attorney general's office to function.

The program may have pinched, but it was effective. The expenses of government during Lamar's three years in office were nearly $5,000,000; during Houston's three years they were to come to slightly more than $500,000, or just over ten percent of his predecessor's extravagant expenditures.

There was sharp contrast, too, between Lamar's and Houston's Indian policies. Houston recommended the establishment among the Indians of trading posts, each protected by a minimal force of twenty-five men. Treaties would be made with the hostile tribes which would restore their confidence in Texas. The trade goods, bartered at the posts for skins and robes, would keep the Indians quiet. Congress supported his plan, and Houston diligently pursued it. Conditions on the frontier demanded attention. "Indians are thick as hops about the mountains in this vicinity and occasionally they knock over a poor fellow and take his hair," complained Jack Snively of Austin.

In July 1842 Henry Scott, Ethan Stroud, Joseph Durst, and Leonard Williams were appointed as special commissioners to negotiate with the Indians, especially the Comanches. Houston kept in close touch with the activities, held conferences in Austin with visiting chiefs, and himself attended several councils of tribal representatives. The Torrey Trading Company, organized by John F., David K., and Thomas S. Torrey, with Sam Houston and George Barnard among the principal stockholders, established important posts along the frontier. Post Number

One at present New Braunfels enjoyed a thriving trade, as did Post Number Two near present Waco. Branches were established the next year on the Navasota River and near the falls of the Brazos. A temporary trading post on the upper Trinity helped quiet the Indians there.

All in all, Houston's peace policy was effective. Depredations continued, but they were somewhat abated. Houston's critics, of course, denied any amelioration of the Indian problem, although they could not debate that the solution was less costly than Lamar's.

In most things the President was patient—willing to give or take with the tide of events so long as he was able to steer toward his goal. But in the matter of the location of the capital, he was stubborn, perverse, and willful. From the time he first took his seat in the Fourth Congress, he had abused Lamar's "seat of empire" with all the invective at his command. And he had continued the attack at every opportunity. In his inaugural address, and again in his message to the Sixth Congress, he abjured the location and recommended a bill to return the capital to the town of Houston. His enemies reviled his vanity—which, indeed, it partly was—and the citizens of Austin waged a passionate fight to defeat the bill. Houston's friends and supporters advised him that it would be more politic to wait until some emergency threatened the frontier capital, but he was obdurate. Unable to push the bill through Congress, he made the removal of the capital the chief issue of the year. In this fight, he was able only to effect a draw with his opponents.

The attention of Congress was diverted from the capital question by the receipt of news of the treacherous capture, the terrible march, and the torturous imprisonment of the Santa Fé Pioneers. Militant speeches blasted the rafters of the halls of Congress, as Texans shook with indignation. Once again, an offensive war against Mexico became the talk of the day. Senator Francis Moore, the eloquent editor of the *Telegraph,* wrote grandly: ". . . the least demonstration on the part of our government to commence or sanction offensive operation against Mexico, would be responded to with joyous acclamations throughout the United States. . . . Let the mandate but go forth. 'Texas has decided to prosecute an offensive war,' and she might in all probability remain almost passive and look on with folded arms to see the great work accomplished."

Houston cautioned restraint but, in the face of the excited war talk, he lost his grip on Congress. Some of his warmest supporters began to drift away from him, to link arms with others in a dream of conquest. He was able to stifle an outright declaration of war—there still was not any money in the treasury—but he could not prevent the passage through both houses of a ridiculous bill, redefining the boundaries of Texas to include all of the territory south of the 42nd parallel—to the Pacific on the west and northern Mexico on the south. This embraced the present states of New Mexico, Arizona, Nevada, Utah, California, Chihuahua, Sonora, Baja California, with parts of Colorado, Sinaloa, Durango, Coahuila and Tamaulipas—an area larger than that of the United States at the time.

With tongue in cheek, Houston vetoed the measure, writing a solemn objection to it with scarcely a hint of the ridicule he surely felt for what he called a "legislative jest." This was the beginning of an ever-widening breach between the executive and legislative branches. Three days after the veto, on February 5, Congress adjourned, the members returning home to continue the fervent talk of military retaliation and to dream of the glorious expansion. The President's popularity began to suffer, and his attitude toward the revitalized navy came in for as much criticism as his anti-war policy.

Houston had not approved the naval contract with Yucatan but, at the time, he was powerless to prevent it. On inauguration day, December 13, 1841, Commodore Moore had sailed out into the Gulf under orders from Lamar. Immediately, on December 15, Houston issued an order recalling the navy. It was too late; the fleet little vessels were on their way, and Moore, too knowledgeable of Houston's attitude, did not stop to let the order overtake him.

By January 6, 1842, Moore and the three ships which he had refurbished—the *Austin,* the *San Bernard,* and the *San Antonio*—were anchored off Yucatan. Moore and his aide went ashore to report to the governor of Yucatan. While they were gone, his second in command, Lieutenant Alfred G. Gray, learned that Santa Anna had succeeded in toppling Bustamante as the head of the centralist dictatorship in Mexico, and that the clever generalissimo had made a truce with the Yucatan rebels. Excitedly, Gray realized that this jolting turn of events made the *Yucatecos* enemies of Texas! The commodore's very life might be in danger. Action was demanded. Gray quickly sent a detachment of Texas marines to take into custody the Yucatecan dignitary, Quintana Roo, and his party. He would hold them hostage for the safe return of Moore and his aide.

Moore, unapprised of the truce and blissfully unaware of his assistant's precipitate action, went straight to the capital. The truce was a shock, but he was informed unofficially that it would not have been signed had Yucatan known that the Texas navy was on its way. Verbally, the governor and his cabinet agreed to continue the $8,000 monthly fee, if Moore would keep his ships at hand as a sword over the head of Santa Anna.

Pleased with the outcome, Moore hardly had time to relax before he learned of Gray's capture of Quintana Roo. Dressing in full uniform, he rushed back to the governor's palace—at 2:00 A.M.—to be the first to give him the news, so that he might explain and apologize. Quick thinking saved the day. The apology was accepted, and Roo was promptly released. Though Moore did not realize it then, this was but the beginning of a long series of disastrous episodes and misadventures which were to keep him in a constant turmoil to rectify.

Near the end of the month, he sent the *San Antonio* back to Galveston, with recommendations that Texas establish a blockade of the Mexican coast, and then took the other two vessels to Vera Cruz. The captain of the *San Antonio* was informed of Houston's recall order— which, by some mysterious circumstance, had not reached Moore—and was instructed to return to the fleet and personally present copies of it to the commodore. At New Orleans, when reprovisioning for the voyage on February 11, 1842, the vessel suffered a full-scale mutiny. Perhaps the contradictory orders had upset the officers and crew, or perhaps it was merely the arbitrary decision of the officers to take shore leave while confining the crew to the ship. Whatever the reason, the mutiny cost the life of Lieutenant Charles Fuller and caused the captain to enlist a new crew.

Probably the most important consequence was the attendant delay in carrying the recall orders to Commodore Moore. The *San Antonio* did not rejoin the fleet until March 10. The news of the mutiny, carried in the newspapers, had preceded the ship's arrival. Moore, in a fit of anger, had determined to "mete out to the rascals the *uttermost penalties* of the law." Two of the mutineers had been caught and were on board the *San Antonio;* Moore quickly convened a court martial which sentenced one mutineer to a hundred lashes (promptly executed) and postponed the trial of the other.

The commodore was less prompt in reacting to the recall order. He later wrote that he was "compelled to disobey," but in none of his dispatches did he make his reasons clear. Two factors probably influenced him: one was the $8,000 monthly stipend; the other was a drastic change in Texas-Mexican relations, which may have prompted him to reason that the order was out of date. The new development was a Mexican invasion of Texas!

After Santa Anna assumed power in Mexico, he remembered the indignity of his capture, but conveniently forgot his protestations of lasting peace and friendship. He ordered the centralist general, Rafael Vásquez, to lead a guerrilla-like raid into southwestern Texas.

General Vásquez was happy to comply, for it was he who had suffered such an ignominious defeat at the hands of the redoubtable Colonel Jordan at Saltillo. With a party, variously estimated to be from eight to fourteen hundred men, he dashed across the Rio Grande toward San Antonio. Detachments hastened to Goliad and Victoria, where they raised the Mexican flag and quickly marched away. Vásquez and the main body of troops reached San Antonio on March 5 and withdrew on March 7. Little damage was done, but it signalled Mexico's intention of renewing her claim to Texas. Too, it illustrated the shallowness of Santa Anna's promises and the Mexican resentment of the naval pact with Yucatan.

Houston's whole policy was predicated on the assumption that Mexico would never invade Texas. The Vásquez raid stripped Houston of his argument, and had he been a lesser man, it would have made his position untenable. As it was, the heated demand for war on all sides left him uncomfortably alone. Even his most loyal followers deserted him in the clamor for retaliation.

As soon as the news reached Austin, Vice-President Burleson, without waiting to seek Houston's approval (which he feared would not be forthcoming), rushed to San Antonio at the head of three companies of mounted men. Houston promptly dispatched a messenger to General Alexander Somervell, militia commander in Bexar County, to assume full command of any troops arriving at San Antonio. He also directed Somervell to take charge of any military action which needed to be meted out to the retreating Mexicans. The order was a blow to Burleson's pride and an effective damper on the more violent spirits.

The volunteers attempted to reject Somervell in favor of the old Indian fighter, but Burleson hesitated over such an open break with Houston. After two weeks of uncertain delay—with the volunteer camp shrinking daily—Burleson returned to Austin. Somervell refused to command the men who did not want him, and the affair ended without incident. Vásquez recrossed the Rio Grande unmolested.

While Somervell and Burleson disputed command, other volunteers, under their own captains, poured into San Antonio. Soon over 3,500 armed and restless men milled about the town, undisciplined and leaderless. Resentment against the Houston-appointed general prevented the men from accepting him as commander. On April 2, with Vásquez long since out of reach, the bulk of the volunteers returned to their homes.

Houston, who had come in for severe criticism for not

compelling prompt action, attempted to appease the war faction by declaring a naval blockade of the Mexican coast on March 26. That he may not have intended the order seriously is evident from the fact that he made no provision for financing it. He thought Moore had received his order to return from Yucatan and, as a consequence, did not believe the blockade would be put into effect. What he did not know at the time, of course, was that Moore had acted on his own initiative, ignoring the order to return, and had already begun to prey on Mexican shipping. He captured two prizes early in April before receiving, on April 18, the notification of the blockade. Houston, through Colonel George W. Hockley, secretary of war and marine, requested Moore to come to Texas to discuss urgent business, after first sending the fleet to New Orleans to be refurbished for the more successful prosecution of the blockade.

With high optimism, Moore complied. It seemed that, after all, Houston was going to promote an aggressive stand against Mexico and to condone a vigorous blockade of the Mexican ports. At his conference with the President, Moore became more firmly convinced of Houston's support; he was soon to reverse his conviction, in the belief that Houston duped him. Arriving at New Orleans, with a scant three thousand dollars remaining from his Yucatan fees, he depended on the President's making $20,000 in appropriated funds available. This Houston failed to do, and Moore finally pledged his personal credit to the amount of $34,000 to reprovision the ships. While he waited anxiously to put to sea, additional troubles stacked up in New Orleans. In desperation, he sent his brother to Texas to seek relief from the President. Two weeks later, the younger Moore returned empty-handed; Houston called a special session of Congress, desiring legislative approval before making further expenditures. Moore was galled—so far he had not gotten a dime from Houston.

In the special session, Houston turned the war talk and the mounting castigation of his policies to his own advantage. He called for Congress to meet in an emergency session to discuss the war with Mexico. But the designated place of meeting was not Austin; it was Houston. The return of the capital to his namesake city was justified on the grounds of the threat of invasion. As a matter of fact, Houston had moved the executive department from Austin in April. Anson Jones felt that the called session was "useless and pernicious," and that "the President convened it for the purposes of making capital for himself."

The proclamation calling Congress to meet on June 27 had cited a crisis "in our affairs with Mexico." Houston's opening message to Congress was a masterpiece of salesmanship. The Vásquez raid was labelled "a demonstration by Mexico" and "a marauding party." The alarm raised throughout Texas was depicted as near panic, although care was taken not to offend. "Violent excitement and commotion . . . brave citizens rushed to the scene . . . without order, regularity, or discipline . . . ready to rush with impetuosity across the Rio Grande . . . . Difficulties arose as to who should lead them; and in the end, they found themselves on examination, totally unprepared for the campaign—inasmuch as they had left their homes upon a momentary summons and were destitute of the means for sufficient and protracted service."

He made a plea for order and discipline in the military service, stating plainly that he was not "an advocate for offensive measures." He boasted that for "an amount comparatively trifling" to the cost of offensive war he could protect the country. He correctly concluded that the Vásquez affair was intended merely to give Santa Anna "a temporary popularity at home and to furnish a pretext for levying contributions and maintaining a large standing army for the purpose of establishing himself permanently in possession of usurped power . . . ."

Then he turned to distract congressional attention with domestic problems of varying nature and especially urged that some additional appropriation for the government be provided with some revenue to back it. Finally, he harangued at length on the danger of leaving the government archives in Austin, and he pleaded that a new seat of government be selected.

Congress dallied for several weeks under a barrage of war talk, while newspapers, especially Francis Moore's *Telegraph,* demanded an aggressive campaign. Finally an elaborate bill was passed authorizing war against Mexico. The hot heads had called Houston's hand.

Houston responded promptly on July 22 with a sturdy veto, commending Congress for its patriotism, but stressing the lack of financial resources in the Republic to carry on a war. He argued that a declaration of war which could not be supported would make Texas a laughing stock of the world and would be injurious to the country itself. "A war of invasion would be the theme of continued conversation—a state of feverish excitement would exist throughout the country—general incertitude would pervade every class, and discontent would be universal. The question would be asked, what is the Executive doing? He has all power given to him . . . . When therefore, will active operations commence? It would be needless for him to respond . . . that he has not a dollar to commence operations with . . . . It would be vain for him to attempt an explanation . . . ."

Although he was forced to veto the idea of making "war

without means," Houston offered a counter suggestion in his veto message: "Texas will be able, for a comparatively trifling amount, to carry on a retaliatory war, or at least to give protection to our Southwestern frontier." His plan involved the use of the militia and the raising of small volunteer companies, "mounted, equipped, and prepared at their own expense." He would rely, he said, on the "chivalry and patriotism of [his] Countrymen."

Before Congress rallied to override his veto, he made public a scheme to raise approximately one thousand such volunteers, even to the details of how many men should come from each county. "The Executive has great reliance upon the zeal of his countrymen," he wrote, but he privately believed that the effort to get such a volunteer army together would probably die aborning. If it did not—if there were a thousand men who would equip themselves for the fight—it was precisely the sort of guerrilla force that Houston knew could be used effectively along the border.

To his great relief the veto message and the alternative scheme "got through," as he expressed it to Anson Jones. "It is the only kind of war the country can sustain," he explained to his secretary of state, who was too ill to attend the meeting of Congress. "Had I sanctioned the war bill, I could not have commanded any means within twelve months . . . I would have been in a state of constant vexation, and threats of revolution would have been constant . . . For my country's sake, and for the credit of those who have been so anxious, I sincerely hope there will be volunteers enough to answer the design of a visit to the Rio Grande. We will see!"

The President's stand, although accepted by Congress—reluctantly—was unpopular. The unbending Anson Jones secretly criticized him for advocating what Jones castigated as "this 'willing war' . . . by volunteers." George W. Hockley, long one of Houston's closest friends, deserted him at this juncture and submitted a bitter letter of resignation as secretary of war and marine. Open threats of assassination were made against Houston, and the editor of the Houston *Morning Star* begged the public to postpone judgment of the President until "the storm of passion and prejudice has subsided." In the midst of these attacks on his position, welcome moral support came from an unexpected quarter. His old friend and former mentor, Andrew Jackson, late fire-eating President of the United States, wrote him: "I approve your veto fully. To make offensive war without ample means . . . would be the height of folly and madness, and must result in defeat and disgrace . . . . If you had not vetoed this bill, it would have led to the destruction of your country . . . . Your true policy is to act upon the defensive, and husband all your means for this purpose . . . . Foster your commerce and revenues . . . . *Stand on the Defensive.*"

Houston had not failed to emphasize the need of bolstering commerce and raising revenue. Even as he fenced with the war mongers, he parried with threats directed at supporting the economy. On July 19, he had submitted a program for this purpose. He asked Congress to reduce the direct taxes, which he deemed oppressive and largely uncollectible; he asked Congress to establish customs houses on the eastern border, empowering the customs collectors to call out the militia if necessary in order to enforce the laws; and he asked Congress to authorize the sale of 400,000 acres of the choicest of the Cherokee lands, for the support of the exchequer bills.

This last suggestion represented a galling retreat on

the Cherokee issue: to be able now to sell a portion of the lands, he had to submit to the passage of a bill revising the statement of ownership of these lands. So great was the government's need for money that Houston did not hesitate to sign the act and commence the necessary public surveys.

On the same day that Congress passed the Cherokee Land Act—July 26, 1842—it also appropriated funds for support of the navy. Moore, who had been frantically trying to repair and provision his ships at New Orleans without any financial support from Texas, had at last made a trip to Houston while Congress was in session. There he had lobbied for an appropriation sufficient at least to cover the amount of his personal pledges for the cost of naval repairs and supplies. Congress responded rather handsomely, with an appropriation of nearly $100,000. Moore was elated and went to call on President Houston personally.

To the commodore's distress, he discovered that the naval bill was like an appropriation of blue sky. Houston smilingly "expressed his gratification" over the congressional support of the navy, and handed Moore an open power of attorney to charge his costs against the Republic, explaining that it was against his policy to issue any more exchequer bills. Moore flew into a rage. He had received two such bonds from Houston before, in lieu of appropriations which Congress had made. Moore said, "A power of attorney from the President of Texas for *one million dollars* would not bring in New Orleans *one hundred dollars!*" He told Houston that the President "need not try to *humbug* me with another bond or power of attorney, for I would not be *humbugged* by him."

Houston calmly asked him when he intended to return to the fleet at New Orleans, and Moore replied testily that he would take the next steamer from Galveston and "would disband the navy and leave the vessels to rot." Then he stormed out of the office to make good his word.

Up to this point, Houston had entertained no feeling of personal animosity toward Moore, but he had always been opposed to the extravagant navy. Now he resorted to trickery to prevent the onus of ruining the navy from falling on him in the midst of turmoil over his veto of the war bill. He sent word to Moore that if he would delay his departure, exchequer bills in the amount of $18,812 would be signed for his use. Several days later, Moore was handed a packet containing the exchequer bills and sealed orders, which were to be opened after he arrived in New Orleans.

Believing that these were orders to put to sea, Moore triumphantly returned to his fleet. He and all the war party, as Houston intended, thought that Moore had outfoxed the old chief. When he opened the sealed orders he found that they authorized him—not to spend the exchequer bills, but to use them as collateral for a loan! It was an impossible plan. As money, the $18,812 was worth only about $9,000 in New Orleans; as collateral, he could borrow less than a fourth of the amount.

But the commodore was ingenious. He resolved not to let Houston sink the navy. His first step was to request permission to sell the *Zavala,* the steamship which Houston had previously ridiculed. Suddenly, however, the President found constitutional scruples against authorizing the sale. Moore now knew that Houston was deliberately trying to keep the navy from putting to sea. Using the small amount he could borrow on the exchequer notes, he provisioned the *San Antonio* and secretly sent her to Yucatan to offer to let the rebels there hire the Texas navy again.

While the *San Antonio* was gone, the *San Bernard* was caught in a violent Gulf hurricane, which hit Galveston in September 1842, and was washed ashore. Her captain could not get funds to put her back afloat. This captain and the remnant of his crew—two seamen, two cabin boys, and five officers—moved over to the *Archer*, which was lying at anchor with seams in her hull wide enough to put a hand through. Finally, with no money with which to get supplies, the little band was literally starved out and the men quit.

In New Orleans, Moore was doing little better with the three remaining ships. The *Zavala* was, of course, incapable of putting to sea. The *Wharton* and the *Austin* hung weakly at anchor with skeleton crews. Between June and September, nineteen men deserted for want of pay, and the next month Moore was forced to discharge fifteen others for the same reason.

Anxiously, Moore awaited the return of the *San Antonio*. Rumors began to reach him that she was destroyed in the September hurricane. None of the vessels entering New Orleans had sighted her, nor had she reached Yucatan. Finally, in despair, Moore was forced to report to the secretary of war and marine that the schooner was apparently lost.

On October 29, 1842, he was ordered to return to Galveston with the remaining ships. In reply, he submitted the muster rolls of his crew, showing that he did not have enough men to take one ship out of the harbor, much less all of them. The war department's answer was a cold reiteration of the order to return to Galveston and instructions to the Texas agent in New Orleans not to furnish the navy with any more supplies. Poor Moore! The end was near. The navy would soon be gone and his own career ruined. Unwarranted disgrace would follow his disillusionment. But until the next year, he struggled against Houston and his destiny like a firmly hooked fish against a stout line.

Meanwhile, fate was perilously close to ruining Houston, himself. The special session of Congress had adjourned on July 23, leaving the President to face the storm of protest, which blew up over his veto of the war bill. Hardly had the angry winds abated when the worst of all possible disasters to Houston's policy occurred—Texas was invaded a second time by Mexico!

On September 11, 1842, General Adrian Woll, a French soldier of fortune in the employ of Santa Anna, appeared suddenly on the outskirts of San Antonio with an army of fourteen hundred men. At dawn, the citizens heard the sound of cannon, but an unusually heavy fog covered the movements of Mexican troops around the town. As the sun cleared the atmosphere, the inhabitants found themselves surrounded, without a chance to escape or resist.

Three members of Congress and the entire membership of the district court, which was then in session at San Antonio, were among the prisoners taken by Woll. The Mexican general raised his flag on the plaza, announced the conquest of Texas by Mexico, and made pretensions of permanent occupation. His victory, however, was short-lived.

Encamped outside of the town was Captain John C. (Jack) Hays and a small band of Texas Rangers. As the news of the invasion spread, volunteers rushed to the scene and placed themselves under the command of this unusual leader—then a mere twenty-five years old. Within a few days, Hays had nearly six hundred eager, if undisciplined, men; and the usual dispute arose over who should command. The young captain deferred to old Matthew Caldwell, a renowned Indian fighter; but it was Hays and his men who enticed Woll out of San Antonio and into ambush on Salado Creek, a few miles away, on September 18.

The victory at the Battle of Salado was short of complete, although Woll licked his wounds over a loss of sixty men (against one Texan), and decided to retreat from San Antonio. Unfortunately, as the Mexicans had fought their way back to San Antonio, they had captured and massacred almost an entire company of volunteers from La Grange, under Nicholas Mosby Dawson. The few remaining Dawson prisoners, together with several civilians and the personnel of the district court, were taken back to Mexico, where they were incarcerated in Perote Prison—the same dungeons from which, only a few months earlier, the Santa Fé prisoners had been released.

Cry havoc and let slip the dogs of war! Houston's peace policy was shattered. Fiery editorials, and more caustic comments, bombarded him at every turn. He could not dismiss this invasion lightly, as he had the Vásquez raid. Nor, apparently, did he desire to do so. On September 16, he directed his new secretary of war, Morgan C. Hamilton, to call out the militia—ordering companies from the counties nearest San Antonio to converge on that place. Three companies were to rush to the defense of Austin, and if they found it necessary to evacuate, they were to burn the town and the government archives. He feared the possibility of a general invasion.

Four days later he reasoned that the enemy intended only to take San Antonio and merely to threaten Austin. He ordered a concentration of troops at San Antonio to force the removal of Woll. Not until September 22 did he learn of the Battle of Salado and Woll's withdrawal. As he received communications indicating the number of companies in the field, he decided to order Woll pursued to the Rio Grande.

Command of the Texan forces was given to Alexander Somervell, who was ordered to harass the enemies' retreat and to follow them across the Rio Grande, if he deemed it advisable. Houston warned Somervell not to take into his command any troops who might later prove insubordinate—the constant plague of Texas' fighting forces. "You may rely upon the gallant Hays and his companions," Houston noted. He urged Somervell to send reports on the situation as often as possible, and he cautioned him to treat Mexican civilians gently. "You will be controlled by the rules of the most civilized warfare, and you will find the advantage of exercising great humanity toward the common people." Houston clearly feared turning loose an undisciplined horde of *"los diablos Tejanos"* to ravish the Mexican countryside. Loot and plunder were not the objectives of invasion.

Not until November 22 did Somervell get his command organized and become able to set out for the Rio Grande. Reaching Laredo on December 8, he found the town evacuated of Mexican troops. Unfortunately, some of his men fell like wolves on the homes of the Mexican population. Unable to control them effectively, he moved his camp several miles away from town. General discontent prevailed. A large number of the Texans wanted to cross the Rio Grande and live off the land in a vicious retaliatory raid. Somervell was undecided. Seven hundred men—the extent of his command—were insufficient to accomplish anything other than guerrilla tactics.

During the remainder of the month he marched down the river to clear the valley of enemy troops. At Laredo two hundred men were dismissed and returned home. At

Guerrero, Mexico, on December 15, Somervell crossed the river and encamped. Four days later, he issued an order to return to Gonzales to be disbanded. This was met with open rebellion, and about three hundred men organized themselves under Colonel William S. Fisher to continue the military *entrada*. The remaining two hundred followed Somervell back to Texas. Again the specter of dissension in command haunted the Texas forces; the results were to prove tragic.

Fisher and his men, although their behavior was outright mutiny, may be looked upon as symbols of the widespread hostility toward Sam Houston and his policies. The rebellious men, positive that Houston had privately ordered Somervell not to invade Mexico, simply decided to take matters into their own hands. With rafts to carry their meager supplies, they moved downriver to the town of Mier, which they entered on December 23. They demanded that the town furnish supplies and ransom money and, taking the *alcalde* and the local priest as hostages, they withdrew across the river to make camp.

While the ragged band of Texans awaited the delivery of their supplies, the centralist general, Pedro Ampudia, slipped into the town with over two thousand men. Learning that the town had been garrisoned, but not knowing the extent of its strength, Fisher decided to attack. On Christmas afternoon, with 261 men, he reentered Mier. Bedlam broke loose. The Texans soon discovered they were outnumbered nearly ten to one, but they fought like demons. The battle raged into the night, falling off after darkness, but breaking out fiercely again the next morning, to continue until after noon.

Ampudia and the centralists, when their powder was nearly exhausted and their bodies almost broken with hunger and thirst, sent out a white flag. They boldly demanded the surrender of the Texans as prisoners of war and, in hopeless desperation, the Texans decided to capitulate. The irony of their defeat was, that if they had not given up, Ampudia himself undoubtedly would have surrendered the town. The Mexican losses had been over six hundred killed and several hundred wounded, against the total Texan loss of thirty! The remaining Mexican troops were at the point of panic—and every bit as tired and hungry as the Texans. A few hours longer, and victory would have been the Texans'.

The promise to treat them with "consideration," and as prisoners of war, was promptly violated as soon as the Texans laid down their arms. They were immediately sentenced to execution as brigands, but the next day Ampudia commuted their sentence to imprisonment. From Mier they were marched to Matamoros, and then toward Mexico City. At Salado, on February 11, 1843, the prisoners overthrew their guards and scattered in a vain attempt to escape back to the Rio Grande. Losing their way in the mountains, many died of exposure and starvation; and all suffered extreme torment. Finally, they were forced to surrender again, singly and in groups. One hundred seventy-six were thus recaptured.

When he learned of the escape, Santa Anna ordered all who were retaken to be executed. The governor of Coahuila refused to obey, and Santa Anna reduced his order to the execution of one man out of ten. This meant that of the 176, 17 must die. What followed at the little Mexican village of Salado was one of the most dramatic moments in history—the drawing of the black beans.

In order to determine who among the prisoners were to receive the death sentence, it was decided to mix 17 black beans in an earthen pot with 159 white beans. With dignity and courage the men filed up to the jar, reached their hands into its small mouth, and drew out their destiny. William A. (Big Foot) Wallace, who was among the prisoners, drew a white bean. He later related humorously that he "figgered" the black beans were larger and he fingered the beans until he located the smallest one he could find.

The seventeen doomed men were led into a separate courtyard, where they were blindfolded, then shot. The cold-blooded horror of the execution startled the civilized world. Resentment against the men, who were clearly unauthorized filibusterers, changed to sympathy; and this additional evidence of Santa Anna's butchery added another spark to flames of the Alamo and Goliad in the hearts of Texans. The remainder of the prisoners were taken to Perote Castle and thrown into cells with Woll's prisoners from San Antonio. A few escaped; a number died of privation and disease; and on September 16, 1844, those remaining were released by Santa Anna, under pressure from foreign diplomats in Mexico.

Meantime, Sam Houston struggled—against increasing unpopularity, public indignation, depression, debt, and Indian depredations—to hold the Republic intact and to secure peace on its borders. Circumstances made his policy seem capricious in 1843; his disposition made it seem tyrannical. One of his last acts in 1842, which was certainly the arbitrary application of a personal whim, was to negate the harsh law ordering free Negroes out of Texas. Although he could not cancel an act of Congress, he could as President issue pardons. So he published an official proclamation, remitting in advance any punishment assigned under the law against free Negroes—thus totally destroying the effectiveness of the law.

9

1843

A CAPRICIOUS KIND
OF PEACE

DRUNK OR SOBER, Houston had risen to heights of greatness during his first year back in office. He had also been mean, vindictive, treacherous, and vacillating. In his attitude toward the capital city he had been persistently petty.

Determined to move the seat of government from "that d - - - - d hole called Austin," as he put it, he used the Vásquez raid of March 1842 as an excuse to establish his headquarters back in the town of Houston. Then he decided to transfer the government archives there for safety. The President had a "high and sacred obligation," he stated grandly. "Should the infinite evil which the loss of the national archives would occasion, fall upon the country through his neglect of imperious constitutional duty, he would be culpable in the extreme, and most justly incur the reproach of a whole nation."

The people in Austin had no doubt about Houston's true intentions. Without the archives, Austin would have little chance to remain as the capital, or even to continue to exist as a city. The citizens held a mass meeting to organize the town to fight the removal of its only hope for the future. A vigilante committee was appointed to guard the archives; and a lookout patrol was established at Bastrop to report on any wagons which Houston might send after the records and to detain any wagons leaving the area carrying them.

W. D. Miller, Houston's private secretary, informed the President that Austinites "would rather take up their rifles to prevent a removal than to fight the Mexicans." Thwarted, Houston convened the special session of the Sixth Congress at Houston rather than at the capital. But Congress refused to redesignate Houston as the seat of government. Unquestionably there was a strong element of vanity motivating Houston. The Woll invasion in September, however, gave strength and validity to his arguments about the security of Austin. The capital was indeed in an exposed position and was clearly threatened.

Again it became Houston's sacred duty to protect the seat of government. Realizing that there was too much resistance to the city of his choice, he relocated the executive offices at Washington-on-the-Brazos, birthplace of Texas independence. Based on the constitutional provision that the capital might be moved "in case of emergency in time of war," he proclaimed it the new capital of the Republic.

Austin in 1842

In truth, Washington was not a very good choice. Its normal population was less than 300 people; it had few buildings suitable for government use; and there were scant accommodations for departmental personnel or for members of Congress. The British *chargé d'affaires,* Charles Elliot, noted that Houston himself had written to him privately that "he finds things at Washington rather raw, and as he has been accustomed to the elaborate comforts of an Indian wigwam, I presume he must be living in a commodious excavation."

Nevertheless, Houston pursued his course. In October he called for the Seventh Congress to meet at Washington on November 14, nearly a month earlier than the previously scheduled date. The response was feeble; only a few members straggled to the capital which Houston had selected for them, and there was much grousing about both the early date and the location. On November 21, the President issued an angry second call for Congress, and three days later, the House had a reluctant quorum, although the Senate did not have enough men in attendance to conduct business until after December 1.

In his annual message, instead of asking Congress to relocate the capital, he announced what he had done and why he had done it. Before Congress had a chance to take any action, he determined once again to move the government archives from Austin. This would be the final step in a *fait accompli* which Congress and the nation would have little choice but to accept. Confidential orders were given to Colonel Thomas I. Smith and Captain Eli Chandler to effect the transfer of the records. "The manner . . . will be left to your own sound judgment and discretion . . . . Be prepared to act with efficiency. Do not be thwarted in the undertaking."

Smith and Chandler were circumspect. On the morning

of December 30 they entered Austin quietly, with three wagons and twenty men. With the help of one-legged Thomas William Ward, commissioner of the General Land Office, they almost got the wagons loaded before anyone in town realized what was happening. It was Mrs. Angelina Eberly, manager of the Bullock Hotel, who discovered the stealthy activities. Quickly she spread the alarm, rushing to Congress Avenue where a small cannon was kept loaded in the event of an Indian attack. The muzzle was turned in the general direction of the land office, and she applied a torch to the breech.

Shot splattered harmlessly against the walls of the building without doing serious damage or harming anyone. Smith hurried the wagons out of Austin. They headed northeast in order to circle the patrol at Bastrop. Some twenty Austin men rallied to rush after them. Although the Smith party was held back by the slowness of the ox-teams, they had gotten a head start of several miles before the defenders of the archives were organized. The Austin guard impeded their own progress by trying to drag the cannon with them, and some of the volunteers lacked horses.

The chase lasted all day and into the night. A wet norther blew in and a hard rain fell. Both parties were miserable. Smith decided to make camp at Brushy Creek; at dawn he found himself surrounded. Mark B. Lewis, in charge of the Austin men, gave Smith the choice of fighting or surrendering. With the little cannon pointed directly at his camp, Smith had no alternative. On their return to Austin, he and his men were hospitably received and then entertained with a New Year's eve dinner prepared by the ladies of Austin. Thus ended the bloodless "Archives War," and thus did the city of Austin cling to its pretensions as the capital of the Republic. In fact, however, the seat of government was to be divided between Washington-on-the-Brazos and Austin until annexation; for President Houston, even though he was censured by Congress for his attempt to gain control of the archives, stubbornly refused to return to Lamar's "seat of empire."

Meanwhile, the Seventh Congress proceeded, in a desultory fashion, to the business of legislation. Houston's message was not designed to conciliate the congressmen, who were already angry with him. Like an irate father to a wayward son, Houston lectured the nation through Congress. "We find the proceedings of Congress too frequently characterized by acts of selfishness," he told them. "The public good has too often been disregarded, and the national interests left out of view. . . . The chimera of a splendid government administered upon a magnificent scale has passed off and left us the realities of depression, national calamity, and destitution." He turned from castigating past Congresses to lambasting the undisciplined volunteers who "rushed to the frontier on the first alarm given of the enemy's approach." Insubordinate and impetuous, the men had eaten the frontier settlers' meager supplies, permitted the enemy to escape without chastisement, and "returned to their homes, leaving behind them an exhausted country."

The only remedy to the nation's ills was for its leaders to stop acting like children and concentrate on finding some economic salvation. "Go home and plant corn," Houston had told one East Texas war party sternly; "sustain the credit of Texas," he now urged Congress.

His admonitions were delivered to a House which barely had a quorum and a Senate that had not yet organized, for want of members in attendance. Houston's message failed to stir much response except antagonism. According to the editor of the San Augustine *Red-Lander,* Congress, "with an utter recklessness of purpose displays a marked hostility to every measure proposed by the President."

Another newsman, the editor of the Houston *Morning Star,* described the legislative impasse three weeks later:

> The Speaker was sitting listlessly in his chair, and before him were a few members, some sitting, some standing, and some leaning against the posts, apparently waiting for a quorum. The Door Keeper was sitting on a log outside the House. Finding little here to interest me, I proceeded to the Senate, which is held in Bailey, Gay and Hoxey's old store, where I found the President looking at the Senators, and the Senators looking at him. The Senate, I learned, was waiting for the House to progress with business, and the House, I suppose, often waits for the Senate, and in the mean time certain members steal away occasionally, and *'consult the book of prophecies'* alias a pack of cards. Thus do our legislators labor for their country.

The result of such a situation was a minimum of effective legislation. Congress did provide for a new issue of exchequer bills to defray the cost of government; it passed (over Houston's veto) an act to raise a regiment of volunteers for the protection of the frontier; it failed, by one vote, to express official thanks to the residents of Austin; it enacted a few relief measures; and it satisfied Houston's desire to abolish the navy, by authorizing the sale of the ships. On his part, Houston was nearly successful in stopping the pay of congressmen for the days when they were not in official attendance.

The act to sell the navy, Commodore Moore later declared, was secured by trickery. In a secret message to the

Senate, Houston reported that Moore had spent every cent which Congress had appropriated; that Yucatan had defaulted her payments; that it would cost $300,000 a year to sustain the navy; and that Moore would not go to sea to enforce the blockade. Houston painted Moore as incompetent, disloyal, and insubordinate. The President's naval message was an artful distortion of the facts, but it was basically true. Even the navy's advocates recognized the futility of trying to support its continued operation without funds. The only solution was to sell the ships and pay off the debts. Moore, unfortunately, was made the scapegoat of the situation by an irate Houston.

Moore, now fully aware of Houston's animosity and "chicanery" as he called it, energetically tried to save the navy. Even before Houston signed the act to sell his ships, the commodore had chartered a boat and made a quick deal with the Yucatan rebels to furnish them two ships at $8,000 a month.

But before James Morgan and William Bryan, who had been appointed commissioners to enforce the sale, could arrive in New Orleans, Moore shipped on new crews for the *Wharton* and the *Austin.* Houston had expected that the commissioners would relieve Moore of command and promptly sell the ships; instead, Moore was so convincing in defense of his position that he gained the confidence of the commissioners, especially Morgan, and seemed to win them both over to his point of view. Their long report, supporting Moore's plan to sail for Yucatan, hit Houston like a bombshell.

He responded with one of the most vindictive acts of his career—an executive proclamation ordering Moore's arrest and inviting the navies of the world to cooperate in seizing "the said Post Captain E. W. Moore, the ship *Austin* and the brig *Wharton* with their crews and bring them, or any of them, into the port of Galveston that the vessels may be secured to the Republic and the culprit or culprits arraigned and punished by sentences of a legal tribunal." Branding Moore a pirate, he added, "The Naval Powers of Christendom will not permit such a flagrant and unexampled outrage."

The proclamation was delivered to Morgan to publish or not, as he saw fit, but to use to bring Moore to heel. Moore had no option. With Morgan aboard as surety for his good behavior, he pulled anchor and eased out of New Orleans harbor for Galveston.

Then came a startling piece of news: Santa Anna was about to force the capitulation of the *Yucatecos* and use their army to invade Texas. Morgan quickly decided—with some effective prodding by Moore—"to save the Republic, if I could." Since virtual control of the navy's destiny was in his hands, he ordered Moore to proceed at once to Yucatan, to give battle to Santa Anna's new warship, the *Moctezuma,* and to try to save the Yucatan rebels.

Moore cleared the mouth of the Mississippi on April 19, 1843, headed "to make *one desperate struggle* to turn the tide of ill luck." On April 28, he reached Sisal, Yucatan, where he was warmly received by the rebellion's leaders. They promptly broke off truce negotiations with Santa Anna, while Moore and his two little ships sallied forth to engage the Mexican fleet, now consisting of two armed steam frigates, two brigs-of-war, and two schooners.

Outnumbered and outgunned, the ready little remnant of the Texas navy did not hesitate. They found the centralist fleet off Campeche and sailed into it at 6:30, the morning of April 30. The Mexicans upped anchor and made south; a running battle ensued, lasting two hours. Then the wind temporarily died down, leaving the Texans at the mercy of the enemy's steam ships. As the Mexicans bore in for the kill, luck filled the Texas sails with a stiff breeze. Moore flung his starboard batteries full at the *Moctezuma,* receiving a 68-pound shot in an exchange that nearly killed the commodore. By noon, the Mexicans had been driven away, and the siege of Yucatan had been triumphantly lifted. Moore reported the Texas loss as two; the Mexican, as twenty, including the commander of the *Moctezuma.*

But Moore was not through. On May 16 he ran down the Mexican flotilla and engaged it again in a two-hour, fourteen-mile chase. Again the Mexicans fled, this time, however, leaving the *Austin* badly damaged. Both Moore and the Mexicans claimed a victory. Moore's casualties were five killed, twenty-one wounded; the Mexican loss was unknown, but according to one observer, seventy men had been killed on one of the vessels.

Moore ran into harbor to repair the *Austin,* with no intentions of giving up the war. There, on May 28, he learned that Houston had published the "Piracy Proclamation." Still he would have stayed on, but Yucatan decided that it could not afford to continue the monthly stipend. A month was consumed in settling the final accounts but, in the end, Yucatan gratefully paid all the bills, including the carpentry work on the *Austin,* plus a $2,000 bonus.

Regretfully, Moore agreed with Morgan, who had been an enthusiastic and excited spectator at the stirring events, that they must return to Galveston. On July 14, 1842, the Texas navy dropped anchor in Galveston Bay for the last time. It was the end, but it was a glorious finale.

Moore immediately demanded a court-martial, to try him on the piracy charges and any other allegations of misconduct or incompetency. So great was his popularity, however, that Houston was much too shrewd to give him that satisfaction. Instead he ordered Moore dishonorably discharged. The embittered former commodore, feeling certain that he would be exonerated, continued to demand a trial. Finally, in frustration, he published a 201-page book addressed *To the People of Texas*—recounting the entire story from his point of view. The book was widely read, especially by Houston's enemies, and the following year Congress undertook an investigation of the affair. Moore was cleared on all but four minor points and was restored to his rank. Years later, his accounts against the Republic were audited at $44,655, of which he apparently received some $41,000 in cash, plus a 320-acre land grant in Burnet County. Moore County in the Texas Panhandle was named for him in 1876.

All that remained of the once proud little navy was decommissioned at Galveston. The *Archer* and the *Wharton* were auctioned off for a total of $935; the *Austin* was towed to Pensacola by the United States navy in 1846, but three years later it was broken up as being unworthy of repairs. All told, the navy had cost Texas nearly half a million dollars in ships, salaries, and supplies. Houston was probably right from the outset, that the game was not worth the candle; but his behavior in the affair did him little credit.

He was stung to the quick, though, by criticism from one of his closest friends, William A. Christy of New Orleans. To him, in a rare moment of self-revelation, Houston wrote a passionate defense of his own conduct.

> You are one of the last men on earth that I could have supposed would excuse, countenance, or sanction mutiny, treason, or piracy, and call them 'slight disobediences.' They have all been perpetrated by Moore. . . . My dear Christy, my indignation is *called* into action by acts of outrage, piracy, and murder added to mutiny and sedi-

tion! . . . How could I sanction the acts of Moore? . . . I have but one maxim: *'Do right and risk the consequences.'* I have done it, and . . . it is in accordance with the principles which have united us by bonds of friendship for the last twenty-seven years. . . . I have acted— let this rest. Why, my dear Christy, what cloud has come over the sunshine of your reason?

Houston implied to his friend that he had received secret assurances, through the British *chargé d'affaires*, that Santa Anna would release the Texan prisoners in Perote Castle, if Texas forbore from any acts of aggression against Mexico. There was some basis for this idea. One of the Texan prisoners, James W. Robinson, had talked his way out of prison by persuading Santa Anna that he could mediate an agreement between Texas and Mexico. Robinson represented to Santa Anna that Texas was willing to recognize Mexican sovereignty if it could come back into the Mexican nation as a separate state with representatives in the Mexican Congress.

Whether Robinson actually believed Texas would accept such an impossible proposal, or whether he merely used it as an excuse for his own release, cannot be known. Freed by Santa Anna, he delivered the proposition to Houston. The President was condemned just for listening to it. Houston ridiculed the idea but did see in it a possibility for an armistice, which he asked the British ministers to attempt to arrange. For this reason, he had deplored so vehemently the activities of Moore and the Texas navy, which might upset the negotiations. Referring to the Texan prisoners, Houston wrote: "My rule is, when your hand is in the lion's mouth, do not strike him on the nose!"

Despite the naval battles (or perhaps because of them), Santa Anna succumbed to the blandishments of the British minister and agreed to an armistice until a satisfactory peace treaty might be arranged. Houston proclaimed the armistice on June 15, 1843, knowing full well that a treaty on Santa Anna's terms would be impossible. He appointed Samuel M. Williams and George W. Hockley as commissioners to meet with a Mexican delegation at the town of Sabinas. After long discussion, a wholly unsatisfactory agreement was drafted and signed by the commissioners on February 18, 1844. It was a meaningless document, since ratification by both governments was necessary. On the part of Texas, Houston said: "I did not deem it necessary to take any action upon the agreement signed by our commissioners further than to reject it silently." As far as Houston was concerned, the whole maneuver was made to gain time, which it succeeded in doing.

While the truce arrangements were going forward, in seeming inconsistency, Houston commissioned two armed incursions into New Mexico: the Warfield Expedition and the Snively Expedition. The first, under Charles A. Warfield, is shrouded in mysterious circumstances. Some time in July 1842, William Christy wrote a letter to his friend Sam Houston, outlining a plan advanced by Warfield for leading an expedition through New Mexico and into Chihuahua. Warfield had, for some years, been engaged in the Santa Fé trade out of Missouri, and he had taken caravans to Chihuahua City. He believed that while the government of New Mexico was under the control of the centralists, the bulk of the population would welcome a release from the dictatorship. It was essentially the same analysis of the New Mexico situation that had been advanced to Lamar in 1840.

Warfield claimed that a determined expedition to Santa Fé, and then to Chihuahua, could overthrow the governments there and win the allegiance of the population. It could be done with volunteers, at no cost to Texas. Warfield was certain that he could get at least five hundred men to join him. Houston did not meet the instigator of this scheme; Warfield's character and honesty were vouched for by Christy. Nor, in all probability, did Houston realize the almost inevitable results of such a project. He warned that "civilized and honorable warfare" must be conducted, and he told Christy: "The character rendered of him by you is all the guaranty which I require." Houston also agreed to Warfield's desire for haste and secrecy and apparently instructed Secretary of War George W. Hockley to issue the necessary authorization.

It was virtually Hockley's last act as a cabinet officer before his resignation. He had become greatly embittered by Houston's inaction in the face of Mexican aggression, and he seems to have fallen in with Warfield's plans without objection. Hockley commissioned the adventurer—for such he was—a colonel in the Texas army, authorized him to raise 500 volunteers, and empowered him to prey upon Mexican commerce in the name of the Republic, to levy contributions, and to capture Mexican property. Warfield was to be allowed to keep fifty percent of the spoils; the other half was to be sent to Texas.

No doubt Hockley thought he was acting in the best interests of Texas to issue such a blank check for brigandage, for he was a sincere and honorable man. But because of future events it must be said, in all fairness, that the Warfield Expedition was not authorized by the Texas government—it was licensed by George W. Hockley, who exceeded Houston's instructions as well as his intentions. The expedition was, of course, unknown to the rest of the government because of Warfield's injunction of secrecy, and it was not sanctioned by Congress.

Nevertheless, Colonel Warfield had a legitimate commission. He went directly to Missouri, where he enlisted a number of frontiersmen for the venture. Establishing a rendezvous at Point of Rocks on the Santa Fé trail for May 15, 1843, he headed for the Rocky Mountains, where he recruited two dozen fur trappers. An incident on his return to Point of Rocks indicates that Warfield may have been the honorable man that Christy depicted. The contingent of mountain men overtook and captured a caravan carrying a large quantity of gold and silver. When the wagon train was found not to belong to Mexican citizens, it was promptly released, unmolested.

Early in May, while waiting for the group from Missouri, Warfield and his small band attacked the village of Mora, New Mexico, on the edge of the Sangre de Cristo Mountains, killing five soldiers and taking eighteen prisoners. He was forced to abandon the town almost immediately, though, because of the reported presence of a large detachment of Mexican troops in the vicinity. He lingered for two weeks at the rendezvous point, but neither the Missourians nor an expected company from Texas arrived. Dejectedly he disbanded his party and, with a half-dozen men, headed east across the plains for Texas.

Some of the men, led by John McDaniel, whom Warfield had commissioned as a major, attacked another wagon train and murdered a New Mexican trader. Because of this act, for which neither Texas nor Warfield was really responsible, the entire affair has been enveloped in an odor of ill repute.

Back in Texas, meanwhile, a respected Texas army officer and former paymaster general of the army, Jacob Snively, petitioned the government for permission to lead an expedition into New Mexico—for the purpose of intercepting Mexican caravans on the Santa Fé trail when they crossed territory claimed by Texas. His scheme was authorized by the war department on February 16, 1843. Whether there was any collusion between Snively and Warfield is not known, nor is it known whether the Snively Expedition is the Texas group which Warfield awaited at Point of Rocks. On the other hand, the Snively Expedition was not masked in the secrecy or mystery of the Warfield Expedition. As Houston later said, "The command of Colonel Snively had all the official sanctions of this government."

In April, with a force of about 150 men, Snively set out toward the Santa Fé trail from Fort Johnson on Red River. He reached the crossing of the Arkansas River, in present Kansas, on May 27. There he was joined by Warfield and three or four of his followers. For several weeks the Texans shifted their campsites about, hoping to sight a Mexican caravan. On June 20 they were attacked by a force of about one hundred Mexicans, seventeen of whom were killed and eighty-two captured, with no loss to the Texans. Still no wagon trains appeared, and the days of waiting became dreary. Finally, on June 28, the prisoners were released and the expedition broke up. One group, under Eli Chandler, struck toward the Arkansas; the other, under Snively, turned toward the Cimarron branch of the Santa Fé trail. Two days later, Snively's band was surrounded by a dragoon company of the United States army, under Captain Philip St. George Cooke.

Cooke believed, or said he believed, that the Texans were in United States territory, despite the fact that he had to cross the Arkansas (the international boundary) to accost them. Snively protested, to no avail. Cooke disarmed the Texans, leaving them but ten muskets with which to hunt game. Rather than face the hostile plains country underarmed, some of the Snively men elected to return to Missouri with Cooke; the remainder rejoined Chandler. The disintegration of the expedition continued when, as Chandler readied to leave for Texas, a small remnant expressed a desire to remain. Electing Warfield their commander, these men, totalling about 70, turned back to the Santa Fé trail, still hoping to fall upon a Mexican caravan. Sighting a large body of Mexican troops on July 13, the diehards finally abandoned the scheme; and they, too, headed back for Texas.

Neither the Snively nor the Warfield expedition accomplished anything constructive. The principal result was to arouse a resentment and antagonism among the people of New Mexico that lingered well into the twentieth century. Of some significance is the fact that the United States government later paid a small indemnity to Texas for Cooke's actions, thus tacitly acknowledging the Texas claim to that part of New Mexico east of the Rio Grande.

While pursuing his unpopular and (at least on the surface) inconsistent policy toward Mexico, Houston tried to keep peace along the Indian frontier. The fundamental plan which had been adopted in 1842, calling for treaties, trading posts, and small ranging companies, was maintained—in sharp contrast with Lamar's previous warlike approach. In January 1843, at Houston's request, the Seventh Congress provided a broader base for his Indian program. A bureau of Indian affairs was created and attached to the war department; the President was authorized to appoint special agents and interpreters responsible directly to him; five new trading posts were created, and the President was empowered to license the government traders; and an attempt was made to establish a line to separate the Indians from the settlements.

Thus, it was made unlawful for any person to cross the

"line of trading posts" into Indian country, without express permission of the President. At the same time, no Indian could come east of the line unless accompanied by an Indian agent. Houston hoped to cure most of the ills by keeping these natural enemies separated from each other. Congress also provided that no person could sell or trade either intoxicating spirits or warlike supplies to the Indians.

The line of separation was a logical solution—so logical that every Anglo-American government had attempted it since 1763, when Great Britain established the Proclamation Line along the Appalachian Mountains. And, like every line so established, Houston's "line of trading posts" was doomed to failure. The white men could not help coveting the Indian lands; the Indians could not resist the temptation to raid and plunder the white settlements, where livestock and other essentials could be obtained so easily by stealing.

Houston's first move was to send agents among the Indians and invite the tribes to a great council, where he would explain the new arrangements. The Shawnee, Caddo, Ioni, Anadarko, Tawakoni, Waco, Wichita, and Keechi tribes were represented at the council, which assembled on Tehuacana Creek on March 28, 1843. George W. Terrell, John S. Black, and Thomas I. Smith, all trusted men, attended for Texas. Pierce M. Butler was present as representative of the United States, since some of the tribes roamed back and forth across Red River at will.

George Terrell made a dramatic appeal for peace between the Indians and the white men, and he couched it in the figurative language which has always so distinguished formal relations with the Indians. "The path between us has long been red with the blood of the white and the red men. The bones of our brothers and kindred have been strewed along the path we have travelled. Clouds and darkness have rested upon it. . . . The bow has been strung, and the rifle kept loaded too long. The white and the red man belong to the same great family; therefore we should all live together in peace and friendship. . . ." He then explained carefully the basis of the peace policy, while the Indians listened in dignified silence. On the following days, various chiefs rose to address the council in their own colorful language. Finally, an agreement was reached for a truce, until a "Grand Council" of all the Indian tribes in Texas could be held to arrange a lasting treaty of peace.

In the months that followed, Houston and his agents worked assiduously to gather the tribes again the following year. With presents and interpreters, the Texas Indian commissioners went from village to village, and from campsite to campsite, carrying the word of the forthcoming peace council and, like apostles of the faith, explaining the new Texas policy. Houston, himself, made several such excursions and received a number of Indian delegations at Washington-on-the-Brazos. Few men in the course of history were ever his equal in dealing with the red men. He understood their unsophisticated minds and he respected their mature dignity. He sympathized with their resentments and he could accept their savage morality without approving it. He could explain the white men's views, and he could reach their hearts as few have ever done. For example, the Lipans could not help being moved by the following letter Houston sent on learning of the death of their chief:

My heart is sad! A dark cloud rests upon your nation. Grief has sounded in your Camp. The voice of Flacco is silent. His words are not heard in Council. The Chief is no more. His life has fled to the Great Spirit. His eyes are closed. His heart no longer leaps at the sight of the buffalo! The voices of your camp are no longer heard to cry: Flacco has returned from the chase! Your chiefs look down on the earth and groan in Trouble. Your warriors weep. The loud voice of grief is heard from your women and children. The song of birds is silent. The ears of your people hear no pleasant sound. Sorrow whispers in the winds. The noise of the tempest passes. It is not heard. Your hearts are heavy.

The name of Flacco brought joy to all hearts. Joy was on every face! Your people were happy. Flacco is no longer seen in the fight. His voice is no longer heard in battle. The enemy no longer make a path for his glory. His valor is no longer a guard for your people. The right arm of your nation is broken. Flacco was a friend to his white brothers. They will not forget him. They will remember the red warrior. His father will not be forgotten. We will be Kind to the Lipan. Grass shall not grow in the path between us. Let your wise men give the counsel of peace. Let your young men walk in the white path. The grey headed men of your nation will teach wisdom. I will hold my red brothers by the hand. Thy Brother. Houston.

The peace movement gained momentum during the summer of 1843. Most of the tribes were receptive, but it was no surprise to anyone when the fierce Comanches proved recalcitrant. In the summer, J. C. Eldredge, who had been appointed general superintendent of Indian affairs, visited the Comanche country. These nomads were like wild mustangs—hard to catch and hard to hold. According to Eldredge they still remembered the Council House Fight and were suspicious. They would not come to Tehuacana Creek, but might meet the Texans on the upper Red or Trinity rivers. And they wanted to deal with the "Chief of Texas himself," not his commissioners.

On the few occasions when Eldredge was able to talk directly to Comanche leaders, he found them deceitful and treacherous. His attempts to secure the release of white prisoners consistently met with failure, and he despaired of getting any Comanches to attend the council. Even if some came, it was doubtful that they could be considered representatives of their tribe. Near Red River, on August 4, he encountered a large band whose chief received him in friendship. Eldredge remained there several days, in growing uneasiness. Many of the braves advocated retaliation for the Council House massacre, but their chief kept them under control. Finally, on August 9, the chief agreed to come in for a council with representatives of all the Comanche bands. The soonest this could be done was "four Moons from the present full moon," or roughly about the middle of December. Eldredge and the chief made a truce to keep the peace until that time.

The following month, on September 28, General Terrell, E. H. Tarrant, and other Texas agents met at Birds Fort, with headmen of the Delaware, Chickasaw, Waco, Tawakoni, Keechi, Caddo, Anadarko, Ioni, Biloxi, and Cherokee bands of Texas. There, a formal treaty of peace was signed, stipulating the basic conditions of the peace policy and the "line of trading posts." This treaty was ratified and proclaimed by Houston on February 3, 1844.

The past year had been a turbulent one for a government whose policy was dedicated to maintaining peace—internal strife, a war over the archives, naval battles, filibusters into New Mexico, and Indian raids. What grand or tragic events might have transpired had Houston not been such a peaceful man is beyond the scope of history. The Republic could now turn in amiable contentment to thoughts of elections and annexation to the United States.

10

1844-46

STRIFE
AND ANNEXATION

FIRST IN DAZED SILENCE, then with clamorous excitement, the little group of musicians in Louisville, Kentucky, learned that the Republic of Texas had passed a law, on February 4, 1841, permitting them to establish a colony between the Trinity and Red rivers. Having had little expectation of receiving the grant for which they had petitioned, they were totally unprepared to take any action. W. S. Peters was proud and pompous; his son Henry, a music teacher, had his head in the clouds as did Timothy Cragg, a piano maker. Another son, William Cummings Peters, although also a musician, was something of a businessman; and perhaps it was he, together with Samuel Browning, who finally urged the group to act. Dreaming was so much more pleasant.

But not until August 1841 did the Kentuckians take advantage of the colonization law to enter into the contract with Texas, which assigned them an area just north of the present city of Dallas, into which they must introduce two hundred families a year for the next three years. A hasty calculation showed that the area granted was not large enough, and in November 1841 a second contract, extending the colony reservation southward, was signed.

The Louisville contractors organized themselves into a grandiose company, the Texas Agricultural, Commercial and Manufacturing Company, and sold a few shares of stock; but they had little idea of how to initiate a colonization program. Time passed, and it became apparent that if an extension was not granted, they would lose their rights. Thus, a third contract, enlarging the area and extending the time limits, was made in July 1842. With a sigh of relief, the empresarios began advertising their land. Several hundred immigrants answered the call during 1842, and most of these located in the colony the ensuing year.

Meantime, the Sixth Congress decided that a general colonization program, based on the Peters Colony law, would be the best way to induce migration to Texas. Passed on February 5, 1842, this general law authorized the President to enter into contract with any colonization company which desired to introduce settlers into the vacant lands of Texas on the same terms the Peters group had received.

Several new contracts were made. On February 15, 1842, Henri Castro, a French citizen, received two grants for settling six hundred Europeans in Southwest Texas. Between 1843 and 1847, he chartered some twenty-seven ships and brought nearly five hundred families and a like number of single men, mostly from the Rhine provinces of France, to his colony. Located on the Medina River, the center of settlement was named Castroville; other villages he established were Quihi, Vandenburg, and D'Hanis.

More important than Castro's Colony were the contracts which Houston made with Henry Francis Fisher and Burchard Miller. (A third partner, Joseph Baker, soon dropped from the venture.) On February 8, 1842, Fisher and Miller contracted to bring one thousand German, Dutch, Swedish, Danish, and Norwegian settlers to Texas. The contract was increased on January 6, 1844, to six thousand immigrants, and the grant, located on the southwest frontier, was enlarged to nearly three million acres. The partners found a great interest in Texas among German intellectuals, who were dissatisfied with political conditions at home. By December 30, 1845, they had completed the sale of their grants to the *Adelsverein*, a society organized for the purpose of promoting German immigration to Texas. In 1844, Prince Carl of Solms-Braunfels became the society's director, and came to Texas to inspect the Fisher-Miller grants. His retinue made a picturesque entourage in its journey from the coast to the frontier, but the prince, although a little ridiculous to Texas frontiersmen, was a man of great vision and imagination. In addition to the Fisher-Miller lands, he purchased extensive acreage northwest of San Antonio for his society, and he bought a tract on Matagorda Bay to establish a port and receiving station for German immigrants, naming it Karlshafen (later Indianola).

The *Adelsverein's* first settlers arrived in December 1844, and they were brought to the Comal River north of San Antonio in the spring of 1845. There they built homes and established a village, named New Braunfels in the prince's honor. From that time on, German emigration to

Texas was extensive, and Solms-Braunfels' foresight in acquiring sufficient land was rewarded. He returned to Germany, where he published a book about Texas in 1846. His successor was the Baron Ottfried Hans Freiherr von Meusebach, who gave up his title to become Texas citizen John O. Meusebach.

Meusebach was even more energetic than Prince Carl. Under his supervision the German settlements in Texas multiplied and prospered. It was Meusebach who, two years later in 1847, met with twenty Comanche chiefs on the San Saba and negotiated the only durable treaty ever made with those Indians. With peace assured, he established the town of Fredericksburg on the outermost frontier. After he resigned as director of the *Adelsverein*, he married a former Tyrolean noblewoman and settled in this region at Loyal Valley.

Early House in a
German Settlement

Success of the German colonization ventures was due as much to the character of the people as to good leadership. The Germans worked industriously to build permanent homes on the frontier. Thrifty and hard working, some of them were at first a little incongruous in the raw surroundings. For example, a former professor insisted for years on dressing completely—even to a frock coat—before leaving his house to plow his fields. Musicians, scientists, educators, and other persons of cultural and intellectual attainments made up a large portion of the immigrants. Had they not tended to cling so rigorously to their own language and habits and had they not been so clannish in their outlook, they might have contributed greatly to the development of Texas. As it was, their effect on the state was inconsiderable, despite the emergence of insular pockets of Germanic environment.

A fourth colonization project in the Republic was initiated by Charles Fenton Mercer, a former United States congressman from Virginia, who had settled in Florida. Through English connections he became interested in the Peters Colony venture. Although the original grant to the Peters group had included the names of eleven Englishmen, these people had been totally inactive in the promotion of the colony. In October 1842, they assigned their hypothetical interests to a group, which included Mercer and a flamboyant promoter named Sherman Converse.

Converse went directly to Louisville where, with grand phrases and eloquent salesmanship, he persuaded the Kentuckians to assign to him their control of the colony. Mercer, too, seems to have authorized Converse to act for him. The promoter hastened to Texas, where the Seventh Congress was in session. He artfully persuaded Congress to pass a joint resolution on January 16, 1843—fantastically enlarging the Peters Colony grant and providing for unbelievable concessions to the colonizing company. The time limit was extended for five years and the President was empowered to increase the size of the colony reservation to accommodate as many as ten thousand families. Furthermore, title to the 640-acre tracts was to be given to the company instead of to the individual settlers, and the company was to be permitted to buy additional land at the phenomenally low price of $12 per section, or less than two cents an acre.

The whole resolution was preposterous and a flagrant violation of common sense, of the Republic's trust in Congress, and of the general trend of Texas land policy. Houston's approval of the resolution was equally surprising. And then, four days later, he extended the boundaries of the colony to include ten million acres. The limits of the colony then ran roughly from the Red River to present Ellis County, west nearly to present Abilene, then north to the Red River at about present Vernon. The new contract was made by Houston, for the Republic, and Converse, as agent for the new London associates including Mercer. No mention was made of the Louisville men.

While Converse was returning to England, apparently to raise money on the strength of his miraculous success in Texas, the Louisville group waited with increasing impatience for some word of their venture. Notice came in a newspaper story of February 4, 1843: "The contract of Messrs. Peters . . . and others . . . has been declared forfeited, and another contract with the government has been entered into by Dr. Sherman Converse. . . ." Slowly it dawned on Peters and his associates that they might have been duped, but they were uncertain just what to do about it. Months passed as they waited hopefully for confirmation from Converse of the formation of the £100,000 corporation of which he spoke so grandly in

Louisville. Finally they held an indignation meeting and published a denunciation of Converse. Then they sent Major E. B. Ely to Texas to present their problems to the Texas government.

Upon hearing of this action, Converse hurried to Louisville again to show the Kentuckians, as he put it, "the great error they had committed." And that is just what he did. They welcomed him as the prodigal returned, repudiated their denunciation, and handed back to him entire control of the venture. What a glib tongue the man had! But with victory in his grasp at Louisville, the prize was to be snatched from him in Texas.

When Mercer learned of the rejection of Converse, he headed to the Texas capital at Washington-on-the-Brazos, where he slyly petitioned for a separate colonization grant for himself alone, cutting out both the Louisville men and Converse. The Eighth Congress was then in session, and under discussion was the wild extension which Houston had granted to Sherman Converse. Many angry voices were raised against Houston, the Peters Colony, and all colonization contracts.

The principal objection, other than irritation over the Converse contract, was that Houston had placed within colony reservations all of the best vacant public domain. No land certificates could be located in these areas, and the holders of land paper of various kinds, from military bounty to scrip, were incensed because they were prohibited from making locations in these choice regions. The scandalously huge grant made to Converse for the Peters Colony came in for the most abuse because it covered "the garden spot of Texas," as one editor phrased it. By mid-January 1844 both houses had passed a bill to stop all empresario contracts and to nullify those in existence if the colonizers had not fulfilled every obligation of the contract.

President Houston vetoed the measure, and on January 29, one day before Congress passed it over his veto, he signed a new contract with Charles Fenton Mercer, authorizing him to settle an area adjacent to the original Peters grant in the heart of North Texas. Obtained by a trick, the Mercer Colony was never successful. Fewer than a hundred families moved into the grant and these were unsure for years whether the title to their homesteads would be verified.

When he learned of Mercer's move, Converse bowed out of the picture and returned control of the Peters Colony to the Louisville men, who reorganized as the Texas Emigration and Land Company and then plunged frantically into efforts to settle enough people in Texas to fulfill the terms of the contract. After countless conflicts with the settlers themselves, with the government of Texas, and with a group of land hungry speculators, the colony ceased to function on July 1, 1848. The company could prove nearly two thousand families had been settled, but claimed to have brought twice that many to Texas. Finally, as a premium for its work, the company was granted over a million acres located in West Texas, and the remainder of the colony reserve was opened for the locating of other certificates. The cities of Dallas and Fort Worth, and a score of smaller settlements, were in part the result of the company's activities.

The Eighth Congress, which put an end to the colonization program despite Houston's protest, was a great disappointment to the anti-Houston party. Before the election Houston's enemies had tried to arouse sentiment for the impeachment of "Sam the First." The editor of the New Orleans *Picayune* wrote scathingly: "An inspired people can certainly devise some constitutional means to rid themselves of an incubus so destructive of their interests." Let Vice-President Burleson convene Congress and have Houston impeached "either as a traitor or an imbecile—one or the other of these charges can certainly be sustained."

It was an embittering experience for a man like Thomas Jefferson Green, recently released from Perote Prison and newly elected to Congress, neither to be able to persuade Houston to give him the satisfaction of a duel nor to enlist congressional help to oust him from office. Green was not alone. Former Commodore Moore was also said to be clamoring for a duel. William Cazneau, Vice-President Burleson, Francis Moore, Moseley Baker, Burnet, Lamar, and a score of others yearned to discredit Houston.

The docility of the Eighth Congress left these men frustrated; adroitly Houston steered it away from such controversial matters as Indian affairs, foreign policy, and finances—and into consideration of domestic matters. Concentrating on such legislation, Congress chartered schools and businesses, fixed county boundaries, set the time for court meetings, and passed an unusual number of private relief acts. One of these was to reimburse Jack Hays for funds he had advanced in support of his Ranger company. Congress also authorized him to enlist a new company of forty men to patrol the frontier from Refugio to San Antonio. In the long run, the Eighth Congress was little more active than the desultory Congress of the year before.

There was a pressing domestic problem which Congress ignored. Perhaps it was too explosive for the legislators to deal with, for it was an outbreak of violent lawlessness in East Texas that threatened the homes and families of many of the members. The festering evil, which grew to proportions of open rebellion in 1844, had its origins several years earlier.

The area of the old "Neutral Ground," once the haven for lawless men from Texas, Louisiana, and Arkansas, had continued to harbor unsavory elements long after the boundary dispute had been settled. After the Texas Revolution, the region sheltered bands of outlaws who had operated without detection for several years. Into the area had come Charles W. Jackson, a fugitive from justice who ran for Congress in Shelby County in 1840. He was defeated. Blaming his failure on other unscrupulous characters in the county, he openly accused them of forging fraudulent land certificates—which, in fact, they were doing. Joseph Goodbread, who headed the faction responsible for Jackson's defeat, threatened immediate and dire retribution. Jackson did not wait for Goodbread to act; he promptly gunned him down in cold-blooded and premeditated murder.

Goodbread's cohorts demanded revenge. The case was taken into the recently created district court in Shelby County where Judge John M. Hansford presided. The courtroom was packed with Goodbread men, armed to the teeth and determined to see "justice" rendered, and with Jackson's followers, similarly armed and equally determined to free their leader. Hansford refused to hold court in the presence of so many explosive spectators, but the belligerent parties refused to leave. The judge dismissed the court, transferring the trial to Panola County.

There Jackson was tried and acquitted, despite the attendance of angry men from both factions. After the trial, Jackson men attempted to murder James Strickland, a Goodbread man who had killed a Jackson follower named McClure. Strickland fled, but his home and that of another man were burned. Known earlier among themselves as the Freebooters, the Goodbread party came out into the open, organized under Edward Merchant, took the name of "Moderators," and began a systematic hunt for Jackson. This soon degenerated into a series of raids on the homes of their enemies.

By 1841, several more men had been killed, the sheriff had fled the county, and the citizens were lined up in one camp or the other. At a public meeting, Jackson organized his forces as the "Regulators," promising to impose law and order on the "Moderators." Murder, theft, and arson followed, with many of the better citizens being drawn into both gangs. The Moderators soon shot Jackson down; but, rather than ending the feud, this only spurred it on. Charles W. Moorman was elected to his place, and the Regulators now sought their revenge.

For a short period Moorman and the Regulators were able to overawe the Moderators. Indeed, so strong did the band become that Moorman defied the courts and threatened a rebellion against the Republic. A virtual dictator by the summer of 1842, he ordered twenty-five families to leave the county. They fled, but they appealed to Houston, who was then enmeshed in the issue of war with Mexico. The President brought the matter to the attention of Congress and ordered Shelby County to mend its ways. In September 1842, the Moderators declared open war on their tormentors; two pitched battles occurred in which the losses were extremely heavy on both sides, perhaps totalling as many as fifty dead.

Houston now called out the militia from adjoining counties to restore order in Shelby County. When the disturbance seemed at an end, the militiamen were sent home. But trouble erupted again in the spring of 1843, and a new reign of terror ensued. Crops went untended, homes were burned, men were ambushed, and shortly the two parties reorganized, with about 150 men on each side. These lawless conditions prevailed for nearly a year, the contagion spreading to adjacent counties, where smaller bands of Regulators and Moderators were formed.

Finally, in August 1844, Houston issued a proclamation ordering the people to put down their arms. To enforce it, he sent a regiment of six hundred militiamen into the area under General Travis G. Broocks. The leaders were arrested and brought before Houston himself. Knowing that the imprisonment of the principals would not stop the bloody vendetta in which so many had already lost their lives, he persuaded the factions to draw up a peace treaty. M. T. Johnson and John H. McNairy signed the articles of truce for the Regulators; and for the Moderators, James Truitt and John Dial signed. A militia company was garrisoned in Shelbyville until the end of the year to assure the reestablishment of law and order. Thus, after an unaccountably long delay, ended this tragic and sanguinary insurrection—the Regulator-Moderator War, which cost innumerable lives, wrecked hundreds of homes, and disgraced the history of Texas.

Perhaps Houston had not realized the extent of the strife in Shelby County, or perhaps he was more concerned in keeping peace on the Indian frontier than in settling civil discord in East Texas. During 1844 his cherished peace policy was meticulously followed by his agents, even though it was often deplored by the settlers who claimed there was no lessening of raids and depredations. The chief offenders were the Wichitas, who had not come in for any of the councils, and the bellicose

Comanches, who had made a truce and only promised to attend one.

Through some misunderstanding, the meeting with the Comanches, which Eldredge, the Indian agent, had arranged for December 1843 on the Clear Fork of the Brazos, did not take place. A messenger, who was sent to the Comanches to find out why, returned in March 1844 with a (dictated) letter from Chief Mopechucope stating that the Comanches had been at the meeting place and waited for the whites to show up. This may or may not have been true, but the Indians professed a desire to arrange another council.

The Tehuacana Creek site had become an established council ground, and it was there that the Comanches were instructed to come in May. The new superintendent of Indian affairs, Thomas G. Western, frequently repaired to Tehuacana Creek to meet with delegates from the various tribes; and in preparation for a series of councils that spring, he erected several log buildings. By the end of April, Western took up residence at the council grounds. Several bands of Indians began arriving the last part of April and early in May. A council was held with Caddo, Ioni, and Keechi chiefs on April 27; another with the Waco and Tawakoni on May 4 and May 11; one with the Delaware, Shawnee, and related tribes on May 12, which was enlarged the following day to include some Keechi, Tawakoni, and Waco chiefs; and then, on May 13, the Grand Council of all the Texas Indians was officially opened.

The big question had been—would the Comanches attend? They did not, but representatives from most of the tribes in northern Texas were present. It was a three-day affair in which, once again, both the Indians and the Texas agents expressed continuing desires for peace. The

Indians querulously demanded the presents that had been promised them; and the Texans presented a list of horses which had been stolen since the making of the Birds Fort Treaty. The Indians promised to try to locate these horses. (Most of the knavery of course was blamed on absent bands.) Altogether, except for the absence of the Comanches, it was a fairly satisfactory council.

Not until October 7, 1844, were the patient commissioners able to effect a meeting with the Comanches. On that day, the largest Indian council yet assembled met at the falls of the Brazos. Sam Houston himself attended, at his dramatic best. On October 9, a treaty was jointly signed between Texas and the twelve different tribes which were represented—including the Comanche—guaranteeing a lasting peace predicated on the trading posts and the separation of Indians and whites. Two articles, originally included in the treaty to delineate Comanche territory, were omitted because of objections of the Comanches.

The councils, the trading posts, and the treaties were valiant but hopeless efforts. The peace policy prevailed through the remaining years of the Republic, but the Indian problem was not solved. At best, the menace was only abated. Even while Houston and his agents talked peace with one band, another would go on the war path. When the commissioners took the chiefs to task for violation of the treaties, it was always blamed on "bad men" who were not connected with the tribe, or on Indians from across Red River in United States Indian Territory.

Slowly and inexorably in the ensuing years, white men pushed into Indian hunting grounds. Houston's "trading post line" was of brief duration. Soon most of the tribes were to be crowded onto reservations in Oklahoma, until only the Comanche, the Apache, and the Kiowa were left at war with the whites. It was to be long after the Civil

War before these savage bands were completely subdued.

Most of the settlers along the frontiers put little faith in Houston's treaties. They preferred to depend on those fearless young men in the ranging companies who, by 1843 and 1844, were being consistently referred to by the proud name of Texas Rangers. The best-known leader was Captain John Coffee (Jack) Hays, the same young man who had rallied the volunteers to defeat Woll at the Battle of Salado. One of the most remarkable stories of Texas history revolves around Jack Hays's company.

The tale began in New York in 1841 when the purchasing agent for the Texas navy met a young inventor who was trying to sell a patented pistol with a revolving cylinder. The inventor was Samuel Colt. The United States army had turned him down, but the naval agent bought a gross of these weapons for the Texas navy. The naval officers had little use for them and, according to tradition, only unpacked one or two. Jack Hays discovered them in storage at Washington-on-the-Brazos. To him, the immense possibilities of a repeating weapon in Indian warfare were immediately apparent.

Heretofore, the Rangers had been at a tremendous disadvantage in the running fights with the plains Indians, especially the Comanches. These warriors, who could ride like a whirlwind, were armed with a short bow which they could shoot so rapidly that one Indian, it was said, could keep as many as twelve arrows in the air at one time. Against such firepower, the Rangers had single shot weapons, for the most part muzzle-loading. Consequently, the only tactic the Rangers knew was to form a circle, crouch behind their horses, and fire alternately—one man shooting while two more loaded. Around them would ride the Comanches, shrieking like demons and showering them with arrows.

Hays "borrowed" the abandoned revolvers and rushed back to his camp outside of San Antonio. There he and his men practiced for months, loading, aiming, and firing from horseback. Like children with a new toy, they could hardly wait to use them in battle. Then, in the summer of 1844, a band of Comanches got the surprise of their lives when they met Hays and his men in a canyon of the Nueces River. The Rangers, as usual, dismounted and fired their rifles. As the Indians began to circle them, the Texans suddenly leaped back into their saddles and rode headlong at the Comanches, firing their "six-shooters." The startled Comanches turned and fled in panic. Amid a wild confusion of stampeding horses, popping pistols, and yelling Rangers, the Indians were chased for three miles. The Comanche chief who was in this engagement said years later that he never again wanted to fight the men who had as many shots as they had fingers on one hand. He claimed that over half his warriors had been mortally wounded and that his band did not check their flight until they reached Devils River.

The actual date that Colt's Patent Revolvers—dubbed "six-shooters" by the Rangers—first came into Texas or were first used against the Indians is not known. By some accounts, the Rangers had secured a few pistols as early as 1839. In 1842, Samuel Walker, a Ranger captain, helped Colt improve the design; the first reported uses of the weapon were at the Battle of the Pedernales in June 1844 and at the Nueces canyon fight a few weeks later.

Notwithstanding the seriousness of Indian affairs, of colonization, and of civil commotion, the most important development of 1844 for Texas was a shift in attitude in the United States, favoring the annexation of Texas. This was brought about by the growing feeling there that Texas was becoming too friendly with Great Britain. Britain had taken a hand in trying to arrange a truce between Texas and Mexico, and it was believed by many that the British foreign office would force Mexico to sign a treaty and recognize Texas independence. Then, Texas might even become a British protectorate! Expansionists in the United States, slave interests in the South, and even merchants in New York and Boston could hardly bear the thought.

Houston did not fail to take advantage of this fear. In July 1843, he instructed Isaac Van Zandt, who had succeeded James Reily as Texas *chargé d'affaires* in Washington, to reject any discussion of annexation with the United States state department. The reason he was to give was that Houston hoped to secure a treaty with Mexico through British mediation. Naturally, Van Zandt was not told to keep his instructions secret, and the rumor spread through political circles that Houston was far too friendly with the British.

The climate for annexation improved, and it seems certain that the United States President drew the inferences that Houston intended. President John Tyler, elected on a Whig ticket with William Henry Harrison, whom he succeeded when old "Tippecanoe" died one month after his inauguration, was a supporter of Texas annexation. His first two years in office were tumultuous ones because of a split with Whig party leaders, but finally he ridded himself of their unwanted advice and replaced Harrison's cabinet with one of his own choosing. Daniel Webster, secretary of state, was the last to resign, his position being filled by Abel P. Upshur. The Whigs had been opposed to the annexation of Texas; Tyler was now free to try to arrange it.

Upshur informed Van Zandt in September 1843 that Tyler believed it was possible to secure the two-thirds majority needed in the Senate to ratify a treaty of annexation. He asked Van Zandt to explore the possibilities of negotiations. Through Van Zandt, Houston played coy. He informed Washington that a discussion of annexation would cause Britain to withdraw her support and would break off the truce arrangements with Mexico. Therefore he wanted some solid assurance that such a treaty would pass if negotiations were opened, and he wanted the United States to guarantee to protect Texas from a possible Mexican invasion while the negotiations were in progress.

Tyler could not give him this officially, but the United States navy was shortly sent to cruise in the Gulf off the Mexican coast, and Andrew Jackson Donelson, the United States *chargé d'affaires* in Texas, promised, without authorization to do so, that such a defense would be made. Upshur asserted that the passage of the treaty through the Senate would be a certainty. Houston consequently agreed to open the discussions and sent J. Pinckney Henderson, the most accomplished diplomatist in Texas, to aid Van Zandt. "Now, my venerated friend," Houston wrote to Andrew Jackson, on February 16, 1844, "you will perceive that Texas is presented to the United States as a bride adorned for her espousal. But if now so confident of union she should be rejected, her mortification would be indescribable."

Upshur was killed in an accident before Henderson reached Washington. His place was taken by John C. Calhoun, determined defender of the Old South. It was with Calhoun that Henderson and Van Zandt signed a treaty of annexation on April 11, 1844. The treaty would bring Texas into the American union as a territory, guaranteeing it the right to progress to statehood. The United States would assume the staggering Texas debt, but in return would take possession of the vast Texas public domain—really a poor bargain, if Texas had but half an eye on the future. The United States would take Texas with the boundary she claimed, including the Rio Grande all the way through New Mexico to its source, with the stipulation that she could make adjustments with Mexico.

Tyler promptly transmitted the treaty to the Senate, emphasizing all the advantages it contained for the United States, and he warned that "if the boon now tendered be rejected, Texas will seek for the friendship of others." The Senate hesitantly postponed the question. Days became weeks and weeks, months. A vote was finally taken on June 8. Texas was rejected 35 to 16. At least fifteen senators that Texas' supporters had counted on voted against the treaty, many of them from the South. The reason: it was the summer of 1844—election year—and the nation was entering its quadrennial madness. Southern Whigs feared antagonizing northern abolitionists.

Tyler withdrew all the papers regarding annexation of Texas from the Senate and two days later, on June 10, sent them to the House, requesting annexation by an act of Congress. Since the adjournment had already been set, such an act was an impossibility, but it made the annexation of Texas the chief issue of the 1844 election in the United States.

Martin Van Buren, who had served as President from 1837 to 1841 before being defeated by Harrison and Tyler in 1840, was due to be the Democratic candidate in 1844. His cool stand on the Texas question caused even those delegates pledged to him at the party convention to switch. The Democratic nomination went to James K.

Polk, a Tennessean and something of a dark horse, but a forthright proponent of Texas annexation. The Whigs nominated Henry Clay, a man who deserved a chance at the office if any person ever did. But Clay's temporizing on the Texas issue made the extremists in both sides of his party only lukewarm supporters.

Polk came into the fight advocating expansion—not only the "re-annexation of Texas" (alluding to the old claims that the Louisiana purchase included Texas), but also the absorption of Oregon. As Texas historian Eugene C. Barker has written: "The play on 're-occupation' and 're-annexation' begged important historical questions, but they were good slogans with which to excite the voters." Polk and Vice-President George M. Dallas were elected, 170 electoral votes to 105.

Meanwhile Texas, too, passed through the heat of a presidential election, but annexation was not an issue, since both sides favored it. As a matter of fact, there were no issues, and the campaign was even more a personality contest than that of 1841—except it was not the personalities of the candidates so much as it was that of their backers. Houston was represented by Anson Jones, his petulent and narrow-minded secretary of state. Lamar, himself, selected General Ed Burleson who had been cast out of the Houston *coterie* for his near-mutinous actions at the time of the Vásquez raid. Other persons had been suggested by both parties, any one of whom, the candid historian must remark, would probably have made a better executive than either of the two candidates.

The campaign got under way by the Lamar party's trying to pose that Burleson did not really represent Lamar's former administration or his policy, but it was to no avail. Then they tried to depict Jones as a mechanical robot controlled by Houston. Slander of all types, the coarser the better, marked the election fight. Typical was an editorial in the La Grange *Intelligencer:*

> Caligula, the depraved and worst of all the tyrants that ever ruled Rome, after having trodden the spirit of his people into the most abject slavery, showed his contempt for them by making his *horse* a Consul. Gen. Houston, thinking the people of Texas in a like condition, evinces a much greater contempt for them, by wishing to impose Dr. Anson Jones upon the Republic as President—*a less noble animal.*

It was a bitter pill for the egotistical Dr. Jones, a physician by profession, that he had to run on Houston's coattails, although ambition made him keep his antagonism to himself until years later. It was additionally galling that, in keeping with Houston's policy, he had to pretend to be disinterested in annexation and friendly with the British. Jones of course was elected, polling over ten thousand votes. James Morgan characterized it perfectly: "He had no popularity of his own—rode in on Old Sam's Shadow! . . . Old Sam can beat the D———l himself when he tries and make anyone president."

Jones had the good sense to continue to follow Houston's lead, although privately he filled his "Memoranda Book" with snide remarks about his mentor, and later he came to fancy himself the "Architect of Annexation." Most of Houston's cabinet were retained. To fill the vacant office of secretary of state, Jones recalled Ashbel Smith from Europe where the doctor had so capably represented Texas to England and France. Reily was returned to Washington to replace Van Zandt, whose wife forced him to resign, and Henderson continued as the Texas negotiator on the scene in Washington. George Terrell, who had served Houston well as Indian commissioner, was given

Smith's post in Europe, joining William Daingerfield who remained as minister to Belgium, the Hanse towns, and Holland, all three of which had recognized Texas during Houston's second administration. With his team in control of the executive departments, Houston sat back to await the inevitable. The outcome of the election in the United States had made annexation certain. The only question was how soon. If Congress did not take action before Polk's inauguration, it certainly would later, for there was a clear mandate from the people.

"It is the will of both the people and the states," Tyler told Congress in December 1844, "that Texas shall be annexed to the Union promptly and immediately." Tyler not only feared that there was a very real danger of losing Texas through British designs to sustain its independence; he also wanted the deed accomplished before he left the presidency. Several bills for annexation were introduced in both houses. The one ultimately passed was a resolution initiated in the House to annex Texas directly as a state with its consent, and amended in the Senate to give the President the option of offering Texas immediate annexation by resolution or negotiating a new treaty.

There was little question which alternative Tyler would take, or which Texas preferred. On March 3, 1845, as virtually his last act in office, the President sped Congress' offer of annexation to Texas for the Republic's approval. The resolution for direct annexation was far more advantageous to Texas than the defeated treaty had been. It provided, in addition to Texas' admission as a state, (1) that the United States would adjust boundary disputes with foreign nations, (2) that Texas must submit a republican constitution for the approval of Congress prior to January 1, 1846, (3) that Texas would give the United States all fortifications, barracks, ports and harbors, navy and navy yards, and any other property pertaining to public defense, (4) that Texas would retain the ownership of its public lands (the only state other than the original thirteen so doing), (5) that Texas was to pay its own public debt (in return for being allowed to keep its lands), and (6) that four additional states might be formed out of the Republic's lordly dominions, if Texas consented, with the stipulation that any north of the parallel of 36°30' (the Missouri Compromise Line) automatically would be free states. To clinch the matter, Congress appropriated $100,000 to cover the costs of carrying on the necessary negotiations.

Despite the obvious desires of the people of both nations for union, the administration's fears of British intervention were well grounded. Her Majesty's foreign secretary, when he learned of the offer, wrote: "The dignity and prosperity of Texas are more secure in its own keeping than under the institutions of any other government." Charles Elliot, the ubiquitous British representative in Texas, undertook to fight Texas' acceptance of the American offer with every means at his command. He believed that many prominent men in Texas would reject annexation if they were assured of Mexican recognition and British protection. From President Anson Jones he secured a statement of the demands which, should Mexico accede to them, might defeat annexation. He thereupon rushed aboard a British man-of-war and sailed for Vera Cruz.

This was the end of March 1845. Could Jones delay the anxious bride (as Houston had so aptly phrased it) from her nuptial vows until she got another proposal? It was May 17 before Elliot and Pakenham got their answer from Mexico. ("It is a matter of regret," Pakenham wrote, "that so much time has elapsed . . . , but you are too well acquainted with the dilatory habits of Spaniards and

Spanish Americans not to be able to explain this.") The Mexican government would recognize Texas independence and submit any boundary dispute to arbitration if Texas would reject annexation. However, with the most exasperating lack of logic, Mexico would continue to claim the Sabine River as its boundary if Texas accepted annexation. Indeed, Mexico's whole attitude was punctured with inconsistencies. On the one hand, she agreed that Texas was a nation with whom she could make a treaty, but on the other hand, Texas did not exist at all, except as a province in rebellion. The Mexican minister in the United States, Juan N. Almonte, had withdrawn his passports, breaking off diplomatic relations because the United States proposed to annex Mexican territory. This was the same Almonte who had, with Santa Anna, agreed to work for Mexican recognition of Texas nine years earlier. The fact that Texas had existed as a nation for nine years and was recognized by all the leading powers was not considered in the construction of Mexican policy.

Under Houston's prodding, Jones had successfully postponed Texas' acceptance of annexation until the Mexican offer arrived. The tactic was simple: he just refused to convene Congress. Pressure grew quite intense, however, and threats were made in several counties to initiate a convention. The majority believed Jones would try to block annexation. It was Houston, of course, who was stalling. He wanted Texas to reject annexation, secure recognition from Mexico, and then inveigle an even more generous treaty from the United States.

There was no stemming the tide, however, and events moved at as rapid a pace as possible after Jones called the Ninth Congress to assemble in special session on June 16, 1845. Meeting at Washington-on-the-Brazos in a twelve-day session, Congress accepted the joint resolution of annexation and rejected the Mexican offer unanimously. It also approved the convention which Jones had called to meet in Austin on July 4. The reasons for the convention were two-fold: (1) acceptance of the annexation offer would be more properly done by a specially elected convention than by Congress; (2) a convention would be needed to draft a constitution for Texas as a state.

The convention met as scheduled in the capital built for Lamar. With only one dissenting vote it adopted an ordinance of annexation on the first day. Then for the next two months the delegates labored to prepare a state constitution for Texas. On October 13, 1845, the constitution and the annexation ordinance were submitted to popular vote. Since the result was certain, the turn-out at the polls was small. The vote was 4,254 for annexation, 267 opposed; and 4,174 for the constitution, 312 against.

Quickly, then, the constitution was forwarded to the United States. Both houses of Congress approved it, and President Polk signed the Texas Admission Act on December 29, 1845. Texas was officially in the union—but the new state had yet to be organized.

11

1846-50

THE NEW STATE

THE INAUGURATION of the new state officers took place in Austin, "seat of empire," on February 19, 1846. Spring had not yet painted the countryside with the brilliant abstractions of bluebonnets, Indian paintbrush, and other wild flowers; the dominant colors were the greens of the cedars and stately live oaks and the grays of the rocks and weathered log buildings. Against a backdrop of lovely Colorado hills, a large group of well-dressed men gathered somberly before the sprawling little capitol building whose rough hewn planks blended appropriately into their surroundings. Above the building, in stark contrast to the gray and green, floated the bright red, white, and blue banner of the Republic of Texas, the Lone Star seeming a resplendent supernova on the verge of bursting into flame.

Raising the United States Flag

As President Anson Jones ended a dramatic speech, he loosened the rope which held the flag, and it slowly fluttered downward. "The final act in this great drama is now performed; the Republic of Texas is no more," he intoned. Breaking from the assembled crowd, the tall figure of Sam Houston strode forward and gathered the flag to his breast before it reached the ground. There were tears in the eyes of many of the spectators, and the momentary hush that followed the ending of the ceremony was soon broken by a honking of noses blown vigorously to hide the sentiment.

State elections had been held on December 15, 1845. J. Pinckney Henderson was the new governor, supported by Albert C. Horton as lieutenant governor. The First Legislature met in the old halls of Congress and promptly elected Sam Houston and Thomas Jefferson Rusk to the United States Senate, with only three or four dissenting votes. Despite the vocal animosity against the President, John S. Ford was undoubtedly right when he stated: "It might be justly said that . . . Texas . . . had two friends on whom she could lean with equal trust and confidence. The impression of a large majority of the people of Texas was that these two great men placed country above self."

The great majority of Texans, too, looked with contentment and relief on their new status as citizens of the United States. A few, however, were regretful. James Morgan, the effervescent speculator from Galveston, voiced the adventurous nature of the Republic when he said: "It seems that 'the long agony is over' and Texas is to be tacked on to the fag end of the U States. . . . Well, all my projects, I fear, are knocked in the head—and I shall die for want of excitement of some kind."

In this he was wrong. The excitement was just beginning. Before statehood was many months old, Texas was plunged into a war with Mexico, *los diablos Tejanos*—from Jack Hays to Governor Henderson—fighting under the Stars and Stripes.

The causes of the Mexican War are among the least understood and most misinterpreted of any episode in American history. Too often, the United States is depicted as a bullying aggressor who, having just robbed Mexico of Texas, turned to provoke a war of conquest so that she might grab California and the Southwest. Too often, the glittering and nearly meaningless phrase *Manifest Destiny* is used to "explain" the "shameful" behavior of the American nation toward the "good neighbor to the south." And too often, the honor of Texas is blackened because of a vague boundary dispute, largely created by historians years after the war. So grossly distorted has the popular concept of this war become that in 1962 the attorney general of the United States joined the ranks of the apologists by saying: "I don't think that this [war] is a very bright page in American history."

His opinion of course is well supported by thoughtless statements from scores of American historians who have mistaken the political tracts of the Whigs and abolitionists of the time for honest "source" material and who have interpreted the facts to disparage Polk, Texas, and the Democratic South. It is tragic that the political propaganda of the last century should be utilized by American scholars to besmirch the image and honor of the nation.

To trace the origin of the war between the United States and Mexico, it is necessary to review the relations between these countries from the time of Mexican independence. The United States promptly recognized the newly formed Mexican nation but was soon bewildered by the rapid changes taking place there. A revolution in May 1822 overthrew the government and made Augustín Iturbide the emperor of Mexico in July. A subsequent revolution in the fall and winter of that year unseated Iturbide, and in 1824 a republican constitution was adopted by Mexico. The government appeared to achieve some stability, but the first national election in 1828 provoked a new revolution, and the presidency was filled by strength of arms rather than decided by votes.

The following year, the United States minister in Mexico attempted to open discussion of the claims question, based on debts owed to United States citizens by the Mexican government. The Mexican foreign minister refused to discuss it, telling him it was a matter for the courts, to which Joel Poinsett then referred the briefs. When the party in power was overthrown by another revolution, the claims cases were indefinitely sidetracked. In 1833 Santa Anna emerged from the fray as the successful leader of Mexico and began to establish his dictatorship. Anthony Butler, then United States *chargé d'affaires,* tried unsuccessfully to dig the claims cases out of the courts. Failing this, he attempted to trade the claims for the Mexican territory of Texas, but failed.

In 1834, Santa Anna abrogated the Constitution of 1824, dissolved Congress, and substituted his personal appointees as officials ranging from governors to *alcaldes.* His dictatorship was complete—except for the outbreak of rebellion throughout the nation. The worst insurrections occurred in California, Texas, Yucatan, and northern Mexico, and continued for years. In Texas, the fighting against Santa Anna became a battle for independence in March 1836. In California, young Manuel Alvarado established an independent government, drove the centralists out, and proclaimed that California would remain separate from Mexico until the Constitution of 1824 was re-established.

At this point, Powhatan Ellis resubmitted the claims issue to the Mexican foreign minister and received such a runaround that he finally left Mexico in disgust. Almost simultaneously, the Mexican ambassador left Washington charging that General E. P. Gaines had violated neutrality by taking United States troops into Texas. The charge was unfounded in fact, although some historians interpret the circumstantial evidence to hint that Gaines may have intended to fight Santa Anna or to support Texas. Indeed, the whole web of degradation thrown about American action is woven from alleged intentions and motivations rather than from facts and actual events.

Early in 1837, President Jackson reviewed the relationship between the United States and Mexico for Congress and suggested that one more attempt be made to collect the claims by diplomacy. It was no real surprise to anyone that this failed. But after France collected her claim by occupying Vera Cruz in the "Pastry War" and Britain negotiated hers by a show of force, Mexico, then headed by Bustamante's party, agreed to submit the United States claims to an international arbitration commission, umpired by the king of Prussia or his delegate.

Internally Mexico was rife with dissension for the next three years as Santa Anna began his rise back to power. Unable to pacify the *Yucatecos,* the centralists did succeed in winning over Alvarado in California, and held onto the government of Armijo in New Mexico. The "Republic of the Rio Grande" failed to dislodge centralist appointees in the northern provinces, and by 1841 Santa Anna was again dictator of Mexico.

Meanwhile, the arbitration of the claims bogged down. Mexico delayed eighteen months before taking action on the agreement, procrastinated four months over procedure, and amid tantrums and table-poundings which thoroughly revolted the Prussian umpire, finally settled less than a third of the cases.

Santa Anna rejected even this partial settlement made by his delegates and refused to pay the $2,000,000 which the commission had agreed upon. Waddy Thompson, United States minister, then offered to trade the claims for territory; but Mexico peremptorily dismissed this. By June 1843, Thompson finally persuaded Santa Anna to begin installment payments on the claims that had been settled and to submit the remainder to another arbitration convention. Signed in November 1843, after months of wrangling, the new arbitration agreement was not ratified by Santa Anna's subservient Congress.

In April 1844, Mexico refused to pay the second installment on the arbitrated claims. By the end of the summer, the United States *chargé d'affaires*, in hopeless exasperation, abandoned any further effort and turned the entire matter over to Congress. Before Congress could take any action, however, the situation changed. A new wave of terror swept over Mexico. Santa Anna was overthrown and exiled; and out of the turmoil, José Herrera emerged as the new leader, a position he held precariously for the next several months. Under the exhortations of extremists, anti-American sentiment swelled, and the disaffected minority tried to turn it against Herrera, who was more moderate. Finally, Mexico broke off diplomatic relations with the United States when Juan N. Almonte, former prisoner of Texas and now the Mexican ambassador in Washington, withdrew, stormily protesting the joint resolution of annexation.

It was this situation that President Polk inherited at his inauguration. Mexico maintained that the annexation of an independent nation now recognized by most of the major powers of Europe was an act of hostility, yet she submitted for the approval of Texas a treaty recognizing the independence of the Republic; the claims issue remained unsettled; and diplomatic relations were suspended. As he debated a course of action with his cabinet, Polk received indirect word that President Herrera would discuss the diplomatic crisis with a minister from the United States having "full power to settle the present dispute."

To Polk it seemed a heaven-sent opportunity. He appointed John Slidell and authorized him to act on every issue, giving him instructions to try to trade the claims for the territory of California—or even to buy California outright and trade the claims for Mexico's deluded pretensions on Texas. If worse came to worst, he was authorized to settle on the Nueces as the southern boundary of Texas. Polk has been accused of sinister duplicity in the California matter. Nothing could be farther from the truth. For nearly ten years numerous Americans had cast their eyes covetously toward the Pacific Coast. Many believed that Californians, themselves, caught up in the dictatorship of the centralists and its accompanying revolutions, would welcome the establishment of American jurisdiction. Polk's offer to buy California was a straightforward attempt to find a satisfactory solution to the dilemma which confronted him.

When Slidell reached Mexico, Herrera refused to receive him and announced that no solution to the claims issue could be discussed until the United States returned Texas to Mexico. The truth is that opposition to the United States was one of the chief elements in the demagoguery of Mexican politics—and that no Mexican politician dared to admit publicly that Mexico had lost

Texas forever. Even the hint that Herrera might receive a United States minister helped to cause his overthrow by revolution and the establishment in power of General Mariano Parades who shouted imprecations against the United States and demanded that Mexico go to war to reconquer Texas.

Meanwhile, annexation proceedings moved to a conclusion, and Polk ordered Zachary Taylor with a rag-tag army of about 1,500 to occupy Texas. Taylor was stationed near present Corpus Christi at the mouth of the Nueces River. With relations strained to the breaking point and war imminent, Polk sent secret dispatches to an American resident in California named Thomas O. Larkin, instructing him to give aid to the liberals there and, in case of a rebellion, to support the establishment of a republican government. John Charles Fremont, a United States army officer with a small detachment, was there for the purpose of exploring the area; his later actions may have been the result of similar instructions from the President, although there is no evidence of this.

When the Slidell mission failed, Polk decided to move Taylor from the Nueces to the Rio Grande to protect the statutory boundary claimed by Texas. The annexation agreement had given him the right to adjust the boundary of Texas with Mexico, but Mexico had refused to discuss it. Instead, Mexican officials stubbornly claimed all of Texas. The accusation is frequently made that the order to send Taylor to the Rio Grande was an act of aggression. This begs the real question, which is: What else could Polk do?

Twenty years of patient (and sometimes impatient) diplomacy had failed to move the two nations any nearer a solution. Mexico had suspended relations over the completely absurd contention that annexation of Texas was tantamount to an act of war. Parades was demanding war against the United States, and Mexican troops were being gathered at Matamoros. Polk was responsible for the defense and safety of Texas. In good conscience, could he have done anything else?

Two points of contention always arise when Polk and the United States are condemned as *provocateurs*. One is that Polk's real desire was to obtain California. There was no secret about his interest in the acquisition of California, but it is utter slander to suggest that he would have waged a war for it. His willingness to bargain was obvious; his hope of a revolution in California was not far-fetched. For all practical purposes California was virtually separated from Mexico at the time.

The second point usually raised is that Polk was morally wrong to support Texas' claim to the Rio Grande and that the Texas claim itself was some kind of shameful and disgraceful skulduggery. It was in truth absurd for Texas to claim the upper Rio Grande in New Mexico as its western boundary, but in the southern region, it was logical. Both Spain and Mexico had shown slight regard for boundaries of any kind in the frontier provinces. The region between the Nueces and the Rio Grande had been opened for settlement as a part of Nuevo Santander in the eighteenth century, but a hundred years later the scattered inhabitants there looked to Saltillo in Coahuila for administration. The only organized municipality, Laredo, operated as part of the state of Coahuila and Texas under Mexico, and this state made colonization grants to John Charles Beales in that area. By the time of the Texas Revolution, the Rio Grande had apparently become the accepted dividing line. In 1835 Cós agreed without question to withdraw his troops out of Texas *across the Rio Grande* after his defeat at Bexar. Likewise, Santa Anna's order to Filisola after San Jacinto was to retreat across the Rio Grande. This was followed by the Treaty of Velasco, stating the same boundary on the south.

Then in 1836, Texas declared its boundaries based on the right of successful revolution. In New Mexico the declaration was, of course, a farce. In the lower Rio Grande valley it was meaningless. The people still looked to Saltillo. From time to time Mexico garrisoned a few troops there, but both Vásquez and Woll had scampered to safety south of the Rio Grande. Finally, in 1845, the Mexican offer to recognize Texas independence (if Texas would refuse the United States) stipulated the Rio Grande as the boundary.

Since the territory later alleged by historians to have been in dispute is that in southern Texas between the Nueces and the Rio Grande, not that in New Mexico, the insinuation that Texas did not have a valid claim is rather weak. It must be remembered that at no time did Mexico officially demur over the Rio Grande boundary—instead, she claimed all of Texas to the Sabine.

General Taylor, after much fumbling, reached the mouth of the Rio Grande on March 23, 1846, encamping on the north bank. Across the river, massed Mexican troops, whipped to a frenzy by their officers, looked on this as an insult. On April 4, President Mariano Parades ordered an attack on the United States Army. A week later, General Ampudia arrived with several thousand additional men to direct the attack. The next day he demanded that Taylor withdraw across the Nueces—the first official mention from Mexico of this river. To protect his encampment, Taylor blockaded the mouth of the Rio Grande.

For nearly a fortnight, the Mexicans continued to send threats to the American commander. Then, on April 24, a detachment of Mexican cavalry crossed the river and attacked the small command of Captain Thornton, quickly withdrawing again across the river. On Sunday and Monday, May 8 and 9, Mexican troops crossed to the Texas side once more where the opening battles of the Mexican War were fought—Palo Alto and Resaca de la Palma.

Polk promptly asked Congress for a declaration of war, which was voted before the week was out. Abolitionists declared the action to be another manifestation of the conspiracy of the slavocracy, but the bulk of the nation supported it. The war was conducted in three major offensives. One, led by Taylor across northern Mexico to capture Monterrey, was probably the hardest fighting of the war. A second, led by Winfield Scott, was an expeditionary force that landed at Vera Cruz and met little resistance in a march to Mexico City. The third, led by Stephen Watts Kearny, entered New Mexico from Missouri, then divided to invade Chihuahua on the south and conquer California on the west. New Mexico capitulated without firing a shot, and by the time Kearny reached California, the liberals there, fighting under the "Bear Flag" (with some support from Fremont), had already turned out the centralists.

Texans fought with Taylor and with Scott. The legislature granted Governor Henderson a leave of absence to command the Texas militia, and the old Ranger leaders put together a small regiment under Jack Hays who was given a commission as colonel. In all, approximately 5,000 Texans saw service in the war.

Henderson returned to office after the Monterrey campaign but refused to run for reelection. George Thomas Wood, a respected Trinity River planter who had gained fame as a regimental commander in the Mexican War, was elected to the office over Dr. J. B. Miller. The lieutenant governor was John A. Greer. It was during Wood's administration that Texas became involved in a dispute with New Mexico over her western boundary. After Kearny occupied Santa Fé and established a military government there, Governor Henderson, on June 4, 1847, reminded Secretary of State James Buchanan that Santa Fé lay within the area claimed by Texas.

Buchanan assured Henderson that the Texas claim would in no way be jeopardized by the temporary government there; but after the Treaty of Guadalupe Hidalgo, ending the Mexican War, was ratified, there was still no acknowledgment from Washington of the Texas claim. In the treaty the United States purchased all the land from the Rio Grande to the Pacific lying between the 42nd parallel and the old southern boundary of New Mexico along the Gila and Colorado rivers. This included all or parts of the following states which were later created: New Mexico, Arizona, Nevada, California, Utah, Colorado, and Wyoming. Mexico was paid $15,000,000 for this territory, the sum being retained in the treasury until the claims question was settled. Vilifiers of the United States' course in relation to Mexico call this (as well as the amount later paid for the Gadsden Purchase) "conscience" money, but the territory was in fact acquired by an almost bloodless occupation, such fighting as occurred taking place for the most part between Mexican factions in California. In the treaty Mexico also renounced all claims to Texas.

Did the Treaty of Guadalupe Hidalgo verify Texas' paper claim to eastern New Mexico? Texans believed it did. On March 15, 1848, the Texas Legislature created

Santa Fé County encompassing most of the region, and sent Judge Spruce M. Baird to Santa Fé to organize the civil government there under the laws of Texas. The legislature also called on the United States to support Judge Baird and the Texas government through the military staff already in occupation.

Texas and Baird were to be disappointed. Colonel John M. Washington, the army commander in Santa Fé, had aligned himself with certain businessmen in New Mexico and was determined to circumvent the Texas government. Threatened even by physical violence—tradition says he would have been tarred and feathered—Baird left New Mexico to the dubious ministrations of Washington and the petty *grandees.*

However absurd the Texas claim to New Mexico might have been originally, Texans now took it as a personal affront that their efforts to gain control were thwarted. Governor Wood, in November 1849, told the legislature that Texas should press its claims "with the whole power and resources of the state." By this he meant, or at least was understood to mean, that Jack Hays and the Rangers could handle the situation.

The legislature responded by re-creating Santa Fé County in a smaller size and establishing three additional ones in the area: El Paso, Worth, and Presidio. Robert S. Neighbors was then appointed to journey into the west to perfect the organization. In theory, he was to organize one county at a time, thus breaking into smaller bites the chunk which Baird had not been able to manage.

Neighbors was an excellent choice. He combined the courage of a Texas Ranger (which he had been) with the diplomacy of a Stephen F. Austin, and the humanity of a Houston. Furthermore he had just returned from the area where, with John S. Ford, he had laid out a trail from

Austin and San Antonio to El Paso—a route soon used by many of the gold seekers to California.

Neighbors had no difficulty organizing El Paso County. Across the river from the old villa of El Paso del Norte, now Ciudad Juarez, the indefatigable Magoffin brothers had established a trading post, and a little American village called Franklin had risen at the foot of the mountain of that name. The people there welcomed the Texas government. This action—organization of El Paso County— unquestionably did more to preserve Texas' claim to the Rio Grande than all other measures put together, for later when the United States Congress began to whittle on the size of the new state, the congressmen stopped short at El Paso.

From there, Neighbors moved into New Mexico. He encountered hostility at nearly every turn. Colonel Washington had issued orders that no army officer or detachment was to assist him in any way. About half way to Santa Fé, desperately in need of supplies for himself and forage for his horse, he stopped overnight at a bivouac commanded by a Major Henry who sympathetically gave him some corn and fed him. For this, Henry received a severe reprimand from Washington, lost six months' pay and allowances, and was transferred out of New Mexico. He returned to the East through Texas; at Austin a gala banquet was held in his honor and the Texas legislature voted him funds equivalent to the losses he incurred for befriending Neighbors.

Neighbors, after leaving Henry's outpost, proceeded on to Santa Fé. There he found the people, supported by the militia, bitterly aroused against him. New Mexico was trying to organize a state government and petition for admission in the United States as a separate state. He returned to Texas and his report to the governor was made public in June 1850.

Great excitement ensued. Newspaper editors raised a hue and cry over the high-handed behavior of the United States—Texas would have been better off out of the Union, etc., etc. Mass meetings were held in various towns, and the people talked of secession and declaration of war. A new governor, meanwhile, had taken office: Peter H. Bell.

Bell was a veteran of the San Jacinto campaign, an officer in the Mexican War, and a well-liked politician. A native of Virginia, he was a staunch proponent of slavery and states' rights. In the election of 1849, he had won easily over Lieutenant Governor Greer, M. T. Johnson (the old Regulator leader who was involved with John H. Reagan in an attack on the Peters Colony company), T. J. Chambers (who was to become a perennial candidate for office) and B. H. Epperson (one of many staunch Unionists in Texas).

On receiving Neighbors' report, Governor Bell called a special session of the legislature, angrily demanded that Texas assert her rights, and sent a fiery letter to Zachary Taylor who, by reason of his career in the Mexican War, had been elected President of the United States. Taylor was strongly anti-Texas, although the reason for his attitude is not clear. Perhaps it was the beastly climate of the Nueces country that had poisoned his mind; perhaps it was a quarrel he had had with J. Pinckney Henderson over the Monterrey campaign; or perhaps it was his ire against the Texas Rangers. During the war, he had found the Rangers to be the most irritating group of men he had ever dealt with. They refused to submit to military discipline—they would not wear proper uniforms—they sneered at the custom of saluting officers (and indeed were known on occasion to spit a big gob of tobacco juice in the general direction of some of the dandied officers of his staff)—and they had the disconcerting habit of wandering off on their own to pick fights with isolated Mexican bands, or to capture a town, or sometimes to overindulge in the "ardent." But Taylor had not been able to fight the war without them. They were his eyes and ears on the campaign, and it was the *Tejanos* who had stormed the walls of Monterrey. He seems to have parted company with the Texans, a frustrated and bitter man.

Now, he had no intention of permitting the Texans to acquire New Mexico. Under his instructions, the army in New Mexico stood firm, and the people were encouraged to submit a constitution as a full-fledged state. They held a convention, drafted a constitution, and claimed most of West Texas as their territory. It was fortunate for Texas that "Old Rough and Ready" Taylor died.

His successor, Millard Fillmore, reinforced the army in New Mexico and announced that any Texas Rangers coming into the area would be resisted. But Fillmore was anxious to compromise. The whole nation was in a turmoil over the question of slavery in the Mexican Cession. A convention of Southern leaders had been called at Nashville, Tennessee, and threats of secession filled the air around the national capitol.

Through the efforts of the great compromiser, Henry Clay, the controversial elements of the situation in the Southwest were balanced off against each other and an "Omnibus Bill" was submitted to Congress. The chief points were the immediate admission of California as a state (the gold discovery in 1849 having suddenly augmented its population); territorial status for New Mexico and Utah; the question of slavery left for future decision (popular sovereignty was implied); and the boundary between Texas and New Mexico established.

The settlement of the boundary dispute by the famous Compromise of 1850 has, itself, an interesting background. It will be remembered that Texas had retained her public lands, but was to pay her own debts at the time of annexation. A large portion of the debt, especially the bond issue and the sinking fund for the bonds, had been based on a hypothecation of the customs revenue—the only real source of money which the Republic had. That is to say, the Republic had pledged the funds derived from the customs tariff to pay the bonds. Now, cried Texas politicians and bondholders alike, the United States had taken over the collection of the customs. Therefore the United States must pay the bonds.

It was a powerful argument. The mortgage on a house attaches to the property, not to the individual who makes the loan. Texas was willing to pay its ordinary or common debt, and indeed had already begun the auditing of these claims, but the state was unwilling to pay the debt against the revenue of the Republic. Most of the bonds had passed at discount rates into the hands of speculators. A group of these men organized and employed a lobbyist in Washington to try to influence Congress to accept the fiscal responsibility for the bonds. Since the case was strong, their efforts were rewarded.

In the compromise, the United States agreed to pay Texas $10,000,000 to accept a settlement of the Texas boundary running east along the 32nd parallel from the Rio Grande, north up the 103rd meridian, and east again along the line of 36° 30'—approximately where the present boundary of the state is located. Of this $10,000,000, Texas would actually get $5,000,000. The remainder would be held in the United States Treasury for settlement of the revenue bonds.

With such a large sum in sight, the Texan indignation faded rapidly, and the legislature accepted the offer with alacrity. Bell signed the Acceptance Act on November 25, 1850. The money was a great boon to Texas. With the $5,000,000 received, the state paid every conceivable claim against the Republic, scaling down the reimbursement for star money and exchequer notes which had never circulated at par, but paying the face amount on treasury warrants, back salaries, and the like. After everything (except the bonds) was paid, Texas was able to put $2,000,000 in a permanent school fund, and to spend over $1,000,000 for needed projects. The people went virtually tax free until the Civil War.

The bonds, or revenue debt, were not settled until 1855. Added to the $5,000,000 which the United States kept in the Treasury was $1,500,000 interest which Texas congressmen claimed was due by that time (almost a usurious rate), and $1,250,000 that Texas insisted the United States owed it for the damage United States Indians had done in Texas. Thus, there was available $7,750,000 to balance against a total of $10,078,703 in revenue debts. The bondholders were paid at 77 cents on the dollar—much more than most had invested.

With the settlement of the debt, the last vestige of the proud little Republic faded into memory—to become a page in a history book, a symbol of the courage, and glory . . . and foibles of the bold men and women who had thrown off the yoke of a tyrannous dictatorship and established a self-governing republic.

POINT OF VIEW

PUBLISHED SOURCE MATERIALS for the history of the Republic are fortunately quite extensive; *Adventure in Glory* is based almost exclusively, therefore, on these primary materials which include *The Writings of Sam Houston*, edited by Amelia W. Williams and Eugene C. Barker (8 vols., Austin, 1938-1943); *The Papers of Mirabeau B. Lamar*, edited by C. A. Gulick, Katherine Elliott, and Harriet Smither (6 vols., Austin, 1921-1927); *Texan Diplomatic Correspondence*, edited by George P. Garrison (2 vols., Washington, 1908); *The Texas Treasury Papers*, edited by Seymour V. Connor (3 vols., Austin, 1955); *The Texas Indian Papers*, edited by Dorman Winfrey and James Day (4 vols., Austin, 1959-1961); *British Diplomatic Correspondence Concerning the Republic of Texas*, edited by Ephraim D. Adams (Austin, 1918); as well as the various journals of the Senate and House of the Congresses of the Republic of Texas, including those of the Fourth and Sixth Congresses, edited by Harriet Smither, and the *Secret Journals of the Senate*, edited by Ernest W. Winkler; and the session laws of the Republic's Congresses which are most readily available in H. P. N. Gammel, *The Laws of Texas* (10 vols., Austin, 1898).

Good runs of newspapers of the time can be found in the State Library and at the University of Texas; many of these have been available to me at Texas Tech on microfilm. Also to be considered source materials are a scattering of reminiscences published in the *Southwestern Historical Quarterly* and the great work by Henderson K.

Yoakum, *History of Texas* (2 vols., New York, 1856). Of a similar nature and classifiable as original sources are John J. Linn, *Reminiscences of Fifty Years in Texas* (New York, 1883), Thomas J. Green, *Journal of the Texian Expedition Against Mier* (New York, 1845), and *Texas in 1837*, an anonymous journal ably edited by Andrew Forest Muir (Austin, 1958).

Obviously no author, no matter how thorough, is going to be on intimate terms with all this great bulk of material. The best guides to its use are the large number of secondary studies of Republic history which have been issued, especially the biographies. Noteworthy among these are the treatments of Sam Houston by Llerena Friend (*The Great Designer*, Austin, 1952), by Marquis James (*The Raven*, Indianapolis, 1929), and by M. K. Wisehart (*American Giant*, Washington, 1962); and the lives of Anson Jones (New York, 1848) and Mirabeau B. Lamar (Dallas, 1934) by Herbert Gambrell. Some of the most useful secondary studies include *Texan Statecraft, 1836-1845*, by Joseph Schmitz (San Antonio, 1941); *The Texas Republic*, by William R. Hogan (Norman, 1946); *Political History of the Republic, 1836-1845*, by Stanley Siegel (Austin, 1956), and *The Texas Navy in Forgotten Battles and Shirtsleeve Diplomacy*, by Jim Dan Hill (Chicago, 1937). For the navy I found *Commodore Moore and the Texas Navy*, by Tom Henderson Wells (Austin, 1960) quite useful. By no means least of the secondary sources is the great *Handbook of Texas*, edited by Walter P. Webb and H. Bailey Carroll (2 vols., Austin, 1952). To list all of the secondary works available or consulted in the writing of this book would require too much space and would serve no useful purpose. Those named above I consider to have been the most valuable to me.

It is true that this book rests solidly on primary data

as I interpret it, but to imply that I did all the research would be false. I used the secondary works broadly, following the authors' interpretations where they agreed with mine and varying from them when they did not. In almost every instance and certainly for every major point, sources cited by other authors were checked to insure accuracy. Dependence upon the work of other historians should be emphasized, for without them this book could not have been written.

Since no footnotes are used here, the sources for most of the quotations are identified in the text, as are many of the more important parts of the narrative. Some pains have been taken, especially to identify for the reader any reference that might be obscure, such as William Weaver's answer to Gorastiza's attack on Gaines in Chapter I, or the messages of the President to Congress, or Green's *Journal of the Texian Expedition Against Mier,* and so on. I hope that my tracks through the *materia historia* are sufficiently clear that any reader really curious about a point will have no difficulty in locating the basis for it.

For the most part, the interpretations of people and events in this book are the standard accepted versions. Perhaps it would be wise for me to try to point out some of the instances in which my interpretations differ from those of other Texas history writers.

I have made no attempt to whitewash the opportunistic character of Santa Anna nor have I made any effort to disguise my admiration for Sam Houston. My interpretation of the Republic's land policy, which is based on my own research and that of some of my students, differs from other interpretations. The presentation of Mexican politics and foreign policy is largely based upon the work of Justin Smith. However, I have placed more emphasis upon the claims question and upon the personal exasperation of American and European diplomats who were trying to deal with the unstable personnel of the Mexican governments. In treating the issue of the Cherokee Indians, I have tried to stick closely to contemporary opinion rather than to superimpose some of the romanticized morality concepts of the present time. Since I believe that the men of the Republic were on the whole honorable men, I have not attempted to judge their actions; they were much better acquainted with the Indian situation than I will ever be. The idea that the great Comanche raid of 1840 stemmed more from the machinations of Mexican agents than from a belated desire for revenge is entirely my own, as is the explanation of Houston's vacillation on the Cherokee Land Bill.

On the whole, I have written this book with a distinct pro-Texas bias, a point of view which I believe entirely justified by the facts.

INDEX

Abolitionist movement, 228, 251; British, 58-59; opposition to Texas, 21; propaganda on Mexican War, 238

Ad Interim government, 3, 10-11, 16, 28, 108

Adams, Ephraim D., 255

Adams, John Quincy, 40-41; opposition to annexation, 81

Adams-Onís Treaty, 37

Adelsverein, 212-213

Alabama Indians, 69, 73; reservation for, 118

Alamo, 2-3, 8

Alcalde, defined, 36

Alcantra, Battle of, 112

Alguacil, defined, 36

Allen, Augustus C., 42

Allen, Eliza, 14

Allen, John K., 42

Almonte, Juan N., 26, 241; aide to Santa Anna, 3; Mexican envoy to U.S., 233

Alvarado, Manuel, 239, 240

Ampudia, Pedro, 186-187; Mexican commander at Matamoros, 245

Amusements, 43, 89

Anadarko Indians, 206, 209

Anaya, Juan Pablo, Mexican federalist, 111, 136, 139

Andrews, J. D., 141

Annexation of Texas, 224-234; ceremony of, 235-236; convention for, 234; Joint Resolution for, 231-232; Texas vote on, 20, 234; Texas withdrawal of, 81; Treaty of, 227-228; United States rejection of, 59

Anti-slavery (*see* Abolitionist movement)

Apache Indians (*see also* Lipan Apache), 223

Arcas Islands, 137-138

Archer (ship), 134, 182, 199

Archer, Branch T., 13

Archives War, 88, 190-194

Armijo, Manuel, 157, 240

Audubon, John, visit to Texas, 44

Augustine, Henry W., 76

Austin (ship), 134, 138, 139, 171, 196, 198

Austin, Stephen F., 15, 24, 26, 58, 92; appointment as secretary of state, 18; candidacy for presidency, 13; capital named for, 100

Austin, Texas: castigated by Sam Houston, 117-118; establishment of, 101-103; resistance to removal of capital, 190-194

Ayuntamiento, defined, 36

Baird, Spruce M., 248

Baker, Joseph, 212

Baker, Moseley, 34, **218**

Barker, Eugene C., 255

Barnard, George, 168

Bastrop, Texas, charter of, 65

Beales, John Charles, 52; colonization grant of, 244

Bear Flag Revolt, 246

Bee, Barnard E., 26; agent to Mexico, 108-110

Belgium: interest in Texas bonds, 153; recognition of Texas, 131; Texas agent in, 231

Bell, Peter H., 250

Bevilport, Texas, charter of, 65

Bexar (*see* San Antonio)

Biddle, Nicholas, 105

Biloxi Indians, 209

Bird, Jonathan, 127

Birds Fort, 209

Black, John S., 206

Black bean episode, 187-188

Blockade, Mexican, 50

Bonds, Texan, 28, 29-30, 130; French sale of, 152; hypothecation of customs revenue for, 93; offered in Europe, 103-105; sale to Biddle, 105; settlement of, 252-254

Borden, Gail, 29

Borden Dairy Company, 29

Boundaries of Texas: defined by Congress, 37; dispute over with New Mexico, 244-252; expansion proposed, 170; map of, 19; northeast, 81; Nueces River, 244; Sabine River, 60; United States to adjust, 231

Boundary Act, 37, 39

Bowles (Cherokee chief): complicity with Mexican agents, 115; conferences with Houston, 74; death of, 100; duplicity charged by Lamar, 99; involvement in Cordova uprising, 75-76; negotiations with Mexico, 71

Bowles, John, 100

Brazoria, Texas, charter of, 65

Brazos, Department of, 13

Brenham, Richard, 156

Britain (see Great Britain)

Broocks, Travis G., 221

Brown, John Henry, 76-77

Browning, Samuel, 210

Brutus (ship), 33, 50, 51, 52

Bryan, William, 196

Buchanan, James A., 89, 247

Bullock, Richard, 150-152

Bullock's Hotel, 103, 145, 150, 151, 166, 193; description of, 102

Burleson, Ed, 95, 127, 218; attack on Cordova, 96-97; defense of San Antonio, 174; election as Vice-President, 163; presidential candidacy, 229-230

Burnley, A. T., 105, 130, 132

Burnet, David G., 5, 8, 10, 11, 13, 161, 218; acting President, 143; address to Congress, 16-17; conference with Cherokees, 71-72; hatred of Houston, 162-163; messages to Congress, 143, 144, 147; presidential candidacy, 162-163; relations with Santa Anna, 3-4; resignation, 17

Burton, Isaac W., 6

Business and commerce, 66

Bustamante, Anastacio, 108, 133

Butler, Anthony, 239

Butler, Pierce M., 206

Caddo Indians, 69, 73, 206, 209, 222

Caldwell, Matthew, 127; attack on Cordova, 97; defense of San Antonio, 184

Calhoun, John C., 227

California, 154; revolution in, 239; U.S. interest in, 243-244

Cameron, John, 72

Canales, Antonio, 111, 119, 122, 125, 133; re-entrance into Mexico, 121; retreat to Texas, 119; visit to Texas, 112

Canalizo, Valentin, 96

Capital Locating Commission, 65, 100

Capitals of Texas: Austin, 100-103, 169, 176, 190-194; Columbia, 16-17; Houston, 42-45, 176, 189; Washington-on-the-Brazos, 190

Capitol buildings, 42, 44, 102

Cárdenas, Jesús, 120

Carroll, H. Bailey, 256

Casa Blanca, Indian battle at, 127

Castro, Henri, 211-212

Cazneau, Mrs. Jane McManus Storm, 88-89

Cazneau, William, 218

Chalmers, John G., 141, 163

Chambers, Thomas J., 250

Chandler, Eli, 194, 204

'Change Notes, 94

Cherokee Indians, 114-115, 209; attack on Texans, 99; conference with Houston, 43; decree of Consultation regarding, 71-72; dilemma of, 69-71; duplicity of, 74-75; history, 69-72; Houston among, 15; implication in Cordova Rebellion, 97-98; misrepresentation of, 73; removal from Texas, 99-100; treaty with, 72-74

Cherokee Land Bill, 116-117, 145, 179

Cherokee War, 99-100

Chickasaw Indians, 209

Choctaw Indians, 73

Christy, William A., 199-201

Ciudad Juarez, 249

Claims against Mexico: British, 59, 109; French, 79-80, 240; U.S., 25-26, 239-241

Clarksville, Texas, charter of, 65

Clay, Henry, 229, 251

Coleto Creek, army camp, 10

Collinsworth, James: appointment as attorney general, 18; presidential candidacy, 85-86; suicide, 86

Colonization, 147-150

Colorado River, Comanche battles on, 95-96, 129

Colt, Samuel, 224-225

Colt Revolvers, 224-225

Columbia, Texas, 42, 45; charter, 65; first capital, 16-17; Santa Anna in, 3

Columbus, Texas, charter of, 65

Columbus (Georgia) *Enquirer*, 7

Comanche Indians, 69, 221, 223, 224; attack on by Hays, 225; attacks on by Moore, 95-96, 129; attendance at council, 223; captives of, 121-122; Council House Fight, 121-125; hostilities of, 95; Meusebach treaty with, 213; Mexican intrigue with, 125; raid on Linnville, 126-127; raid on Southwest Texas, 125-127; raids on South Texas in 1836, 52; raid on Victoria, 126-127; rejection of peace council, 208-209; treaty with, 77

Common law, adoption of, 118

Compromise of 1850, 251-253

Connelly, Henry, 155

Connor, Seymour V., 255

Constitution of 1824 (Mexico), 239-240

Constitution of 1836, 11-12

Constitution of 1845, 234

Consular Act, 67

Consular service of Texas, 67-68

Consultation, 71

Convention of 1836, 11, 31, 55, 60, 146-147

Convention of 1845, 234

Converse, Sherman, 214-217

Cooke, Philip St. George, 204-205

Cooke, William G., 122; Santa Fe commissioner, 156

Copano Bay, Horse Marines at, 6

Cordova, Vicente: biographical sketch of, 75-76; retreat of, 96

Cordova Rebellion, 76-77, 97-98

Cós, Martín Perfecto de, 39

Council House Fight, 121-125, 129, 208

Coushatta Indians, 69, 118

Cox, Frances, 107

Cragg, Timothy, 210

Creath family, 54

Cuba, 89

Currency and money, 28, 47-48, 93, 141, 167, 195

Customs Act, 29

Customs duties, 47, 119

Daingerfield, William, 231

Dallas, George M., 229

Dalmatia, Duke of, 106

Danish settlers, 212

Dawson, Frederick, 134

Dawson, Nicholas Mosby, 184

Day, James, 255

Declaration of Independence, 11, 47

Delaware Indians, 69, 73, 209, 222

Dial, John, 221

Dolores, English colony, 52

Dolores, Spanish settlement, 38

Donelson, A. J., 227

Dougherty family, 52

Douglas, Kelsey, 99

Douglas family, 52

Dryden, William G., 155
Duels and duelling, 15, 17, 34, 45, 88, 89, 118, 162-163, 218
Dunlap, Richard, 108
Durst, Joseph, 168
Dutch settlers, 212

Eberly, Mrs. Angelina, 88, 166, 193
Economic conditions: (1836), 10-11; (1837), 66-67; (1839), 113; (1840), 140-141; (1842), 167-168, 179-180; Houston's retrenchment program, 166-167; legislation regarding, 146; Morfit's appraisal, 23
Education Act of 1838, 91-92
Edwards, John, 54
Eight Percent Fund, 119
El Paso County, creation of, 248-249
El Paso del Norte, 249
Eldredge, J. C., 208, 222
Elections: (1836), 11-15; (1838), 83-86; (1839), 114; (1841), 161-163; (1844), 229-230
Elliot, Charles, 164, 191, 232
Elliott, Katherine, 255
Ellis, Powhatan, 23, 25, 26, 109, 240
Ellis, Richard, 60
Ely, E. B., 216
England (see Great Britain)
Epperson, B. H., 250
Exchequer Bills, 167, 195
Expansion Bill, 170

Falconer, Thomas, 156
Fannin, James W., 8
Fannin County, creation of, 65
Farnese, Charles, Count de, 57
Fayette County, creation of, 65
Filisola, Vicente, 6, 76, 245
Fillmore, Millard, attitude toward Texas-New Mexico dispute, 251
Finances of Texas, 47-48, 93, 104, 113, 118
Fisher, Henry Francis, 212

Fisher, S. Rhoads, 18, 50
Fisher, William S., 120, 122; Mier expedition led by, 186-188
Fisher-Miller contracts, 212
Five Million Dollar Loan, 29, 104, 118, 151-152
Flacco (Lipan chief), 207
Flood, George, 151
Flores, Manuel, 76, 96-97
Florida Purchase Treaty, 37
Fontaine, Edward, 162
Forbes, John, 72
Ford, John S., 56-57, 83, 237; trail to El Paso, 248
Forsyth, John, 61, 81, 109
Fort Bend County, creation of, 65
Fort Houston, 55
France: claims of against Mexico, 79-80, 240; negotiations with, 57; treaty with, 106-107
Franco-Texienne Bill, 147-148
Franklin, Texas, progenitor of El Paso, 249
Fredericksburg, Texas, establishment of, 213
Fremont, John Charles, 243
Friend, Llerena, 256
Frontier: defense of, 55-56, 94-96, 205-209, 224; posts along, 55, 94; settlement on, 146-150
Fuller, Charles, 172

Gaines, Edmund Pendleton, 240; analysis of 1836 actions, 23-24
Gambrell, Herbert, 256
Gammel, H. P. N., 255
Garrison, George P., 255
German settlers, 212-214
Goliad, Texas, 2, 3, 8; charter of, 65; invasion of, 173
Gonzales, Battle of, 95
Gonzales, Texas: charter of, 65; retreat from, 8
Goodbread, Joseph, 219
Gorostiza, Manuel E., 23
Grand Saline, Ranger post at, 98, 100
Granville, Earl of, 79

Gray, Alfred E., 171
Gray, William Fairfax, 56
Grayson, Peter W., presidential candidate, 84-85
Great Britain: attitude toward annexation, 226, 232-233; claims of against Mexico, 59, 109; mediation promise of, 160; opposition to naval war, 138; rejection of Texas bonds, 153; Texas relations with, 57, 58-59; treaties with, 131-132
Green, Thomas Jefferson, 5, 9-10, 88, 218, 256; opposition to Houston, 34; Santa Anna kidnapped by, 2-3
Greer, John A., 247, 250
Gregg, Josiah, 165
Guadalupe-Hidalgo, Treaty of, 247
Guizot, F. P. G., 153
Gulick, C. A., 255

Hall, Edward, 163
Hamilton, Alexander, 47
Hamilton, James, 33, 119; appointment as Texas bond commissioner, 103; biographical sketch of, 104; heroism of, 105; meeting with Treat, 110; negotiations in Europe, 106-107, 130-132, 151-152; opposition to naval war, 138; return to Texas, 107
Hamilton, Morgan C., 184
Hanse towns, Texas agent in, 231
Hansford, John M., 219
Harbor survey, 145
Harvey family, 54
Hays, John Coffee ("Jack"), 88, 185, 248; defense of San Antonio, 183-184; Mexican War campaigns, 246-247; popularization of Colt revolvers, 224, 225; Ranger company organized by, 218
Headright grants, 31-32, 50, 147
Henderson, James Pinckney, 88, 230; annexation efforts, 227-228; appointment as attorney general,

18; appointment as Texas minister to Europe, 57; biographical sketch of, 57-58; election as governor, 237; marriage of, 107; Mexican War duties, 246-247; negotiations with England, 78-79; negotiations with France, 79-80, 106-107; quarrel with Taylor, 250; return to Texas, 107
Henry, Major ——, 249-250
Herrera, José, 241-244
Hibbins family, 54
Hill, Jim Dan, 256
Hockley, George W., 26, 175, 179, 202
Hogan, William R., 256
Holland: recognition of Texas, 130-131; Texas agent in, 231
Homestead Act, 92
Homestead grants (see Headright Acts; Land laws)
Hornsby's Bend, Indian attack on, 54
Horse Marines, 6
Horse thieves, death sentence for, 94
Horton, A. C., 55, 237
Horton, Alexander, 15
Houston, Sam, 9, 10, 26, 34, 41, 42, 50, 87, 117-118, 199-200, 207-208; alcoholism criticized, 162; anecdote about drinking, 165; anger over Cherokee War, 115-116; annexation tactics of, 225-234; attitude toward duelling, 163; biographical sketch of, 14-15; Cherokee Land Bill by, 116-117, 145, 179; Cherokee negotiations of, 43, 71-72, 74, 77; conflict with Moore, 175-176, 180-181, 196-199; contrast with Lamar, 168; control of Congress, 142; convalescence, 6, 7; courtship of Margaret Lea, 115; criticisms of, 63-64, 174-175, 218; duelling challenges ignored by, 218; election to Texas Congress, 115; election to presidency, 13-14, 17, 163; election to Senate,

237; emotion at annexation, 237; eulogy for Indian chief, 207-208; first cabinet of, 18-19; Indian policies of, 55, 77-78, 168-169, 205-209, 221-223; instructions to Somervell, 185; messages to Congress, 18, 166, 192, 194; negotiations on Sabine boundary, 61-62; negotiations to free prisoners, 200-201; opposition to Austin as capital, 169, 189-190; opposition to Lamar, 116-117; opposition to land acts, 48-49, 62-63; opposition to Mexican invasion, 143-144; opposition to navy, 171-173, 175-176, 180-181, 196-199; opposition to Texas war against Mexico, 176-178; organization of Rangers, 55; problems of in 1842, 188-189; relief of free Negroes, 188; self-defense of, 199-200; speech at Lamar's inauguration, 90; supporter of colonization, 148; Warfield expedition authorized by, 201-202

Houston, Texas, capital at, 42-45, 176, 189; charter of, 65

Houston County, 65

Houston *Morning Star*, 179, 195

Howard, George Thomas, 88, 123-124, 156-157

Hunt, Memucan, 80, 163; Texas agent in U.S., 41, 59; withdrawal from Washington, 81

Huston, Felix, 9-10, 33-34, 49, 88; at Battle of Plum Creek, 127; duel with Johnston, 34; invasion proposal by, 143

Ikin, Arthur, 132

Immigration, 65, 210-217; encouragement of, 146-150; German, 88

Independence (ship), 33, 50, 51

Independence, Texas, charter of, 65

Indians (*see also* particular tribes): campaigns against, 95-96, 145; captives of, 119, 123; councils with, 207-208, 222-225; hostilities of, 24, 52-56, 53 (map), 68-69, 121, 125-127, 168-169, 221-222; Texas relations with, 69, 70 (map), 205-209; trading posts for, 168-169; treaty with, 223; U.S. relations with, 69

Intelligencer (La Grange), 230

Invincible (ship), 1-2, 3, 5, 6, 33, 50, 51

Ioni Indians, 206, 209, 222

Irion, Robert A., 61, 81

Iturbide, Augustín, 239

Jackson, Andrew, 14, 26; attitude toward recognition, 20-21, 41; Houston letter to, 227; letter to Houston, 179

Jackson, Charles W., 219

James, Marquis, 256

Johnson, M. T., 221, 250

Johnston, Albert Sidney, 100, 122, 162; appointment as army commander, 33; cavalcade to Austin led by, 103; duel with Huston, 34; message to Cherokees, 98

Jones, Anson, 162-176; appointment as Texas minister to U.S., 81; biographical sketch of, 82; criticism of Houston, 178-179; presidential candidacy, 229-230; speech at annexation ceremony, 236

Jonesborough, Texas, charter of, 65

Jordan, Samuel W., 112, 132, 173; attack on Sam Houston, 145; filibuster in Mexico, 120-121

Juarez, Mexico, 249

Karankawa Indians, 69

Karlshafen (Indianola), Texas, 212

Karnes, Henry W., 121-122

Kearny, Stephen W., 246

Pawnee Indians, 69
Pedernales, battle of, 225
Peraza, Martin F., 160
Perote Castle, 157, 188, 200, 218
Peters, Henry, 210
Peters, William Cummings, 210
Peters, William S., 149, 210
Peters Colony, 147-150, 210-217, 250
Pig affair, 150-152
Pirson, Victor, 153
Plum Creek, battle of, 127
Plummer, Joseph, 140-141
Plummer, Mrs. Rachel, 54
Pocket (ship): damages for, 80-81; Texan capture of, 50
Poinsett, Joel, 239
Polk, James K., 228-229; Mexican problems of, 241-244
Population of Texas, 22, 65
Postal service, 118
Potomac (ship), 134
Potter, Robert, 167
Presidio County, creation of, 248
Promissory notes, 48, 93, 141, 146
Provisional Government, 13, 28-29, 72-73
Public domain (*see* Land laws)

Quihi, Texas, 212
Quintana, Texas, 3

Reagan, John H., 250
Recognition of Texas: Belgian, 131; British, 79, 131-132; Dutch, 130-131; French, 106; United States, 20-26, 41
Red River settlements, 60
"Redbacks," 94, 119
Red-Lander (San Augustine), 195
Reed, Braman, 54
Reed, Joseph, 54
Refugio, Texas, charter of, 65
Regulator-Moderator War, 218-221
Reily, James, 226, 230

Republic of the Rio Grande, 120-121, 132, 137
Resaca de la Palma, battle of, 246
Rice, James O., 97
Richmond, Texas, charter of, 65
Rio Grande, basis for Texas boundary on, 38-39, 244-245
Robertson County, creation of, 65
Robinson, James W., 200
Roo, Quintana, 171-172
Ross, Reuben, 112
Rusk, Thomas Jefferson, 8, 10, 13, 162; acting commander of army, 6-7; appointment as secretary of war, 18; conference with Cherokees, 76; election as senator, 237; presidential candidacy suggested, 83-84

Salado, Battle of, 184
Saligny, Count Alphonse de, 80, 150-152
San Antonio (ship), 134, 138, 139, 171-173, 181
San Antonio, Texas: army post at, 10; charter of, 65; Council House fight at, 121-125; invaded by Woll, 183-185
San Augustine, Texas, charter of, 65
San Bernard (ship), 134, 138, 139, 171, 182
San Felipe, Texas, charter of, 65
San Gabriel River, Indian battle of, 97
San Jacinto (ship), 134, 138, 139
San Jacinto, Battle of, 1, 7, 8, 13, 14, 15, 21, 75; anniversary celebration of, 42-43
San Juan Bautista, 38
San Patricio, Texas, army camp at, 10
Santa Anna, Antonio López de, 8, 11, 13, 20, 26, 75, 177, 187, 188, 197, 200; dictatorship of, 239-240; imprisonment of, 1-5; public feeling toward, 3-5; renewal of popularity, 108; Vera Cruz